PAKISTAN

A Global Studies Handbook

GLOBAL STUDIES: ASIA

PAKISTAN

A Global Studies Handbook

Yasmeen Niaz Mohiuddin

A B C 〰 C L I O

Santa Barbara, California • Denver, Colorado • Oxford, England

Copyright © 2007 by ABC-CLIO, Inc.

Library of Congress Cataloging-in-Publication Data

Mohiuddin, Yasmeen Niaz.
  Pakistan : a global studies handbook / Yasmeen Niaz Mohiuddin.
    p. cm. — (Global studies. Asia)
  Includes bibliographical references and index.
  ISBN-13: 978-1-85109-801-9 (hardcover : alk. paper)
  ISBN-10: 1-85109-801-1 (hardcover : alk. paper)
  ISBN-13: 978-1-85109-802-6 (ebook)
  ISBN-10: 1-85109-802-X (ebook)

  1. Pakistan—Handbooks, manuals, etc. I. Title.

DS376.9.M64 2007
954.91—dc22   2006029904

09 08 07 06   10 9 8 7 6 5 4 3 2 1

This book is also available on the World Wide Web as an eBook. Visit www.abc-clio.com for details.

ABC-CLIO, Inc.
130 Cremona Drive, P.O. Box 1911
Santa Barbara, California 93116-1911

Production Editor   Alisha Martinez
Production Manager   Don Schmidt
Media Editor   Ellen Rasmussen
Image Coordinator   Ellen Dougherty
Media Manager   Caroline Price
File Manager   Paula Gerard

This book is printed on acid-free paper. ∞
Manufactured in the United States of America

In loving memory of
my father, Niaz Ahmed Siddiqui and
my mother, Dr. Bismillah Niaz Ahmed
whose knowledge of, insights into, and passion for Pakistan
served as a guiding light for me in writing this book.

Contents

Series Editor's Foreword

It is imperative that as many Americans as possible develop a basic understanding of Asia. In an increasingly interconnected world, the fact that Asia contains almost 60 percent of all the planet's population is argument enough for increased knowledge of the continent on our parts. In addition, there are at least four other reasons why it is critical that Americans become more familiar with Asia.

First, Americans of all ages, creeds, and colors are extensively involved economically with Asian countries. U.S.-Pacific two-way trade surpassed U.S. trade with Europe in the 1970s. American companies constitute the leading foreign investors in Japan. With the world's second-largest economy, Japan is also the second-largest foreign investor in the United States.

The recent Asian economic crisis notwithstanding, since World War II, East Asia has experienced the fastest rate of economic growth of all the world's regions. Recently, newly industrialized Southeast Asian countries such as Indonesia, Malaysia, and Thailand have joined the so-called Four Tigers—Hong Kong, the Republic of Korea, Singapore, and Taiwan—as leading areas for economic growth. In the past decade China has begun to realize its potential to be a world-influencing economic actor. Many Americans now depend upon Asians for their economic livelihoods, and all of us consume products made in or by Asian companies.

Second, it is impossible to be an informed American citizen without knowledge of Asia, a continent that directly impacts our national security. America's war on terrorism is, as this foreword is composed, being conducted in an Asian country—Afghanistan. (What many Americans think of as the "Mideast" is, in actuality, Southwest Asia.) Both India and

Pakistan now have nuclear weapons. The eventual reunification of the Korean Peninsula is fraught with the possibility of great promise or equally great peril. The question of U.S.-China relations is considered one of the world's major geopolitical issues. Americans everywhere are affected by Asian political and military developments.

Third, Asia and Asians have also become an important part of American culture. Asian restaurants dot the American urban landscape. Buddhism is rapidly growing in the United States, and Asian movies are becoming increasingly popular. Asian Americans, though still a small percentage of the overall U.S. population, are one of the fastest-growing ethnic groups in the United States. Many Asian Americans exert considerable economic and political influence in this country. Asian sports, pop music, and cinema stars are becoming household names in America. Even Chinese-language characters are becoming visible in the United States on everything from baseball caps to T-shirts to license plates. Followers of the ongoing debate on American educational reform will constantly encounter references to Asian student achievement.

Fourth, Asian civilizations are some of the world's oldest, and their arts and literature rank as some of humankind's most impressive achievements. Anyone who is considered an educated person needs a basic understanding of Asia. The continent has a long, complex, and rich history. Asia is the birthplace of all the world's major religions, including Christianity and Judaism.

Our objectives in developing the Global Studies: Asia series are to assist a wide variety of citizens in gaining a basic understanding of Asian countries and to enable readers to be better positioned for more in-depth work. We envision the series being appropriate for libraries, educators, high school, introductory college and university students, businesspeople, would-be tourists, and anyone who is curious about an Asian country or countries. Although there is some variation in the handbooks—the diversity of the countries requires slight variations in treatment—each volume includes narrative chapters on history and geography, economics, institutions, and society and contemporary issues. Readers should obtain a sound general understanding of the particular Asian country about which they read.

Each handbook also contains an extensive reference section. Because our guess is that many of the readers of this series will actually be traveling to Asia or interacting with Asians in the United States, introductions to language, food, and etiquette are included. The reference section of each handbook also contains extensive information—including websites when relevant—about business and economic, cultural, educational, exchange, government, and tourist organizations. The reference sections also include capsule descriptions of famous people, places, and events and a comprehensive annotated bibliography for further study.

—*Lucien Ellington*
Series Editor

Preface and Acknowledgments

Pakistan matters. Its stability, prosperity, and modernization have far-reaching implications for the region and for the world. It is bordered on the east and northeast by two of the world's emerging economic powers, India and China, and on the west and northwest by two of the world's political hot spots, Iran and Afghanistan. Pakistan occupies a position of great geopolitical strategic importance for the United States. It has been a staunch ally in the fight against Soviet expansionism and occupation of Afghanistan during the Cold War in the 1980s, and in the war against terrorism after September 11. It has increasingly become a strategic player on the world stage and a truly critical country for the United States in maintaining security in a polarized world.

Yet Pakistan is a country largely misunderstood in the West, and often depicted unfairly and incorrectly, flashed across newspaper headlines and television screens as a country dominated by religious extremism. But the reality is that most Pakistanis want their country to be a moderate, prosperous, and modern state, informed by the true Islamic values of peace, justice, and tolerance, in consonance with universal values. In many ways, Pakistan is such a state, with high growth rates, a significant middle class, a relatively free press, high levels of scientific capabilities, a cohesive military, a western-educated political elite and bureaucracy, and a politically conscious electorate. The western paranoia that Pakistan could transform into a radical and militant state—or that religious hard-liners could take over and Pakistan could become a theocracy like Iran, or that it could fall apart with severe implications for nuclear proliferation—are not well-founded. The concern and fear is partly a result of the superficial knowledge in the United States about Pakistan.

Although many Pakistanis are devout Muslims, they are not attracted to religious authoritarianism. Thus, despite its religious identity, Pakistan did not veer toward a theocracy as did its western neighbors, Iran and Taliban-era Afghanistan. In fact, through most of Pakistan's history, religious parties have had few electoral successes despite their street power.

Pakistan: A Global Studies Handbook is an attempt to tell the Pakistan story in an objective manner while, at the same time, conveying the feelings of Pakistanis. It is written from my outsider-insider perspective—with the eyes of an outsider and the feel of an insider. As an academic living and teaching in the United States for the last twenty-five years, I am a distant observer, not committed to any specific group or political party. I am also an insider to Pakistan, having been raised and educated there, then teaching as a university professor at Karachi for ten years. This gives me an insider's understanding, insight, and instinct. I also travel to Pakistan at least once a year in connection with my research, to present a conference paper, or as a member of a World Bank or United Nations mission, giving me an opportunity to interact with a diverse group of Pakistanis from all walks of life. It is their voices, particularly the voices of the common men and women, that I have tried to capture in telling the Pakistan story. The story of Pakistan is the story of Muslims in India—of their arrival as conquerors; of the blending of Central Asian, Middle Eastern, and Indian cultures; of the spread of Islam in India; and of the Muslim struggle for independence from British colonialism and Hindu domination leading to the creation of Pakistan. It is also the story of the courage, perseverance, and accomplishments of the ordinary people of Pakistan—of how a newly born, asset-poor nation handled the 1947 partition holocaust and the resulting influx of millions of refugees; of how, for ten years in the 1980s, it bore the brunt of the confrontation with the USSR for their occupation of Afghanistan, including the burden of millions of Afghan refugees; and of how it developed nuclear capabilities to maintain the political and military balance in the Indian subcontinent. At the same time, it is also the story of a nation grappling with unresolved political and institutional issues such as the role of Islam in a nation intentionally formed as a religious homeland; of sharing of power between the center and provinces; of the strong hold of feudalism; of a culture of divisive tribal, ethnic, and regional loyalties and factional politics; of the establishment of democratic institutions; of the Kashmir dispute and relationship with India; and of a sub-culture of sectarian violence and corruption.

These are serious challenges. But Pakistanis have overcome serious challenges before and have triumphed in the face of heavy odds against them. Several factors bode well in this regard. Pakistan's economy has once again become a success story, as it did in the 1960s. Growth rates are up and poverty is down. Both corruption and sectarian violence seem to be declining. Democratic and military governments have alternated during Pakistan's entire history, but, in both cases, many political freedoms have been maintained. Pakistan remains a very open country willing to tolerate the scrutiny of local and foreign media, and even the hostile media coverage that often contributes to its image problem. Its strength is its people, their optimism and resilience in the face of the most severe challenges. Pakistan has a committed workforce, an informed middle class, and a strong pool of scientific and technological talent. Its recently developed nuclear capabilities can be harnessed for peaceful purposes and serve as a deterrent to a war with India. There is both hope and evidence that Pakistan has embarked on a road to recovery and that, one day, the high expectations of its founding fathers will be met.

I am deeply grateful to Lucien Ellington, the series editor, for asking me to write *Pakistan*, for his helpful comments on the earlier drafts, and for his constant encouragement throughout the process. I would especially like to thank Dr. Alex Mikaberidze, the submissions editor, for his detailed comments and insights, and for his patience. Both Lucien and Alex have been a great help in the quest for clarity. I would also like to thank Ellen Rasmussen for her remarkable efforts and success in obtaining the most appropriate photographs for the book, and Mansoor Suhail of the Pakistan Mission to the United Nations for providing important photographs. My thanks also go to Alisha Martinez, the associate production editor, for her understanding and for making the production process smooth and stress-free for me.

My deepest thanks go to my husband, Mohammad Mohiuddin Siddiqi, without whose constant advice, insights, patience, and encouragement, I would not have been able to complete this book. I am grateful to my son, Umar Mohiuddin Siddiqi and his wife, Cathy, for their advice along the way; to Saeedul Hasan Burney for his comments and encouragement; to Ghazi Salahuddin and Farid Siddiqui for their comments on Chapter 1; and to Zeenut Ziad for her valuable comments and editing of some chapters. My students, Omair Ahmed and Prashant Shukla, were helpful in locating some of the material used in the book.

My thanks also go to the multitude of average Pakistanis in all walks of life whose voices and views have informed my writing, including waiters, taxi drivers, vendors, shopkeepers, domestics, clerical workers, bankers, journalists, teachers, students, and housewives. The views expressed, and any errors and omissions, are entirely mine.

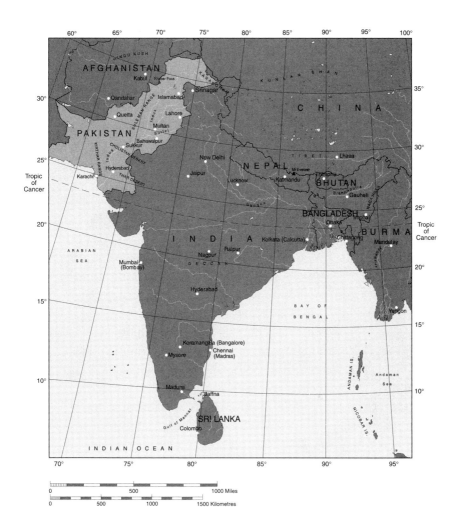

Map of South Asia

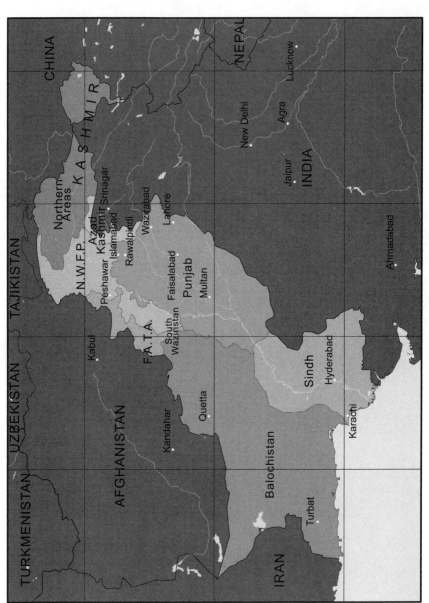

Geopolitical Map of Pakistan

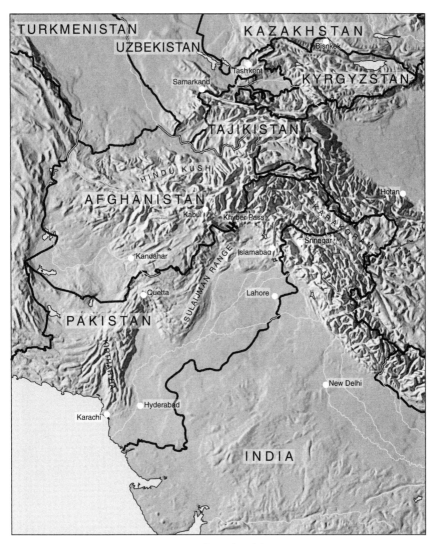

Topography of Pakistan

PART ONE
NARRATIVE SECTION

CHAPTER ONE

Geography and History of Pakistan

Pakistan stands at the crossroads of the world where the cultures of Central Asia, the Middle East, and South Asia meet and become one, creating a unique Pakistani identity. For centuries, the "Silk Route" through Pakistan was not only the main route between Europe and Asia for trade in silk and spices but also the route for skills, ideas, and religion to travel across the Eurasian continent, shaping the course of European and Asian cultural development. Geographically, it is a land of contrasts where the majestic mountains and arid steppes of Central Asia extend toward the fertile lowlands of the Indian subcontinent. Historically, Pakistani society has reflected a blending of great cultures—Buddhist, Mongolian, Greek, Muslim, and Hindu— while at the same time maintaining a strong Islamic identity. Currently, it is a society in transition where tradition and modernity coexist. In this period of change, Pakistanis have not abandoned their traditional traits of great hospitality, warmth, and friendliness, and retain their deep sense of dignity.

Bordered by Iran, Afghanistan, China, and India, Pakistan also lies in one of the world's political "hot spots," where it has often found itself in the center of some of the most serious conflicts of modern times. Since its creation in 1947, Pakistan has been a staunch ally of the West. Since then, it has occupied a position of great geostrategic importance for the United States, being a frontline state during the Cold War and in the fight against Soviet expansionism. As a direct consequence of its primacy in the fight against the Soviet occupation of Afghanistan in the 1980s, Pakistan became home to millions of Afghan refugees. The burden of supporting refugees increased significantly when the international community, including the United States, discontinued help in rehabilitating and reconstructing Afghanistan's war-devastated economy following the withdrawal of the Soviet forces in 1989. For a developing country with limited resources, the burden of supporting millions of refugees within its borders without any significant external assistance, coupled with the refugees' easy access to weapons, led to a serious socioeconomic upheaval in the country that gave rise to a *Kalashnikov* or weapons culture, ethnic violence, and religious extremism.

After the September 11, 2001, attack on the United States, Pakistan became a frontline state in the war against terrorism. It has once again become one of the most critical allies of the United States. The refugee burden has only increased, however. Pakistan now has the dubious distinction of having the largest number of refugees in the entire world—18 percent of the world's total, 25 percent of the developing countries' total, and about as many as in the combined regions of the Arab States (excluding Palestinian refugees), East Asia and the Pacific, Latin America and the Caribbean, Central and Eastern Europe, and CIS countries (Commonwealth of Independent States, formerly the Soviet bloc) (Human Development Report 2003, 306–307).

Soon after India detonated a nuclear bomb in May 1998, Pakistan also became a declared nuclear state in order to maintain the political and military balance in the Indian subcontinent. Pakistan's geographic location; its history with its neighbors, particularly Afghanistan and India; and its historic alliance with the United States have created many serious internal and external challenges for the government of Pakistan.

PHYSICAL AND HUMAN GEOGRAPHY

Pakistan is located in the northwest of the South Asian subcontinent. Moving clockwise, it is bordered by Iran on the southwest, Afghanistan on the west and north, China on the northeast, India on the east and southeast, and the Arabian Sea on the south. It is separated from Tajikistan, one of the Central Asian Republics of the former Soviet Union, by a narrow strip of Afghan territory in the northwest called the Wakhan Corridor. The Arabian Sea, a part of the Indian Ocean, forms the country's southern border with 650 miles of coastline. The boundary with Iran is about 565 miles long, with Afghanistan some 1,510 miles, and with China about 325 miles. The boundary with India is about 1,810 miles long, extending from the Karakoram Pass to the Arabian Sea, with some borders more contentious than others. The boundary that is formally disputed runs from the Karakoram Pass west-southwest to a point about 81 miles northeast of Lahore. This mutually agreed boundary, or the Pakistan-India cease-fire line, known as the Line of Control, is about 478 miles long.

Pakistan covers an area of 307,374 square miles, about one-tenth the size of the United States, not counting Alaska and Hawaii. It is slightly smaller than the U.S. states of Texas and Kansas combined, or slightly smaller than twice the size of California. Its population was estimated to be 159 million in 2004, compared to 293 million in the United States. Pakistan is divided into four provinces and a federally administered area. The four provinces are Balochistan, North-West Frontier Province (NWFP), Punjab, and Sindh. The government has designated about one-fourth of the land within the NWFP, bordering Afghanistan, as the Federally Administered Tribal Areas (FATA), where the central government has only limited authority and the local council of tribal chiefs, known as the *jirga,* handles most governmental affairs. This makes it difficult for the federal government to pursue fugitives who may seek shelter in these areas. The Tribal Areas include North and South Waziristan, Wana, and Parachinar.

In addition to the four provinces, Pakistan controls the northern and western parts of the former princely state of Jammu and Kashmir. Pakistan's portion of Kashmir consists of

Azad (Free) Kashmir, covering 4,494 square miles, and the Northern Areas, covering 27,985 square miles, which include the Gilgit Agency and the Baltistan Agency (so called because these areas were administered by a "political agent" during British rule). India controls two-thirds of Kashmir. The Indian state of Jammu and Kashmir includes southern and southwestern Kashmir and the Vale of Kashmir. Ladakh, the easternmost part of Kashmir, is partly under Chinese control. India and Pakistan have fought three wars since 1947 to seize or retain control of the disputed territory of the Kashmir region in the northeast. Initially, Pakistan also included the province of East Pakistan, separated from the rest of the country by 1,000 miles of Indian territory, which became the independent state of Bangladesh in 1971.

Regional Division

Pakistan is a land of contrasts not only in climate and topography, but also in life-styles. Life in the high mountain valleys seems like a page out of a medieval book, whereas the life-style in the big cities is modern. Physically, it is a country with a vast range of climatic zones and topography that encompasses almost all those found on the whole continent of North America. Its elevation ranges from sea level to the second highest point on the earth. Pakistan's landscape includes towering mountain ranges, jagged and snowcapped peaks, vast glaciers, gushing rivers, dry plateaus, fertile plains, lush valleys, arid deserts, and hundreds of miles of almost uninhabited sandy beaches. Flowing from north to south is the Indus River, which nourished one of the world's earliest civilizations. Pakistan can be divided into five major geographic regions according to land features, topography, and climate: the northern and western mountains, the Balochistan Plateau, the Indus River Plain, the Thar and Cholistan deserts, and the high mountain valleys.

The Northern and Western Mountains. Over the past eighty million years, massive natural forces have shaped what

Diran Peak at 23,838 feet is among the forty highest peaks in Pakistan. (Pakistan Mission to the UN)

are now the oceans and the continents, created mountains and glaciers, and carved gateways and passes into those mountains. An arc of these mountains—the Himalayas, the Karakorams, and the Hindu Kush Range—now forms the northern and northwestern borders of Pakistan, separating Central Asia and the Indian subcontinent. The western ranges of the Himalayas and the Karakoram Range extend across the northern end of the country, running through Pakistan's Kashmir region. The Karakoram Mountains form one of the world's highest mountain ranges and contain some of the most dramatic scenery in the world. This region is rightfully called the roof of the world. The Karakoram Range is part of the Himalayas that run between Pakistan and China. Many of the world's tallest mountains are found in these ranges, including K2, Pakistan's highest mountain and the world's second highest after Mount Everest. Peaks higher than 21,300 feet are commonplace, and many remain unconquered by climbers. Massive glaciers rise among the mountains, too. The three largest glaciers outside the polar regions—the Baltoro (36 miles long), Biafo, and Hispar—are all in the Northern Areas of Pakistan, which is why they have sometimes been called the third pole. The Hindu Kush Mountains in the northwest form part of Pakistan's border with Afghanistan. A chain of low ranges lies on Pakistan's west side. The Sulaiman and Kirthar ranges define the western extent of the province of Sindh, forming a natural border between Pakistan's land regions. The lower ranges are far more arid than those in the north and run to the southwest across the province of Balochistan.

Pakistan is a mountain climber's paradise. Of the world's fourteen mountains that are higher than 26,246 feet, five are in Pakistan. These are K2, second highest at 28,250 feet; Nanga Parbat, ninth highest at 26,660 feet; Hidden Peak, eleventh highest at 26,469 feet; Broad Peak, twelfth highest at 26,400 feet; and Gasherbrum II, thirteenth highest at 26,352 feet. Moreover, seven of the sixteen tallest peaks in Asia and forty of the world's fifty tallest peaks are in Pakistan. There are at least fifty peaks that are over 21,300 feet, and more than 50 percent reach above 14,800 feet. By contrast, the tallest peak in North America is Mount McKinley in Alaska, at 20,320 feet, and the highest peak in Africa is Kilimanjaro, at 19,340 feet in Tanzania. The highest Alpine peak, Mont Blanc, only reaches 15,771 feet and is a mere hill compared to the taller peaks in Pakistan.

At several points on the Hindu Kush, which forms part of the boundary between Afghanistan and northern Pakistan, mountain passes cut through the tall peaks, providing gateways to invaders, refugees, fugitives, and nomads. The name "Kush," meaning death, was probably given because these passes are dangerous. Among the more important ones along the border with Afghanistan are the Khojak Pass, fifty miles northwest of Quetta in Balochistan; the Baroghil Pass in the far north, providing access to the Wakhan Corridor; and the Khyber Pass, perhaps the most famous mountain pass in the world, twenty-five miles west of Peshawar and leading to Kabul in Afghanistan. Since ancient times, the Khyber Pass has been the point of entry to the subcontinent for invading armies, partly because it is the widest and lowest of mountain routes from Afghanistan into the subcontinent. Invaders, including the Aryans, Persians, Greeks, Huns, Mongols, Turks, and Mughals, entered the subcontinent through this pass. At the same time, it is believed that the majority of invaders did not use it or used it only once and not again because of the fierce and brave Afridi tribe who have inhabited the pass for centuries.

The rugged topography of the northern and western mountains and the rigors of the climate have shaped the everyday life of the mountain people and the sources of livelihood for them. They are typically farmers, herders, and traders. They grow crops such as wheat, corn (maize), barley, mustard, nuts, and fruits. The inhabitants of these mountains are courageous and dignified people, who are fiercely indepen-

The 56-kilometer long Khyber Pass was the point of entry to the subcontinent for Alexander the Great, Genghis Khan, Tamerlane, and Babur, among others. (Pakistan Mission to the UN)

dent, resilient, and tough. Their harsh and unrelenting code of honor matches the harshness of their terrain.

The Balochistan Plateau.   The mountain chains change direction, about midway down Pakistan's western border, running south to the Arabian Sea. To the west of these mountains is the rocky, arid Balochistan Plateau, and to the right is the Indus River. The Balochistan Plateau covers roughly the same area as the Balochistan Province. It is described as one of the most desolate landscapes on the face of the earth, resembling the moon, an inhospitable land of dry lakes and riverbeds interspersed with steep hills and barren mountains. Alexander the Great and his army nearly perished here in 323 BCE on their way back from the Indus to Persia. Few conquerors have chosen the route since. The Balochistan coastline on the Arabian Sea is little more than 300 miles of deserted beaches because the steep hills of the Makran Coast Range in the south isolate it from the rest of Pakistan.

The Balochistan Plateau receives less than 5 inches of rainfall each year. The lack of water makes Balochistan the least populated region of Pakistan where only about 5 percent of the total population of Pakistan lives in an area that represents about 44 percent of the nation's land. The harsh topography and lack of water make economic activities extremely arduous. As a consequence, there is little agriculture except for wheat and minor crops. Water is channeled to the fields through underground tunnels using a centuries-old irrigation method for farming called the *karez,* which minimizes water loss through evaporation. But almond groves and grape and apricot orchards abound in the valley near Quetta. There are virtually no industries in Balochistan, but Pakistan's most important source of fuel, natural gas, comes from the Sui gas fields at the south of the Sulaiman Range and is transported by pipeline to several cities. Although oil, gas, coal, copper, chromite, iron ore, limestone, gypsum, marble, and onyx are mined here, the mineral potential of Balochistan remains largely unexplored. The Makran coast supports fishing villages.

The Indus River Plain. The mighty Indus River is one of the most important rivers of the world in terms of both the power of its flow (it is three times as powerful as the Nile and ten times as the Colorado River) and its length—about 1,900 miles from headwaters to mouth. It begins high in the Himalayas in southwestern Tibet from a spring known as the Mouth of the Lion, flows down through the Karakoram Mountains into the Northern Areas of Pakistan, and then continues southward and westward, traversing the entire length of the country, and finally flows into the Arabian Sea. All five of Pakistan's major rivers—the Kabul, Jhelum, Chenab, Ravi, and Sutlej—flow into the Indus. It has supported and nourished agricultural settlements for more than 4,000 years and gave the Indian subcontinent its name. The Indus is also the source of one of the largest irrigation systems in the world, providing silt-enriched waters to the agricultural plains of Punjab and Sindh. The catchment area of the Indus is about 390,000 square miles. The Indus River basin is a large, fertile alluvial plain formed by soil and silt deposited by the Indus River and its tributaries.

The Indus Plain encompasses an area of about 200,000 square miles, about two-thirds of the area of Pakistan. The northern part, or Upper Indus Plain, covers most of the Punjab Province, the most densely populated region in Pakistan. It is the most fertile farming region because the main tributaries of the Indus River—Jhelum, Chenab, Ravi, Sutlej, and Beas—flow through these plains. In fact, these five rivers gave the Punjab its name, which means the land of five rivers. Without the Indus and its tributaries, Pakistan would have been a desert. In 1960, Pakistan and India signed an agreement, one of the few solid and successful ones between the two countries, regarding the use of these rivers. Under the Waters Treaty, it was agreed that Pakistan would have exclusive use of the waters of Jhelum, Chenab, and Indus, and India would have exclusive use of the waters of Ravi, Sutlej, and Beas. The "land of five rivers" is almost as flat as a table, which has allowed its people to transform it into the most extensively irrigated area in the world. The southern part, or Lower Indus Plain, covers most of the Sindh Province. Near its mouth, the Indus branches out into a fan-shaped delta that rivals the Lena delta in Siberia and the Mississippi delta south of New Orleans. In fact, the Indus River delta is one of the world's largest, occupying an area of about 3,000 square miles.

In Pakistan, land is fertile not because of rain as in most of the world, but primarily because of an extensive irrigation system built during British rule and because of the hard work of the Pakistani people in building and maintaining over 85,000 canals and irrigation ditches. The fertile land produces major crops, including wheat, rice, cotton, sugarcane, tobacco, and other minor crops. However, in recent years, water has seeped through the soil of many irrigation canals in Sindh, raising the water table and creating the twin problems of waterlogging and salinity, making thousands of acres uncultivable monthly, not only in Sindh but also in Punjab. The Indus and its tributaries are also used extensively for the generation of hydroelectric power. The Tarbela Dam, located northwest of Rawalpindi, is the world's largest earth-filled dam, with a capacity to generate 3,478 megawatts of electricity.

Deserts. The major features of southeast Pakistan are the Thar Desert in Sindh and the Cholistan Desert in the south of Punjab. The Thar is Pakistan's largest desert region, extending over the border from India into southeastern Sindh and parts of eastern Punjab. Sandy dunes cover most of the region. Dust storms are common in the hot months. People use irrigation to farm land near the Indus River and draw water from underground wells. Very few people live here. The Cholistan Desert spreads across southeastern Punjab. Dry winds sweep across the desert, creating sand waves and sand dunes. Crop cultivation is very difficult here because the soil is very dry and sandy.

High Mountain Valleys. Mountain valleys lie high in the Karakoram and Hindu Kush ranges that border Pakistan's Northern Areas. Lying at high elevations ranging from 3,200 to 14,000 feet above sea level, these valleys are surrounded by soaring peaks, impressive glaciers, ice-blue lakes, gushing rivers, and beautiful waterfalls. These valleys are also home to tribes that are different from Pakistan's five main ethnic groups of Pathans, Sindhis, Baluchis, Punjabis, and Muhajirs. These tribes include the pagan Kalash, the Kohistanis, and the Hunzakut. Many of these valleys were tiny kingdoms at one time, and some still are a journey back into another era. Some were designated as princely states under British India, and to a limited extent under the Pakistan government until 1974. Because of their remoteness, few outsiders have seen these visually stunning valleys and the rich heritage of their people. Moving clockwise, some of the more important ones are the Hunza, Skardu, and Gilgit valleys in the Northern Areas; and the Kaghan, Swat, and Chitral valleys in the North-West Frontier Province.

Hunza Valley, at an elevation of 8,000 feet, lies in the Pakistan-controlled part of Kashmir near the border of China and Afghanistan, beyond which there are no further settlements of any size. Hunza remained a tiny, self-contained, isolated state ruled by a *mir* for hundreds of years, then became a princely state, and finally came under the full control of the Pakistan government after 1974. The grandeur of snow-capped mountains, the fragrance of poplar trees, the rarified invigorating air, the serene view of velvety green wheat fields, and the bright colors of beautiful orchards make the valley breathtakingly beautiful. It is no wonder that the British explorer Eric Shipton called the valley "the ultimate manifestation of mountain grandeur."

The people of Hunza, known as Hunzakuts, are known for their longevity and for a typical life span of ninety years. Hunza water, also called glacial milk, has the reputation of being a fountain of youth. Research has shown that it contains different minerals and a lower surface tension than most other kinds of drinking water, making it more easily absorbed into the body. The valley and its inhabitants are said to be the source of inspiration for the classic fable of Shangri-la, the land of eternal youth in the novel *The Lost Horizon,* by James Hilton. But at the onset of winter, Hunza presents a different sight. John Keay, author of *When Men and Mountains Meet,* described it as a revolting sight, less a valley or gorge than some gigantic quarry.

The *Gilgit Valley* lies at an elevation of about 4,800 feet. The world's second and ninth highest mountains, as well as a hundred peaks of over 18,000 feet, are within a 100-mile radius of Gilgit, which itself is dominated by the 25,550-foot Rakaposhi peak. The bridge over the fast-flowing Gilgit River is 600 feet long and only 7 feet wide. It is the largest suspension bridge in Asia. An aerial view of Niltar Valley near Gilgit shows a chain of small lakes and streams that look like emer-

Baltit Fort in the Hunza Valley. (Pakistan Mission to the UN)

ald and turquoise gems. Polo, described as "the king of games and the game of kings," was born here centuries ago, and the British learned to play it during their stay in the valley.

Skardu Valley, perched 8,000 feet above sea level, is one of the five valleys and the capital of Baltistan, which is known

Satpara Lake near Skardu Valley in Baltistan. (Pakistan Mission to the UN)

as Tibet-e-Khurd (Little Tibet). Baltistan gets this name because it resembles the Land of the Lamas, both because of its location at the "roof of the world" and the life-style of its people. It borders on the Chinese province of Sinkiang and Indian-occupied Kashmir. Baltistan is noted as much for its unusual cluster of mountain peaks and glaciers as for the quality of its fruits.

The *Kaghan Valley,* extending for about 100 miles, lies to the northeast of the Hazara district of the North-West Frontier Province. It varies in elevation from about 7,000 to 14,000 feet. It is known as an unspoiled paradise because its mountains, lakes, waterfalls, streams, and glaciers are still in a pristine state. It is blocked at the end by high mountains, but the Babusar Pass, at 13,700 feet, allows passage into the Chilas Valley. It gives a panoramic view of the valley and glimpses of the 26,660-foot-high Nanga Parbat, the ninth tallest mountain in the world and the second tallest in Pakistan. The most breathtaking view is of Lake Saiful Muluk, which is 10,500 feet high and is in the shadow of the 17,400-foot-high Malika Parbat (Queen of the Mountains). Local legend holds that the lake was a rendezvous for Prince Saiful Muluk of Persia and fairy princess Badar Jamal of Caucasus, and that a jealous *Jinn* guard of the Queen of Parbat tried to drown them, but they escaped.

Swat Valley was an autonomous princely state under a Pathan leader of the Yusufzai tribe, known as the *Wali* of Swat, until 1969. Entry to the valley is through the high Malakand Pass. Swat covers an area of 4,000 square miles at an average elevation of 3,200 feet. It is lush green due to abundant rainfall. The kaleidoscope of colors from trees, bushes, and fields; towering mountains cloaked in perennial snow; rushing rapids; fruit-tree orchards; and flower-slopes make it "the land of enthralling beauty." Several invaders, including Alexander the Great, Mahmud of Ghazni, and the early Mughals, won some of their major battles here before entering the Indus Plain. The Pathan poet Khushal Khan Khattak said that Swat was "meant to give kings gladness." The Buddhists who fled to Swat from the wrath of the Huns in the fifth and sixth centuries called it *Udayana* (the Garden) of the ancient Hindu epics. The famous Chinese pilgrim-chroniclers Fa-Hian and Hiuen Tsang in the sixth and seventh centuries described it as the valley of the hanging chains.

The Swat Valley was once the cradle of Buddhism with more than a thousand monasteries. The ruins of ancient forts and monasteries, and Buddhist stupas and statues are found all over Swat, including the 1,500-year-old seated Buddha carved into a cliff face above the town of Jehanabad. Here, Buddhism did not give way to Islam until the eleventh century, surviving far longer than it did elsewhere in Pakistan, partly because of the remoteness of Swat and the natural barrier of the Malakand. Swat was also the home of the famous

Ushu Valley in Swat. (Pakistan Mission to the UN)

Gandhara School of Sculpture, a combination of Greco-Roman and Buddhist art, which produced the famous statue of the "Fasting Buddha," now 2,000 years old. The Swat Museum contains one of the finest collections of Gandhara art in the world. Pathans inhabit the valley except in the northernmost part, beyond Bahrain, which is the home of the Kohistanis (people of the mountains), who have mixed racial origins and speak many different languages.

The *Chitral and Kalash valleys* of the Hindu Kush Mountains are located north of the Swat Valley in the Chitral district of the North-West Frontier Province and are bordered by Afghanistan on the north, south, and west. The Wakhan Corridor separates Chitral from Tajikistan. It has an elevation of 3,700 feet and a length of 200 miles. Chitral Valley is known for its magnificent scenic beauty. Set against the background of the 25,280-foot-high Trichmir peak, the highest of the Hindu Kush mountain ranges, the Chitral Valley is a dream come true for mountaineers, anglers, hunters, hikers, natu-

Kalash girls wearing ornate headdresses covered with cowry shells. (Julian Calder/Corbis)

ralists, and anthropologists. The Kalash Valley in Chitral is the home of the Kafir-Kalash, or "Wearers of the Black Robes," a primitive pagan tribe. The Kalash of Kafiristan, believed by some to have descended from the armies of Alexander the Great, were the inspiration for Rudyard Kipling's story "The Man Who Would Be King."

The valleys in the Northern Areas are no longer as remote due to the recent construction of the Karakoram Highway, which runs through the Northern Areas connecting Pakistan's capital, Islamabad, to Kashgar, in Sinking Province of China. The 800-mile, dual-carriage road is the highest tar road in the world and runs through some of the world's toughest terrain and across the 15,500-foot-high Khunjerab Pass on the border between China and Pakistan. The road twists and turns through icy mountain passes and high river gorges, cuts repeatedly through sheer rock, and runs along the edge of mountainsides that are almost vertical and hundreds of meters above the thundering waters below. The construction of the highway was a cooperative venture between China and Pakistan and was largely built by the Pakistan Army, in association with Chinese experts and technicians. It has been described as one of the greatest engineering feats in the world, a testimony to the courage and endurance of the people who built it, and even as the Eighth Wonder of the World. The location and the elevation make the air so thin that the slightest physical effort is exhausting, and it is a wonder that it was built at all. In fact, American engineering firms had said that it couldn't be done. It took fifteen years to complete the construction, and it is said that one life was lost for every kilometer of its length due to avalanches, falling boulders, and other accidents. Even now, landslides continue to block traffic daily. The highway is considered to be vital for the military security of Pakistan and as a link to China. It has also opened up the Northern Areas, improving trade and communications and bringing isolated villages closer.

Climate and Rainfall

Pakistan lies in the temperate zone. It has an array of climatic zones, ranging from the Arctic-like conditions on the perennially snow-clad mountains to arid and hot in deserts, and humid in coastal areas. On the whole, the climate is generally dry, with hot summers and cool winters. The annual average rainfall is about 10 inches. But there are wide variations from year to year and between different regions. For example, the southwestern desert area gets fewer than five inches of rain annually (less than the average rainfall of Arizona), while eastern Punjab gets more than twenty inches annually (about that of western Kansas), and the southern valleys of the Himalayas receive about 70 inches of rain annually, the most in Pakistan.

Pakistan's climate is also characterized by wide variations in temperature. Average temperatures vary from one part of the country to another. The mountain regions in the north and northwest have the coolest weather, with an average temperature of 75 degrees Fahrenheit in the summer and often below freezing in the winter. On the Balochistan Plateau, temperatures are hot during the summer and cool during the winter. The average temperature is about 80 degrees Fahrenheit in the summer and less than 40 degrees Fahrenheit in the winter. On the Indus Plain, temperatures range from a high of 90 to 120 degrees Fahrenheit in the summer to a low of 55 degrees Fahrenheit in the winter. In the deserts, temperatures in the hottest months of May and June can reach 122 degrees Fahrenheit, and the coolest temperature averages 41 degrees Fahrenheit in January. Dust storms are common in the summer and frost in the winter. The southern coastal region has mild, humid weather most of the year, ranging from 66 to 86 degrees Fahrenheit in the winter.

Pakistan has three seasons: a cool, dry winter from November through February; a hot summer season from March through June; and a rainy monsoon season from July through September. Monsoons sweep through all of Southern Asia, and the Indus River has its worst floods then. October marks the "retreating" monsoon period when the monsoons are over and temperatures gradually begin to cool. The onset and duration of these seasons vary somewhat according to location and from year to year.

Population

One out of about every forty people in the world is a Pakistani. The population of Pakistan was estimated to be about 159 million in 2004, making it the sixth most populous country in the world, after China, India, the United States, Indonesia, and Brazil. One of its cities, Karachi, with a population of slightly over 10 million, is the fifth most populous city in the world, after Shanghai, Mumbai (Bombay), Buenos Aires, and Moscow.

Distribution, Density, and Growth. The most populated province of Pakistan is Punjab. Among the four
provinces, about 56 percent of people live in Punjab, 23 percent in Sindh, 16 percent in the North-West Frontier
Province, and 5 percent in Balochistan. Most of Pakistan's
population live in rural areas. The proportion of urban population in the total is 33 percent for all provinces taken
together, but there are wide variations, ranging from 17 percent in the North-West Frontier Province to 49 percent in
Sindh. The more urban distribution of Sindh is partly due to
the effect of Karachi, which accounts for about 30 percent of
total Sindh population and about 7 percent of the total population of Pakistan.

Pakistan has about 2.5 percent of the world's population
living on about 0.5 percent of the world's land. It ranks sixth
in the world in terms of population, but thirty-seventh in
terms of area. It has more than half the population of the
United States (54 percent) but only about 8 percent of the
U.S. area. This means that many more people are living per
square mile in Pakistan than in the United States or the world
as a whole. According to the 1998 population census, the
most recent in Pakistan, the population density is about 530
persons per square mile, but there are wide variations among
different regions. Thus the density varies from 60 persons per
square mile in the scarcely populated areas of Balochistan to
1,140 persons per square mile in Punjab (Population Census
Organization 1998).

Pakistan adds about 3.6 million people to its population
every year, which is roughly equal to the entire population
of Costa Rica or New Zealand or Singapore. This means that
the population of Pakistan is growing at an annual rate of
about 2.4 percent per year, higher than the average for
South Asian countries of 1.7 percent, as well as higher than
the average for low-income countries of 1.9 percent. In the
past twenty-five years, the population of Pakistan has
almost doubled, and it is expected that by 2015, the total

will be 204 million; by 2025, 251 million; and by 2050, 344 million.

Historically, Pakistan's population growth rate has been one of the highest in the world, at around 3.1 percent per annum. It consistently increased from 1.79 percent in 1951 to 3.1 percent in 1981, as indicated by the decennial censuses. The government postponed the 1991 census, however, out of fear of ethnic unrest and violent reactions by ethnic groups and minorities who believed that their groups were undercounted (Blood 1995). These groups particularly included the Muhajirs (immigrants from India and their descendants) and religious minorities. The next census, taken in 1998, showed the average annual growth rate between 1981 and 1998 to be 2.69 percent. The average annual growth rate between 1990 and 2003 was estimated to be 2.4 percent per year. The growth rate in 2004 was estimated to be 1.98 percent per year.

The natural growth of population is the difference between the crude birth rate (number of births per thousand persons) and the crude death rate (number of deaths per thousand persons). Unlike most European countries, which experienced declines in mortality prior to fertility declines, demographic transition in most Asian countries has been characterized by mortality and fertility declines in close succession. As Table 1.1 shows, the Crude Birth Rate (CBR) at 33 per thousand is higher in Pakistan compared to the average of other low-income countries at 29 and the average for South Asia at 26. However, the Crude Death Rate (CDR) at 8 per thousand is lower in Pakistan, compared to the South Asian average at 9 and the low-income countries' average at 11. One reason for the higher population growth rates in Pakistan than elsewhere is that death rates have fallen faster in Pakistan than elsewhere. The other reason is that fertility rates, defined as the number of births per 1,000 women in the 15–49 year age group, are very high in Pakistan. In fact, the fertility rate is higher in Pakistan than the average fertility rate both for other low-income countries and for South Asia. Pakistan's fertility rate at 4.5 is also higher than that of other Muslim countries such as Indonesia (2.4) and Iran (2.9) (Population Census Organization 1998).

Pakistan was among the top ten contributors to world population growth during 1995–2000, and its performance on overall population growth rate is worse than other South Asian countries, including India and Bangladesh. Between 1980 and 2002, the annual growth rate decreased from 2.9 to 2.4 percent in Pakistan, compared to a decrease from 2.5 to 1.7 percent in Bangladesh in the same period. This is largely due to the impact of micro-finance institutions (MFIs), which provide credit to the poor without collateral, on women's empowerment. These MFIs include the Grameen Bank and nongovernmental organizations (NGOs) such as the Bangladesh Rural Advancement Committee (BRAC) in Bangladesh. Moreover, the growth rate is lower in the rural areas both because of outmigration (to urban areas in the country and overseas) and a lower natural rate of increase due to higher death rate associated with limited access to and availability of healthcare facilities.

Age-Sex Composition and Dependency Ratio.   Pakistan has a very youthful population age-structure: children under the age of fifteen constitute about 42 percent of the total population compared to about 19 percent in high-income countries. This means that the working-age population in Pakistan has to support more than twice as many people as in developed countries. The dependency burden (the ratio of children under fifteen years of age and persons over sixty-five to all persons between the ages of fifteen and sixty-five years) at 88 percent is very high in Pakistan. The high dependency burden also creates a hidden momentum of population growth because of the large number of youths of reproductive or childbearing age. This momentum persisted for several years in Pakistan, leading to population growth even after birth rates went down considerably.

Table 1.1   Trends in Population Statistics: Crude Birth Rate (CBR), Crude Death Rate (CDR), Fertility Rate, and Population Growth Rate

	CBR 2002	CDR 2002	FR 2002	Population Growth Rate 2002	Change in Growth Rate 1980–2002
Pakistan	33	8	4.5	2.4	−0.5
Bangladesh	28	8	3	1.7	−0.8
India	24	9	2.9	1.6	−0.7
South Asia	26	9	3.2	1.7	−0.6
Low-Income Countries	29	11	3.7	1.9	−0.6
Middle-Income Countries	18	7	2.25	0.95	−0.8
High-Income Countries	12	9	1.7	0.6	−0.2
United States	1	1.1	1.3	1.1	0.1

Source: The World Bank. 2004. *World Development Report, 2004.* http://devdata. worldbank.org/hnpstats/thematicRpt.asp.

Females constitute 48 percent of Pakistan's population. The gender-specific distribution of population is also shown by the sex ratio, that is, the number of males per 100 females. A ratio of 1 shows an equal number of males and females and is considered balanced, whereas a ratio greater than 1 shows that there are more men than women, and a ratio less than 1 shows that there are more women than men. The sex ratio in most countries of the world is less than 1 since typically women outlive men. But South Asia has one of the most distorted sex ratios in the world—1.06 (106 men for every 100 women), as compared to a global ratio of 0.94 (94 men for every 100 women). The sex ratio is more than 1 in every single region of Pakistan, varying from a high of 1.15 in Balochistan to a low of 1.05 in the North-West Frontier Province, where it is lower only because of massive male migration to other provinces. The sex ratio is typically higher for urban than for rural areas because of the internal migration of men from rural to urban areas. The sex ratio is distorted in Pakistan because of high mortality rates among female children under the age of five and among women of childbearing age. Many countries in South Asia, including Pakistan, are among the very few countries in the world where life expectancy at birth of females is less than that of males, which is a reversal of the global biological norm. The distorted sex ratio and higher female mortality rate are generally ascribed to the lower status of women, particularly their more limited access to food, nutrition, and health care.

Religious-Ethnic Composition. An overwhelming majority of 97 percent of Pakistanis are Muslims (77 percent being *Sunnis* and about 20 percent *Shiites*), and Hindus and Christians are about 1.6 percent each. The highest percentage of Christians is in urban Punjab (3.3 percent), and the highest percentage of Hindus reside in rural Sindh (9.8 percent). The distribution of population by ethnicity is based on language (mother tongue). Punjabi is spoken by the largest single majority of people (48 percent), followed by Sindhi (12 percent), Pushto (10 percent), Saraiki (10 percent), Urdu (officially 8 percent), Baluchi (3 percent), Hindko (2 percent), and other less frequently spoken languages in that order. Urdu is the national language and the mother tongue of 20 percent of the population in urban areas and of 41 percent in urban Sindh. Most Pakistanis speak Urdu and one other regional language.

Population Planning. It is imperative that Pakistan's population growth rate be reduced. Higher fertility rates are typically associated with lower literacy and labor force participation rates for women, and with higher infant mortality rates. A high population growth rate is also a drain on education and health services, on amenities such as water supply and electricity, and on the overall infrastructure of the economy. However, population control remains an elusive goal in Pakistan. According to Sathar, Pakistan has not experienced "any notable declines in fertility despite an official population planning program and substantial development accompanied by significant declines in overall mortality" (Sathar 1992,

699). One reason for the failure is that every governmental effort to launch a family planning program has met with strong resistance from religious leaders and has never been effectively publicized. Neither has there been a political will to implement the program. However, other Muslim countries such as Iran and Bangladesh have been more successful in their family planning initiatives, Iran through seeking support of clergy for the program and Bangladesh through the initiative taken by NGOs and the Grameen Bank. It has been suggested that, instead of a narrow family planning focus, a successful population policy must emphasize education and advocacy to overcome the social, religious, cultural, and other demand-side constraints to family planning programs.

Internal and Foreign Migration. In addition to internal migration, both interprovince and intraprovince, Pakistan is a receiving country for migrants, particularly from Bangladesh and Afghanistan, and a sending country to the Middle East and to Europe and North America. According to the most recent census of population in 1998, the total migrant population in Pakistan is about 10.8 million. About 5.7 million are intraprovince migrants who have moved within the same province to a different district, mostly from a rural to an urban area, often in search of better economic prospects. The number of interprovince migrants who move from one to the other province is 2.9 million, most of them also migrating for economic reasons, being "pushed" by lack of income-earning opportunities in their original location and "pulled" by the prospect of such opportunities in the new location. Examples include the Pathans, many of whom have migrated from the North-West Frontier Province to Karachi in the Sindh Province where they dominate the transport sector. An important "push factor" in rural Punjab and Sindh has been the eviction of tenants due to the decision for self-cultivation by landlords, which happened in the wake of higher incomes made possible by the green revolution technologies and mechanization of agriculture. The migrants from other countries total about 2.2 million, most of them being Afghan refugees.

Afghan Refugees. Refugees from Afghanistan started pouring into Pakistan after the invasion of Afghanistan by the Soviet Union in December 1979. Over the next ten years, as anti-Soviet *Mujahideen* (Muslim guerrilla fighters) fought with Soviet forces, about 3.9 million Afghan refugees settled in Pakistan, putting pressure on its meager resources. In 1990, according to the United Nations High Commission for Refugees (UNHCR), there were 345 Afghan refugee villages with 10,000 people in each village. About 68 percent of the villages were located in the North-West Frontier Province, including the Tribal Areas, and most of the rest in Balochistan. After the end of Soviet military intervention in Afghanistan and the Mujahideen victory in 1992, the refugees were encouraged to return home, and the number of refugees fell to 1.4 million by 1994, according to estimates by Amnesty International. But since then, wave upon wave of refugees has fled Afghanistan. The second wave came as a result of factional fighting following the Mujahideen victory and the *pre-Taliban*-era abuses, combined with severe droughts. The third exodus occurred in response to the fighting that took place as the Taliban rose to power and due to the human rights violations by the Taliban. The fourth and most recent wave of Afghan refugees came to Pakistan to escape the air strikes and bombing by U.S. military forces against the al-Qaeda camps, and the related conflict involving Taliban and Northern Alliance forces. It was reported that around 2,000 Afghans were escaping into Pakistan every day at that time. Several thousand continue to flee or attempt to flee Afghanistan.

Current estimates indicate that over 2.5 million Afghan refugees are living in Pakistan. Although the Pakistan government officially closed its border with Afghanistan in November 2000 to stop new flows of refugees, it has granted entry to the most vulnerable. Refugees, who have entered unofficially, partly because of the porous border, have also been allowed to remain inside Pakistan. According to a Human Rights Watch Report (2002, 3), Pakistan's policies on Afghan refugees have been very generous even after the "closed door" period; about 160,000 new Afghan refugees were received from October to December 2001.

The Afghanistan refugee emergency is one of the world's largest and most prolonged. After the withdrawal of U.S. support following the Soviet retreat from Afghanistan and the Mujahideen victory, Pakistan was left with a huge burden. Several international agencies, including UNHCR, the World Food Program, and local and international NGOs, stepped in to help, but the task was massive. Pakistan has continued to shoulder this massive burden over the years despite minimal international interest, financial support, and burden sharing. But the country's generosity has taken its toll, both in economic and social terms. It has imposed a big burden on the Pakistan economy and on its environment. It has also led to conflict between the locals (Pakistanis) and the refugees as they compete for scarce jobs and resources.

Worse still, it has led to a proliferation of weapons, creating a *Kalashnikov* or weapons culture. This happened because some of the arms, channeled to the Afghan Mujahideen by the United States (through the Pakistan government) to help them in their fight against communism, were sold to the local and refugee population in Pakistan. As a result, the crime rate has increased manifold since then, and kidnappings for ransom, armed robberies, looting, and gun battles between rival groups have increased dramatically. This, in turn, has fanned all types of violence—religious, ethnic, and political—and has created a subculture of intolerance and extremism. The Afghan influx also led to a proliferation of drugs and has increased drug use dramatically among Pakistanis. The perception among many Pakistanis is that the country has paid a heavy price for its hospitality to Afghans and for its support of the United States first in the Cold War and now in the war on terrorism in terms of the worsening law-and-order situation in its major cities, rising extremism, and increasing unemployment and inflation.

Migration to the Middle East. The migration of both skilled labor and professionals out of Pakistan has been primarily to the Middle East. It started in the early 1970s, following the construction boom in the Middle East, and reached its peak in the mid-1980s. Around that time, more than 2 million Pakistanis had migrated to the Persian Gulf states, remitting $3 billion every year. The remittances declined to about $1.3 billion by 1989–1990. According to Malik (1994, 57–58), the remittances from the Middle East, at their peak in 1983–1984, "accounted for 86 percent of all remittances, 40 percent of all foreign exchange earnings, and financed 86 percent of the trade deficit." It is estimated that during the peak period, 9.3 percent of all rural and 15.9 percent of all urban households in Pakistan had at least one migrant member (Malik 1994, 57). Similarly, one-half of all working-class families had one close relative working in the Gulf. About 70 percent of these migrants were from Punjab, particularly from the cities of Gujranwala, Jhelum, and Sialkot. The typical worker was a married, working-class man who left his family behind with the extended family. He lived for five to ten years alone, in harsh conditions, often with several other men in a room, so that he could save for his family. Families used the savings accumulated with great sacrifice for consumption goods, particularly TVs. It has been estimated that migrants spent 60 percent of their income on consumption goods, partly because of previous deprivation and the demonstration effect of other migrants doing the same.

The major impact of migration to the Gulf has been that remittances have affected the living of the urban poor, changed their life-styles, and led to an improvement in income distribution. Also, employment was generated locally as a result of increased demand not only for consumer goods but also for services such as travel agencies, hotels, recruiting agencies, health clinics, and secretarial services. Small industries like plastics and toys also expanded, leading to growth of informal-sector employment. Moreover, women became effective household heads and were involved in managing and making decisions, which enhanced their economic and social status. At the same time, migration to the Middle East created a shortage of skilled labor. Moreover, psychologists identified a sort of disorientation, a syndrome, among the male migrants, referred to as *Dubai Chalo* (let's go to Dubai). It happened because of social isolation, culture shock, harsh working conditions, and the sudden acquisition of relative wealth (Blood 1995). The men felt that families did not appreciate their sacrifices and sometimes wanted them to go back to the Middle East help maintain the wealth and life style that their families had gotten used to even when the men wanted to return home.

A large number of Pakistanis also work in Western Europe and North America, either legally or illegally. They work as professionals, clerical workers, small-business owners, and service workers such as taxi drivers. In fact, a recent study reported in the *New York Times* (2004, July 7) indicates that Pakistanis, together with Bangladeshis, constitute the largest single majority of yellow cab drivers in New York City (14 percent each out of a total of 41,624). The push factors for migrants to North America and Western Europe are linked to the current socioeconomic situation in Pakistan: the lack of earning opportunities in the urban areas, uneployment of the educated, deteriorating law and order, and ethnic tensions and violence. The pull factors include the hope of a more prosperous life, the lure of the American dream and stories about its reality narrated by relatives and friends, escape from violence and persecution, and the possibility of eventually enabling the migration of the entire extended family.

Growth of Major Cities and Urbanization. The majority of migrants, from the same province, another province, or other countries, tend to flock into urban areas. While only 33.5 percent of the overall population live in urban areas, as much as 64 percent of the migrants inhabit these areas. It is

Tongas and scooters against the background of Balahisar Fort in Peshawar, a frontier town and the capital city of North-West Frontier Province. (Pakistan Mission to the UN)

no surprise that population growth rates in Pakistani cities have been explosive. Pakistan's cities are expanding much faster than the overall population, as a result of both natural increase and migration. An analysis of the intercensus (1981–1998) average annual growth rates for twenty-three major cities shows that fourteen have grown at a rate of more than 3 percent, five at a rate of more than 4 percent, and only two at a rate of less than 2 percent. Islamabad, the capital of Pakistan and the site of a large number of Afghan refugee camps, experienced a growth of 5.8 percent per year during that period. In absolute numbers, at least seven cities have populations in excess of one million, and the two largest cities, Karachi and Lahore, have populations of over ten and over five million, respectively. Karachi is the fifth and Lahore the twenty-fourth most populous city in the world.

The major cities of Pakistan are Karachi, Lahore, Faisalabad, Rawalpindi, Multan, Peshawar, and Quetta. Located on the Arabian Sea, Karachi is the largest of all and the only port. It is now the capital of Sindh and was the country's capital from 1947 to 1959. Lahore, the capital of Punjab, is the nation's center of culture and learning. Faisalabad is famous for its textile industry. Islamabad is the nation's capital, and Rawalpindi is its twin city. Multan is famous for its old forts and mosques. Peshawar lies at the foot of the historic Khyber Pass. Quetta is the capital of Balochistan.

This increasing urbanization has not been preceded or accompanied by increasing industrialization and economic development, as was the case with the growth patterns of Western Europe, Japan, and North America when they were developing. The increase in the supply of labor due to natural increase in population plus migration has thus outstripped the demand for labor, leading to high levels of open unemployment and underemployment, even for the educated. Most of the migrants and the locals, who are at the lower level of income and education, are thus absorbed by the "informal sector," consisting of petty retail trade and services, and characterized by small firms and labor-intensive methods. Moreover, cities are facing mounting problems in providing basic needs and services, including safe drinking water, sewage and sanitation, electricity, essential health services, and education. They are facing even tougher problems in curbing crime, illegal arms, ethnic and religious violence, and increasing illegal drug use. At the same time, urban slums and squatter settlements are on the increase, where the poor live with minimal sanitary facilities, water supply, and electricity.

HISTORY

Pakistan is a relatively young nation, created as a Muslim homeland in 1947, when it became an independent country in British India. But one of the world's earliest urban centers was here 6,000 years ago, and cultures flourished even earlier. This long history can be divided into the following periods.

Prehistoric Cultures

The area of Pakistan was home to some of the oldest civilizations on earth. This region has been occupied since prehistoric times, dating back to the Stone Age (500,000 to 100,000 years ago). Relics of the earliest Stone-Age man include tools found in the Siwalik Hills near Rawalpindi in northern Punjab that may be 500,000 years old. Paintings on rocks in the Rohri Hills in northern Sindh are considered to be at least 25,000 years old. The Mehrgarh culture of the Balochistan Plateau developed around 7000 to 2000 BCE and is considered the precursor of the Indus Valley civilization. Its people built mud-brick homes and worked as farmers cultivating wheat and barley or as herders raising cattle.

Indus Valley Civilization

The region that is now Pakistan was one of the three early "cradles of civilization." For centuries, it was believed that there were only two such civilizations, one in ancient Egypt along the Nile River and the other in Mesopotamia (present-day Iraq) centered between the Tigris and Euphrates rivers. Archaeological evidence discovered in the 1920s showed that a third major "cradle of civilization" existed along the Indus River between 4,500 and 6,000 years ago, around 2500 BCE, that flourished for about a thousand years. This Indus Valley or "Harappan" civilization stretched from the Himalayan foothills almost to the Arabian Sea, enclosing an area of at least 1,600 kilometers from north to south. It included two large cities, Mohenjodaro in Sindh and Harappa in Punjab, about half a dozen small cities, and more than 100 villages. The population in the cities was about 25,000 to 30,000. Ruins of the two major cities show that both were well

Discovered in 1922, Mohenjodaro (Mound of Dead), forming part of the Indus Valley civilization, was one of the earliest and most developed urban civilizations of the ancient world. (Corel Corporation)

planned, with 30-foot-wide streets laid out at right angles, extensive water supply and drainage systems, sewage facilities, canals for irrigation, public baths, centralized granaries, meeting halls, and many two-storied shops and houses. The residential areas were separate, and houses were made of standardized burnt bricks with flat roofs. Larger homes even had bathrooms with indoor plumbing and drainpipes, a sewage system unparalleled until the nineteenth century.

The Harappans developed an advanced way of life with a diversified social and economic system, a written language, centralized administration, a highly organized government system, extensive commerce, and trade with ancient Egypt and Sumer in southern Mesopotamia. They were the first on earth to grow, spin, weave, and dye cotton. Copper, tin, and bronze were used to make knives, axes, and utensils. Merchants used a standard system of weights and measures. Seals were engraved with pictographic inscriptions showing animals and trade goods. Archaeologists have identified about 400 of these pictographic characters. This Indus script is believed to be the earliest form of writing, but it has not been deciphered yet despite the use of modern technology and the efforts of world-renowned philologists. Archaeologists agree about the unusual cultural uniformity of the Indus Valley civilization. There appears to be no variation in terms of either time or geography in the layout of the streets, the size and style of bricks, the designs on the pottery, and the pictographs on the seals. For example, no seal or pottery has been found with more than seventeen pictographs together.

The Indus Valley civilization declined after about 2000 BCE and was virtually extinct by about 1700 BCE, but historians disagree on the possible causes for its end. Around this time, a nomadic group from Central Asia called the Aryans invaded the subcontinent. Many historians subscribe to the Aryan invasion theory that these conquerors "destroyed" the Indus Valley civilization. But archaeologists have also found signs of recurrent floods, economic hardship, crop failures, and overcrowding of cities. Some historians believe that such major floods and other natural disasters forced people to leave the area. Another theory is that the Indus River changed its course repeatedly, significantly causing the Harappan cities to decline owing to lack of water, desertification, and soil salinity.

Invasions and Empires

Invasions are a recurring theme in the history of the region that is now Pakistan. The route taken by all invaders and conquerors except Muhammad bin Qasim has been through the Khyber Pass. The Aryan invaders from Central Asia entered Punjab through the Khyber Pass between about 2000 and 1500 BCE, and settled in what are now Iran, Pakistan, Afghanistan, and North India. The language of the Aryans, the root of all Indo-European languages, was an early form of Sanskrit, and the Aryans' Vedic or "Brahmanic" religion was the ancestor of Hinduism. Their records were preserved in their hymns, the "Vedas," which come from an oral tradition that developed during the thousand years of Aryan rule in the subcontinent. The rigid four-tiered caste system of Hinduism also developed during that period, dividing people into Brahmans (priests), Kshatriyas (warriors), Vaishyas (merchants), and Sudhras (menial workers). A fifth category, outside the mainstream society, was Panchamas (outcasts or "Untouchables" or scheduled castes or scheduled tribes). It is believed that the Aryans belonged to the three upper classes and that the indigenous people made up the bottom two. Present-day India has retained many of these social ranks, but there is no caste system in Pakistan. Both the Aryan heritage and the Aryan invasion issues have important political ramifications.

The great religious teacher Siddhartha Gautama, later known as the Buddha, or Enlightened One (ca. 563–483 BCE), founded Buddhism during the sixth century BCE, and at the same time, Mahavira founded Jainism. Partly because it was a protest against the unjust caste system, the Buddhist religion took root in India and spread rapidly to what are now Pakistan, Tibet, Burma (now called Myanmar), and China. At about the same time, the Gandhara kingdom emerged in northern Pakistan near Peshawar. The Persians from present-day Iran and Afghanistan conquered Punjab in 500 BCE under Cyrus the Great, making it part of the huge Achaemenid Empire. The Gandhara kingdom came under Persian influence.

From 500 BCE to 700 CE, the Greeks, the Mauryans, the Kushans, the Huns, and the Guptas gained and lost power in the region that is now Pakistan. In 326 BCE, Alexander the Great of Macedonia led his army of 25,000 soldiers from Afghanistan into the Punjab through the Khyber Pass. He fought a fierce battle with King Porus, the Gandharan ruler of Taxila, and defeated him, adding Punjab to his conquests of

Greece, Egypt, and Mesopotamia before he had reached the age of thirty. He stayed in the region for only one and a half years because his homesick troops were weary of a decade of military campaigns and protested to return home. The return march through Sindh and the Gedrosian Desert of Balochistan, one of the most inhospitable places on earth, ended with Alexander's death in Babylon, Mesopotamia, in 323 BCE. The Greek influence in Pakistan was minimal except for the Indo-Greek school of art, which spread as far as Central Asia.

Within thirty years of Alexander's departure, Chandragupta Maurya (ca. 321–297 BCE) conquered the region of Gandhara and founded the Mauryan Empire, which lasted from 321 to 185 BCE. His grandson, Ashoka (r. ca. 274–236 BCE), the most renowned of the Mauryan kings, converted to Buddhism and decided to wage no more wars. Gandhara, particularly Taxila and Peshawar, became the leading center of Buddhist art and learning. Ashoka had edicts and Buddhist beliefs carved on stone pillars in many important cities. The Mauryan dynasty weakened after Ashoka and began to break up after 230 BCE.

During the next several centuries, invaders, mostly from Central Asia, came through the Khyber Pass and established their dynasties. These included the Scythians from southern Russia (known as Sakas in the subcontinent), who came from Afghanistan into Balochistan and Sindh in 100 BCE and ruled for 200 years, replaced by the Parthians (Pahlavas), who were in turn displaced by the Kushans of Central Asia. The Kushan dynasty arose in the first century CE (50–mid-200s CE) and spread from Afghanistan through Pakistan into north India. Gandhara became the center for the Silk Route trade between China and India to the east and Arabia and the Roman Empire to the west, and Peshawar, the Kushan capital, became a major commercial center. The Kushan Empire was overrun by the Huns in the north and taken over by the Guptas in the east and the Sassanians of Persia in the west. Around 320 CE, the Gupta dynasty established its rule over the region, uniting all of North India under Hindu rule from 320 to 500 CE. The period is known as the classical age of Hindu civilization. Around 500 CE, fierce Huns from western Siberia overthrew the Guptas and conquered the empire and destroyed the Greek-Buddhist city of Taxila. However, there are signs of the blending of Greek, Central Asian, and Indian cultures in the ruins of Taxila City, as well as in the current culture and life of the inhabitants of Kalash and Gilgit, Pakistan's high mountain valleys in the north. For the next 200 years, India was politically fragmented and divided into small Hindu kingdoms.

The Arrival of Islam in India

While no conqueror between 500 BCE and 700 CE had a lasting impact on modern-day Pakistan, the invasion by the seventeen-year-old Arab general Muhammad bin Qasim, about 1,000 years after the death of Alexander the Great, was just the opposite: it shaped the subsequent history of Pakistan significantly. Muhammad bin Qasim led an expedition sent by the Umayyad caliph of Baghdad in 711 CE to take the message of Islam to the region. Unlike most invaders who had entered Pakistan through the Khyber Pass, he sailed across the Arabian Sea and marched across the Balochistan coast and into Sindh with an army of 12,000 men and 6,000 horses. His method of warfare was new for the region. Throwing arrows of burning cotton and heavy, far-reaching stone missiles from large, carriage-drawn catapults, he defeated the larger army of Raja Dahir and conquered Sindh. He added Sindh to the vast Arab Empire that stretched westward all the way to Spain, and included Persia and most of North Africa. Once he had effective control over the whole of Sindh and a part of Punjab, he did not expand any further but diverted his attention to administering the conquered territories in the true spirit of Islam—with tolerance and conciliation. He followed the Islamic creed that there should be no coercion in religion and that all men and women are equal in the eyes of God. He came to Sindh with a sword in his hand but won converts through personal example and spiritual persuasion. It is no surprise that during the 300 years when Sindh was the only part of India under Muslim rule, thousands of Buddhists and Hindus converted to Islam. They formed a new language, *Sindhi,* by combining Arabic words with their native words, and introduced the Arabs to the use of zero and decimals, the Arabic numerals, and advances in medicine.

Full-scale Muslim invasions by Turks, Persians, and Afghans came later, beginning in the tenth century and continuing until the sixteenth, through the Khyber Pass. In 997, an Afghan warrior named Mahmud of Ghazni (979–1030) made the first of his seventeen invasions of Pakistan and northern India across the Khyber Pass. Known to many Muslim scholars as a Defender of the Faith but to many others as a plunderer, he established the easternmost part of his large but short-lived empire in Punjab in 1021, with Lahore as its capital. All the territory of what is now Pakistan was under Muslim rule, and it would remain so for the next 800 years. A new language, Urdu, emerged in the army camps of Mahmud Ghazni, which combined words of Persian, Arabic, Turkish, and Sanskrit, and which later became the national language of Pakistan. After a 150-year respite from invasions after Mahmud's death in 1030, Muhammad Ghauri led his army through the Khyber Pass in 1179. Using iron stirrups, which enabled his men to fire crossbows in the midst of a gallop, he conquered Ghazni, Multan, Sindh, Lahore, and Delhi in succession, and all of northern India by 1203. This established the first Turkish rule from Delhi.

The Delhi Sultanate

Before Muhammad Ghauri died in 1206, he put his black slave-lieutenant, Qutb-ud-din Aibak, in charge of consolidating North India, actually implementing the Muslim creed

of equality regardless of race. A few years later, Aibak established a new Muslim kingdom, the Sultanate of Delhi. It
included all of what is now Pakistan and northern India, and
it was ruled for more than 300 years by thirty-five Turko-
Afghan Sultans (rulers). The first was the Slave or Mamluk
dynasty (1211–1290), first ruled by Aibak, then by his slave-
lieutenant (also son-in-law), Iltumush, who was generally
recognized as a very wise leader. Iltumush nominated his
brilliant and dynamic daughter Razia Sultana (r. 1236–
1239) as his successor over his sons. She remains the first
and only woman to ascend the throne of Delhi, the first
female Muslim ruler of South Asia, and among the few in the
world to have ruled such a vast empire. She was a talented,
wise, just, and generous ruler. She was also a great administrator who established law and order in her country in a
short time. She was not only a good leader in the battlefield
but also an excellent fighter herself. She wore no veil and
used to dress like a man when appearing in public, be it in
court or on the battlefield. By 1250, much of Bengal and
central India were under Muslim rule. Faced with internal
conflicts, the Slave dynasty ended in 1290. It is believed that
the greatest contribution of the dynasty was its ability to
militarily defend the subcontinent against potential Mongol
invasion like the one in the Middle East in the 1250s when
Hulagu (Halaku) invaded and massacred entire cities including Baghdad. It was the refugee scholars, poets, and craftsmen who poured from all over the Islamic world into India
that transformed the cities of Delhi and Lahore overnight
into centers of art and culture. The resulting Indo-Muslim
fusion left behind lasting monuments in architecture, music,
and literature.

The Mamluks were followed by the Khiljis (1290–1320),
the Tughlaqs (1320–1413), the Sayyids (1414–1451), and
the Lodhis (1451–1526), in that order. The territory under
the control of Muslim rulers of Delhi expanded rapidly under
Khilji and particularly Tughlaq rule. There were only a

handful of kingdoms independent of Delhi. By 1351, the Tughlaqs had extended Muslim rule to all of South India except one Hindu kingdom in Vijaynagar, which eventually fell in 1565. The Sultanate suffered from the sacking of Delhi in 1398 by Amir Timur (Tamerlane) but revived briefly under the Lodhis before it was conquered by the Mughals, who consolidated Muslim rule over most of India and ushered in an era of political calm and cultural achievement that lasted three centuries.

It was also during the reign of the Delhi Sultanate that the feudal or *jagirdari* system took hold in India. Because the sultans ruled from urban centers, they controlled the rural areas through generals who were given land grants or *jagirs* in return for providing a specified number of soldiers to the sultan when needed. The generals collected a land tax on the sultan's lands, equivalent to about one-fourth of the crop. This *jagirdari* system, substituted by the *mansabdari* system during most of the Mughal period, was revived by the British and vestiges of it remains a problem to the present day in the subcontinent. Peasants, tenants, and small farmers remain under the powerful control of landlords or *jagirdars* and are often denied the free exercise of their right to vote even in democratic elections. The system has also been an impediment to economic and social development.

The Delhi Sultanate was a Muslim state, but it was not a theocracy. The sultans based their laws on the Quran and the *Sharia* and allowed freedom of religion but imposed a tax, the *jizya,* on non-Muslims. *Jizya* was paid by non-Muslims who chose not to join in defending the Sultanate, whereas the Muslims were required to pay *zakat* instead of *jizya*. The period was marked by better relations between Hindus and Muslims, more authority to regional rulers, and equality between races. It was also during the last few decades of the Delhi Sultanate that Guru Nanak, a man of peace, founded the Sikh religion, blending aspects of Hinduism and Islam.

The Mughal Period

Muslim rule was consolidated over most of India by the Mughals whose dynasty lasted for three centuries. The six great Mughals are Babur (1483–1530, r. 1526–1530), Humayun (1508–1556, r. 1530–1540, 1555–1556), Akbar (1542–1605, r. 1556–1605), Jahangir (1569–1627, r. 1605–1627), Shah Jahan (1592–1666, r. 1628–1658), and Aurangzeb (1618–1707, r. 1658–1707). Their rule is considered the golden age of Muslims in the subcontinent. The vastness of their conquests, their military prowess and administrative genius, the grandeur of their architecture, and their patronage of culture and the arts are a source of great pride for Pakistanis who look up to them as their glorious past.

Babur. Babur, who became king of Ferghana (in present-day Uzbekistan, north of Afghanistan) at the age of eleven but lost his kingdom soon afterward, seized the opportunity presented by the internal quarrels of the Delhi Sultanate in the 1520s. After conquering Kabul in 1504, he led his armies through the Khyber Pass, conquering Punjab in 1526 by defeating Sultan Ibrahim Lodhi at Panipat, north of Delhi. Although Ibrahim had an army four times as large as Babur's, with an estimated 100,000 men and 1,000 fighting elephants, a fifth of the army was killed in just one day, as was he, because the elephants panicked at the unfamiliar sound of cannon fire. Babur declared himself emperor a few days later and seized the enormous diamond, *Koh-e-Nur* (Mountain of Light), which he calculated could buy enough grain to feed the entire world for three days. He established the vast Mughal Empire by 1529, which stretched from Afghanistan to Bengal.

Claiming descent from fierce Mongol conquerors like Genghis Khan on his mother's side and Timur on his father's, Babur combined military strength, indomitable courage, and statesmanship with humility and love of beauty. He was a poet, a calligrapher, a connoisseur and composer of music, and a creator of gardens. He was one of the few kings in world history to write an autobiography, the *Baburnama,* which is commended for its truthfulness and charm. Above all, Babur was deeply imbued with the true Islamic spirit of humanism. He believed that defeated enemies should be conciliated, and he prevented, with rigid discipline, his own followers from victimizing the local population (Ziad 2002). This was the vision with which the Mughal Empire began. Babur strongly influenced his descendants by his religious tolerance, as well as his delight in gardens and interest in poetry. His personality gave the Mughal dynasty an image of great patronage of literature, arts, and culture that was very different from the image of his Mongol predecessors.

Humayun. Babur's son, Humayun, inherited his father's sensitivity and scholarly talents but not his military skills and administrative ability. He became emperor in 1530 at the age of twenty-two, but in just ten years, his rule was interrupted by the Afghan Sher Shah Sur, who rebelled against him. He remained in exile for several years. He was eventually able to regain his empire, first conquering Afghanistan in 1545 and then India in 1555, with the help of the Shah of Persia, who supplied soldiers, weapons, horses, and grain. He died six months later in 1556 from a fall in his observatory.

Akbar. Humayun's son, Akbar, was only fourteen when he inherited an empire that was only six months old. He ruled as a boy-king under the tutelage of Bahram Khan for four years, and he assumed direct rule in 1560. Akbar was the greatest of all Mughal emperors. He ruled India for half a century, about the same number of years as his contemporary Queen Elizabeth I ruled England. He extended the frontiers of the Mughal Empire beyond what his grandfather had accomplished, and he conquered much of southern India, Kashmir, Balochistan, and Sindh, bringing most of India under Mughal rule. He is best known not only for his skills in the battlefield, gigantic military conquests, and winning alliances, but also for his administrative genius and statesmanship, as well as for his religious tolerance and enlightenment.

Akbar introduced the *mansabdari* system, which formed the basis of both his military organization and civil administration. It consisted of a ranked imperial service with separate military, political, and revenue collection functions. Selection for the service was based on ability and loyalty rather than on birth or religion, and members were paid with cash rather than land. They were also kept away from their inherited estates, primarily to centralize and protect the imperial power base. Akbar's reign was characterized by prosperity. Farmers paid one-third of their harvest in taxes but no taxes at all when crops were poor. His land revenue system was both efficient and just. Grain surpluses were common and farmers received good prices for cotton and spices. Akbar is also commended for economic prosperity during his reign due to development of a monetary system, building of bridges and canals, and better communication networks.

Akbar was extremely respectful of other faiths. In 1564, he abolished the *jizya* tax on non-Muslims and lifted the ban on temple building and Hindu pilgrimages. He further unified India by recruiting large numbers of Hindus into the Civil Service, the highest ranks of the army, and in his nine-member council of advisors, known as *nau rattan* (nine gems). Four out of the nine council members were non-Muslims. He also married Hindu princesses and allowed them freedom of religion, thus building alliances with the *Rajputs,* who were the warrior class, had their own armies in hilltop fortresses, and could be potential enemies. Akbar greatly encouraged scholarly, artistic, and cultural endeavors. Most of the prominent scholars, painters, musicians, and poets, as well as architects and craftsmen of his time, were attached to his court and benefited from his patronage.

In 1582, Akbar announced his adherence to a new set of beliefs and philosophy called *Din-e-Ilahi* (The Divine Faith), drawing on elements from the mystical strains in Islam, Hinduism, and Zoroastrianism. His new beliefs were deeply influenced by Sufism, an Islamic spiritual discipline that cultivates the individual worshipper's direct and ecstatic experience of the divine presence. He did not, however, try to impose *Din-e-Ilahi* as a state religion, which is indicated by the fact that it had only eighteen genuine adherents and faded away when Akbar died in 1605. However, its content and rituals offended orthodox Muslims and alienated the two sources of challenge to Akbar's power, the Afghan-Turkish aristocracy and the traditional interpreters of Islamic law, the *ulema*. It would not be until 1658 that the reaction against this creeping secularism and *Din-e-Ilahi* by the two groups would fully surface when both would support the pious military commander Aurangzeb against his learned brother in the fight for power. Akbar was succeeded by his son, Saleem, later known as Jahangir (seizer of the world).

Jahangir.   Akbar's son, Jahangir, became emperor at the age of thirty-six. He is best known for his unbiased judgments in disputes and as a just king. A man of exquisite aesthetic taste, he was a great patron of the arts and of architecture. Painting, in particular, reached glorious heights during his reign. Having inherited a stable and prosperous empire, he consolidated his father's achievements. Jahangir is also known for his love for his queen, Mehr-un-Nisa, whom he renamed Nur Jahan (light of the world). She was beautiful, ambitious, and brilliant. She set fashions, designed jewelry and clothes, created perfumes, wrote poetry, and shot tigers. She became the power behind the throne, and her brother and other relatives were given top positions in the kingdom. Nur Jahan played a big role in the power struggle for the throne between Jahangir's two sons (her stepsons), Khurram and Shahryar.

She opposed Khurram, renamed Shah Jahan (sovereign of the world) by Jahangir after he had won several victories against rebels, and supported Shahryar who was married to her daughter from a previous marriage. When Shah Jahan refused to go to faraway Afghanistan on Jahangir's orders in 1624 because he was afraid that his brother would seize the

Portrait of Jahangir, fourth ruler of the Mughal dynasty in India. Jahangir was an ardent patron of the uniquely Mughal style of minia-ture painting, a legacy from his grandfather, Humayun. (Angelo Hornak/Corbis)

The Taj Mahal was built in the seventeenth century by Shah Jahan to honor his wife, Mumtaz Mahal, who died in childbirth in 1631. The construction lasted about 20 years, and the Taj Mahal remains one of the most beautiful buildings in the world and the finest example of Mughal architecture. (Felix Bivens)

throne on his ill father's death, Jahangir sent an army that pursued Shah Jahan across India for three years till Jahangir's death in 1627.

Shah Jahan.   Jahangir's son, Shah Jahan, had to fight for his throne with Shahryar, whom he defeated in 1628. Shah Jahan's reign was the zenith of the Mughal era, marked by economic prosperity, educational advancement, and artistic achievement. He was a significant patron of the arts and had a special genius for architecture.

His architectural contributions include the Taj Mahal in Agra, the Shalimar Gardens and Jahangir's tomb in Lahore, the Red Fort and Jama Masjid (mosque) in Delhi, as well as significant additions to the Lahore Fort, including the Shish Mahal (palace of mirrors). The Taj Mahal is a testament to Shah Jahan's great love affair with his beloved wife, whom he named Mumtaz Mahal (distinguished one of the palace). The Taj is a mausoleum that he built in her memory after she died in childbirth. About 20,000 craftsmen and laborers worked for sixteen years to build the Taj, which is one of the wonders of the world. The monument's paradise imagery is considered, in scholarly discourse, as a symbol of Shah Jahan's view of his power as divinely guided.

Shah Jahan also built the Peacock Throne, a jewel-studded chair under a canopy supported by twelve emerald pillars topped by two golden peacocks whose tails were filled with diamonds, rubies, and pearls. He also initiated a return to Islamic orthodoxy and to the *Sharia;* yet his favorite son, Dara Shikoh, was a great mystic who translated many Hindu religious texts (Ziad 2002). Late in Shah Jahan's life, his four sons fought for succession. He was deposed in 1658 by Aurangzeb on the grounds that he had allowed his other son, Dara Shikoh, to spread Hinduism. Shah Jahan was imprisoned in the Agra Fort where he had a view of the Taj Mahal for eight years till his death in 1666.

Aurangzeb.   Shah Jahan's son, Aurangzeb, proclaimed himself emperor in 1658 and ruled India for forty-nine years,

The Lahore Fort, also built by Emperor Shah Jahan. (Pakistan Mission to the UN)

assuming the title Alamgir (world-seizer) in the latter half of his long rule. He was known for aggressively expanding the empire's southern frontiers. He was an outstanding general who conducted his campaigns with ruthless efficiency. During his reign, the Mughal Empire reached its greatest geographical extent, stretching from the hills in the northwest to the plains of the Deccan. However, he spent so much money on war that the weakened empire crumbled soon after his death. Instead of remunerating high-ranking officials with cash, as in Akbar's time, he once again made land the usual means of remuneration.

Aurangzeb was the last Mughal emperor to keep the empire strong. He was a rigorous administrator, and ruled the empire with an iron hand. He was pious and God-fearing in his personal habits and an orthodox Muslim in his beliefs. To conservative Muslims, Aurangzeb was the greatest of the Mughals because he continued and strengthened the return to Islamic law that had been instituted by his father. He was an unfailing

Built by Emperor Aurangzeb in Lahore, the Imperial or Badshahi mosque is constructed entirely of red sandstone. It has the largest courtyard in the world, and about 100,000 people pray here on Eid. (Pakistan Mission to the UN)

protector of orthodox Islam, and appointed a commission of scholars to compile a code of Islamic jurisprudence relevant to the conditions of life at that time. To non-Muslims, Aurangzeb was an intolerant emperor; yet there was a considerable increase in the percentage of Hindus working in his administration. In 1668, he outlawed Hindu religious festivals, and in 1679, he reimposed the *jizya*, 115 years after Akbar had abolished it. Although it was based on a person's ability to pay and exemptions were provided for the unemployed, the sick, and others, the imposition of *jizya* was one of the causes of the rebellion by Hindus, Jats, Sikhs, and Rajputs in the north and Maratha forces in the Deccan. Aurangzeb crushed the rebellion in the north, but it posed a challenge to central authority. It also reduced agricultural productivity. The costly campaign against Maratha guerrilla fighters continued for twenty-six years till Aurangzeb's death in 1707 at the age of ninety.

After Aurangzeb's death, there was a civil war among his sons and nephews, and fifteen emperors reigned over the next century compared to the six great Mughals of the previous 181 years. Over time, provinces such as Bengal to the east and Hyderabad to the south quit paying taxes and became largely independent of the Mughals. The *zamindari* system replaced the *mansabdari* system, and those who were tax collectors became the hereditary landed aristocracy. Delhi itself was invaded: first by Nadir Shah of Persia, who seized the Peacock Throne in 1739 and took it with him; then by Ahmed Shah Abdali of Kabul; and later by Hindu Marathas from central India, who stripped Mughal tombs and palaces of their precious metals in 1760. As Delhi's control weakened, other kingdoms gained and lost power, thus paving the way for eventual British takeover.

Company Rule, Colonialism, and British Raj

At about the same time that Babur had arrived in India from the northwest in the early sixteenth century, Portuguese sailors and missionaries came by a very long route, around Africa, to the southern part of the subcontinent in search of the spices and wealth of the East. Mughal officials allowed them to build forts on the coast to resupply their ships on their way to the Spice Islands of Indonesia. Other Europeans had their eyes on the region's valuable trade routes too. Mughal officials permitted the new carriers of India's export trade to establish trading posts in India. Soon there were Dutch, Portuguese, French, and British trading companies all along India's coast, some gaining a foothold through attacks. The trading posts (factories) were initially used for transshipment, but increasingly acquired political and military power as the company hired local people to serve in armies to protect company interests.

England set up its first trading post in the Mughal Empire in 1612 through the British East India Company, which became the real beneficiary of the vacuum of power in India around that time. By the 1700s, the company had edged out its trading competitors and become the strongest trade power in India. At the same time, Mughal emperors were losing their grip on the vast empire. Local princes and kings were becoming more powerful than the emperors. As the Mughal Empire weakened, the British saw their chance for territorial acquisition. Little by little they gained political and territorial control of the Indian subcontinent. In 1757, British East India Company forces led by Robert Clive defeated the forces of the last Mughal governor of Bengal, Nawab Siraj-ud-Daulah, at the battle of Plassey, with the help of the treachery of Mir Jaffer, a close relative of Siraj. The British rule, beginning in Bengal, eventually extended to all of India. By 1803, the once-mighty Mughal emperor reigned over only two square miles of Delhi inside the Red Fort. Aside from their superior military power, the British deployed the principle of divide and rule to rise to power, fully exploiting any Hindu-Muslim animosities.

Company rule expanded in the early 1800s both by military conquest, as in most of northern India, and by subsidiary agreements between the British and independent, local rulers. These agreements, under which the local rulers retained some powers but transferred control of foreign affairs and defense to the company, created the princely states, which were ruled by Hindu *maharajas* or Muslim *nawabs*. Sindh in present-day Pakistan was ruled by a group of local Muslim landowners, the Talpur *mirs* (chiefs), until it was annexed by the British in 1843. In the Punjab, Ranjit Singh, a Sikh leader, became the *maharaja* of Lahore and built an empire across the Indus Valley in the first decade of the 1800s. Its control extended beyond Peshawar and included Kashmir. For forty years, this was the only state in India that was not under British control. After Ranjit Singh died in 1839, the British fought two wars with the Sikhs, in

1845 and 1849. After a short but bloody war, the Sikhs were defeated in 1849 and Punjab, including the present-day North-West Frontier Province, was annexed. The newly installed British government lowered taxes, promoted irrigation projects, and allowed religious freedom, winning full loyalty of the region in a few years, which proved vital to the British during the Uprising of 1857.

Assisted by Sikh allies, the company advanced into Afghanistan, taking over Kandahar and Kabul. The subsequent retreat from Kabul was one of the rare defeats suffered by the armies of Queen Victoria. The First Afghan War (1838–1842) saw the virtual annihilation of a British force of more than 16,000 at the hands of Afghan tribesmen outside Kabul. From then on, the British sought to control passes rather than to rule over the Pashtuns, who have never been truly subjugated by any outside power. All these lands in present-day Pakistan, together with present-day India and Bangladesh, were called British India, the most profitable colony of the far-flung British Empire.

The Uprising of 1857 marked the formal end of the Mughal Empire as well as of company rule in India. It is known as the First War of Independence in Indian and Pakistani history (and the Indian Mutiny or Sepoy Rebellion in the British). It was a rebellion against British expansionism, although the immediate spark for the revolt was that Indian troops had to bite the tip off a cartridge allegedly greased with cow or pig fat before loading it into the new Enfield rifle. Both Muslim and Hindu soldiers were outraged since pig fat is forbidden to Muslims and beef fat to Hindus. Rising in revolt against the British, they killed some British officers, and marched to Delhi proclaiming the elderly Mughal emperor Bahadur Shah II as the leader of their revolt. It is a testament to the sway that Mughal rule held over the hearts and minds of Indians that Hindus and Muslims joined hands to rise up against the British Empire and sought the protection of a dynasty that had lost effective control about a hundred years before.

The resistance was crushed with the help of Nepal and of the troops from the Punjab. The Sikhs particularly helped the British to retake Delhi and capture the royal family in 1857. A young British captain executed all nine of the emperor's sons, ending the Mughal dynasty forever. In 1858, a British court exiled Bahadur Shah II to Burma (present-day Myanmar) where he died in 1862. Although it was limited to Bengal and northern India, it took a full year for British soldiers to put down the uprising. The uprising was a severe blow to the British and threatened their rule in India. The subsequent Government of India Act of 1858 abolished the British East India Company, imposed direct rule, and transferred authority to the governor general and viceroy representing the British crown in India. This marked the beginning of official British colonialism in India. Queen Victoria became the empress of India, and India (including present-day Pakistan and Bangladesh) became the "jewel in the crown" of the British Empire, both metaphorically and in reality as the enormous, 108.93-carat, *Koh-e-Nur* diamond of India was put in the Imperial crown. After the uprising, the British Indian Army was also overhauled drastically, using racial criteria to exclude Indians from artillery and technical services and a theory of "martial races" to recruit particular groups. Thus recruitment of Sikhs, Punjabis, Dogras, Gurkhas, and Pakhtuns that were considered loyal to the British was encouraged, while that of Bengalis, high-caste Hindus, and men from the United Provinces (UP) was discouraged.

The British followed a "forward policy" toward the tribal people in the North-West Frontier that was more assertive. In 1876, Sir Robert Sandeman concluded a treaty with the Khan of Kalat, which extended British rule to his territories— including Kharan, Makran, and Lasbela (in present-day Balochistan). In 1879, the British forcibly occupied some districts of Afghanistan, including Pishin and Sibi (in present-day Balochistan). By 1893, Gilgit, Hunza, and Nagar (in present-day Northern Areas of Pakistan) and Chitral came under

British control. The British left the direct administration of these North-West Frontier regions to new appointed tribal chiefs, *mirs* and *maliks,* who upheld local customary law and social customs.

British colonial rule was a mixture of benevolence and despotism. The Sikhs, Muslims, Hindus, Christians, and Zoroastrians had equal status under British law, but a lower status than the British. Segregation was common, and signs of "dogs and Indians not allowed" were often posted at private clubs and even some public spaces, like waiting rooms at railway stations. The British used severe methods to protect their interests. There are numerous reports on the method by which the threat of Indian competition with textile mills of Manchester (England) was handled. It is said that the skilled Muslim weavers of Dhaka, who produced such fine muslin that ten yards of the fabric could fit into a matchbox, had their thumbs amputated by the British.

The overall impact of British colonial rule on the Indo-Pak subcontinent was very deep. Using the labor and taxes of the Indian people, the British built roads, railways, irrigation canals, communication networks, post offices, sewers, hospitals, and educational institutions. The most significant improvement was the building, between 1853 and 1900, of about 25,000 miles of railroad tracks all over India, along with workshops to build and repair locomotives. The expansion of irrigation in the Punjab led to its designation as the granary of India. Between 1850 and 1900, about 8 million acres of dry land were irrigated in the Punjab and Sindh. Similarly, by 1880, about 20,000 miles of telegraph wire were laid (Weston 1992, 60–71).

The British adopted the monetary and revenue collection systems of the Mughal Empire but brought English legal procedures and justice systems, meritocracy-based civil services, the Victorian model of administration, and a parliamentary form of government. They introduced changes in social and economic structures, in systems of production, and in social institutions and relationships that served British interests and were not always in harmony with local needs: the shift to cash crops like cotton to provide raw material for the British textile industry; improvement of transport and communications for strategic, administrative, and commercial reasons; and forms of education based on British classical education rather than on needs of an agricultural country. A new middle class of professionals emerged that modeled itself on the British but was not fully in touch with the domestic problems, a shortcoming that became more evident later. British colonialism brought significant economic change but impoverished and depleted India.

Independence Movements and the Rise of the Muslim League

British distrust of Muslims in the aftermath of the 1857 uprising resulted in their near exclusion from the Civil Service and the officer corps of the army and hence in their powerlessness. The British particularly discredited Muslim leaders and landed aristocracy in the UP in North India for their alleged role in the uprising, pushing them into political isolation. As middle-class Hindus were acquiring British education and becoming upwardly mobile, Muslims were lagging behind in education. They continued to be underrepresented at Indian universities as late as the 1880s, accounting for 25 percent of population but only 4 percent of students. This misery and humiliation combined with rising Indian nationalism and revivalist Hindu movements like *Arya Samaj*—attempting reconversion to Hinduism—all sowed the seeds of Muslim nationalism that would eventually lead about a century later to the creation of Pakistan. The landmark events and people who played a key role in the creation of Pakistan in 1947 include the following.

Sir Syed Ahmad Khan.   An educational reformer and pioneer of English education for Muslims, Sir Syed (1817–1898)

A nineteenth-century educational reformer and visionary, Sir Syed Ahmad Khan launched the Aligarh movement, which later played a crucial role in the creation of Pakistan. (Hafiz Malik, Sir Sayyid Ahmed Khan and Muslim Modernization in India and Pakistan, *1980)*

played a key role in the awakening of Muslims in the period following the 1857 uprising. He advised Indian Muslims to become enlightened and reform society on the basis of true Islamic teachings, modern education, and scientific thought. He set up the Muhammadan Anglo-Oriental College in 1875 at Aligarh in North India, which developed into the Aligarh Muslim University, which later became the focus for Muslim demands for a separate homeland. He hoped that Aligarh would provide a focus for scientific advance among Muslims and produce an educated cadre of leaders. The Aligarh movement changed the attitude of Muslims toward Western education, and slowly the number of Muslim students at all universities began to increase.

Meanwhile, the Indian National Congress, founded in 1885 initially to advocate strictly constitutionalist and gradual reforms for British rule, argued for a quicker end to the rule after World War I. Muslims did not join the party in large numbers because they were afraid that the Congress would not adequately represent Muslim interests. The beginnings of self-government by Indians can be traced back to the Government of India Act of 1909, also known as the *Morley-Minto Reforms,* which modified the rules of membership in the legislative councils (central and provincial legislatures) that advised the viceroy. While the majority of seats on these councils were filled by appointments, the British government announced elections for some of these seats based on a limited electorate of upper-class Indians. Many Muslims worried that Hindu politicians might win all the seats, as they constituted 75 percent of the population.

Founding of the Muslim League. The All India Muslim League was founded in Dhaka in 1906 by seventy wealthy landowners, *nawabs,* and lawyers to protect and advance Muslim interests. The secular leaders of the Congress believed that they could represent Muslims as well as they did Hindus, while the Muslim leaders feared that, without separate electorates, they would be dominated by a Hindu majority that they considered worse than continuation of British rule. The League asked the British to set aside a percentage of council seats for Muslims. Aga Khan III led the Simla delegation to the viceroy to ask for separate electorates, so that Muslim voters could elect their own representatives in separate elections for those seats. Separate electorates were a safeguard against nonrepresentation of Muslims in the legislative councils. As a result of the property and tax qualifications for voting, the Muslim electorate was relatively disadvantaged and would have been unsuccessful in getting Muslims elected to these councils. Hindus objected, but the *Morley-Minto Reforms* granted communal representation and separate electorates to Muslims, incorporating the principle of weightage, whereby the number of seats in the elected bodies allotted to Muslims was slightly higher than their share of the population. The British government held separate elections for Muslim seats in 1910; one Muslim elected to the national council was Mohammad Ali Jinnah (1876–1948), the future founder of Pakistan.

Jinnah and the Lucknow Pact.   Realizing that a joint front with Congress was needed for a fight against colonial rule, the Muslim League invited Mohammad Ali Jinnah, the moderate, nationalist leader of Congress, to join the League and build bridges between the League and the Congress. Jinnah was ideally suited for this task because of his high standing in the Congress. In 1913, he joined the Muslim League but continued his membership in the Congress as well. He believed that Hindu-Muslim unity was the key to India's independence from Britain. In 1916, he negotiated a pact in Lucknow (known as the Lucknow Pact) with Motilal Nehru, president of the Congress. The pact demanded a majority of elected rather than appointed members in legislatures, and sought direct elections by the people and a broadening of the franchise. It also put full Muslim League support behind Congress's demand that India be given dominion status like Australia or Canada. In return, the Congress accepted the separate electorates demanded by the Muslim League. The pact was instrumental in soothing Muslim fears of Hindu domination. It was a triumph for Jinnah, who was described by a leading Congress spokesperson as the "ambassador of Hindu-Muslim unity." Alavi writes, "Jinnah was a unifier and not a separatist. He was to persist in that difficult role, despite setbacks, for a quarter of a century until the point was reached when, despite all his efforts, unity was no longer an option" (Alavi 2002, 7).

The Khilafat Movement. The new dynamic of Hindu-Muslim unity was threatened by two developments in Indian politics between 1917 and 1920: the Government of India Act of 1919, also known as the *Montague-Chelmsford Reforms,* and Mohandas Gandhi's capture of Congress with the help of Khilafat Muslims in 1920. The *Montague-Chelmsford Reforms* demonstrated that the British were not going to grant dominion status to India anytime soon. The British placed restrictions on freedom of the press and movement. Political leaders such as Mohandas Karamchand Gandhi (1869–1948) and Jawaharlal Nehru (1889–1964), son of Motilal Nehru, began a campaign of civil disobedience and peaceful noncooperation in protest of these restrictions. They particularly protested against the *Amritsar Massacre* of 1919. The incident happened at Jallianwala Bagh (Garden) in Amritsar, where British Indian Army soldiers opened fire on an unarmed gathering of people at a Sikh religious festival because it was in violation of the prohibitory orders banning gatherings of five or more persons, a regulation created after several civil disturbances in the city. The hardline Muslim *ulema* of the Deobandi sect and political activists supported Gandhi in the mass demonstrations of 1920 and 1921. In return, Gandhi supported them in their pan-Islamic Khilafat movement against the British over Britain's alleged role in trying to end the Caliphate of the Ottoman sultan in Turkey who had become the symbol of Islamic authority and unity to Indian Muslims after the Mughals. The Khilafat movement overwhelmed the League after 1919 and eventually broke the League–Congress unity that Jinnah had worked so hard to build. It is believed that the movement, "in the hands of Mahatma Gandhi, torpedoed the new political dynamic of the joint struggle of the Muslim League and the Congress against the colonial rule that was set in motion by the Lucknow Pact" (Alavi 2002, 7).

The alliance between Gandhi and the Khilafat Muslims also "undermined the secular leadership of the Muslim League, and, for the time being, established the mullahs in that place. . . . [it] implanted the religious idiom in modern Indian Muslim politics for the first time" (Alavi 2002, 8). Moreover, the methods of the mass-based civil disobedience and noncooperation movement, involving boycotts, protests, demonstrations, and consequent arrests and imprisonments, were counter to the methodology of a constitutional politician like Jinnah, whose legal background predisposed him against any extraconstitutional agitation. He believed that Gandhi's civil disobedience campaign would lead only to chaos. He and other members of the League felt increasingly alienated from a movement that to them seemed spiritual rather than political. Gandhi was a spiritual teacher as well as a political leader. Many Muslims saw his movement as fundamentally Hindu in character, although Gandhi had the deepest respect for Islam. According to British historian Sir Percival Spear, "a mass appeal in his [Gandhi's] hands could not be other than a Hindu one. He could transcend caste but not community. The [Hindu] devices he used went sour in the mouths of Muslims" (Blood 1995, 27). Jinnah resigned from Congress soon afterward. Ziring (1999) notes that Gandhi urged all his followers to adopt noncooperation with the government and particularly called upon the Muslims to migrate en masse to Asia Minor, the seat of the Ottoman Empire, to save the Caliphate. True to Gandhi's urging, Muslims left their work and businesses, and about 20,000 sold off their properties and migrated to Afghanistan. It was only when the Muslims saw that Hindu institutions operated normally during the noncooperation movement and Gandhi himself suspended the movement soon afterward that "even the more gullible among the Muslims realized they had been led astray" (Ziring 1999, 14).

The Montague-Chelmsford Reforms. These reforms provincialized and localized Indian politics, increasing the importance of Muslim-majority provinces like Punjab and Bengal, where Muslims could form provincial governments. Ministers now had the power to dispense patronage and give jobs. The reforms created a wedge between interests of provincial politicians who preferred a weak federal structure with provincial autonomy and centralist, all-India politicians who preferred a strong center. Jinnah was a centralist and opposed the federal scheme because he believed that the real security for Muslims lay not in separate electorates, which he had never favored, but in unity with the Congress at the center. The reforms shifted the center of gravity of power from the Muslim-minority provinces like UP to Muslim-majority provinces and changed the class base of Muslim politics as well. Thus Punjab dominated Indian Muslim politics, and the feudal classes dominated Punjab politics. By the late 1920s, the demand of Muslim provinces, particularly Punjab, had swamped Jinnah's centralist strategy.

The Nehru Report and the Calcutta Convention. Although alienated by the Congress Party, Jinnah still believed that Hindu-Muslim unity was necessary to win self-government from the British. During the 1920s, he tried hard to resolve the differences between the Congress and the Muslim League. He was willing to bargain on the question of separate electorates if Congress was willing to accept other Muslim demands. But his attempts failed, and any hope for unity was shattered in 1928 when Congress issued the *Nehru Report* repudiating its past approval of separate elections for Muslim representatives. However, it recommended reservation of seats for Muslims in the UP and some democratic reorganization of the provinces, which safeguarded Muslim interests to some extent. But at the subsequent Calcutta Convention later that year, the Congress, at the behest of the Hindu Mahasabha, reversed all recommendations that would have safeguarded Muslim interests. It also betrayed the principles of the Nehru Committee. This betrayal by Congress, when Jinnah had abandoned joint electorates for the sake of unity even at the cost of support from his Muslim supporters, convinced him of the Hindu Mahasabha's veto power over Congress in matters concerning Muslims. The report made no concessions at all to Muslims, which led to its rejection by all shades of Muslim opinion. Once again, in 1929, at an all-party conference convened by Motilal Nehru, Jinnah again tried to forge a common front between the League and the Congress by putting forward his *Fourteen Points* that would satisfy Muslim demands, either by retaining separate electorates or by creating safeguards to prevent a Hindu-controlled legislature. His proposals were rejected, and Motilal Nehru thought that Congress could safely "ignore Mr. Jinnah." This marked the near end of Hindu-Muslim cooperation in the independence movement. Disillusioned, Jinnah left India in 1929 to practice law in London.

Sir Muhammad Iqbal.   Their experiences with the Congress in the 1920s and 1930s and the disillusionment led Muslims to begin to think of a separate Muslim nation, which developed into the demand for partition. In his 1930 presidential speech to the Muslim League in Allahabad, Sir Muhammad Iqbal (1877–1938), a great Islamic poet and philosopher, was the first person to put forward the concept of a separate Muslim homeland in the subcontinent. He proposed the establishment of a confederated India to include a Muslim state, saying, "I would like to see the Punjab, the North-West Frontier Province, Sindh, and Balochistan amalgamated into a single State. Self-government. . . . [is] the final destiny of the Muslims, at least of North-West India" (Weston 1992, 75). He considered Muslims to be a nation based on

unity of language, race, history, religion, and economic interests. Three years later, a group of Indian Muslim students at
Cambridge in Britain issued a pamphlet, *Now or Never,*
opposing the idea of a federation and demanding partition
into regions, the northwest becoming the nation of Pakistan.
Chaudhri Rahmat Ali came up with the name, which in Urdu
means Land of the *Paks* or the Pure and is also an acronym:
"P" is for Punjab, "A" for Afghania (referring to the North-
West Frontier Province), "K" for Kashmir, an "I" that occurs
in English but not in Urdu, "S" is for Sindh, and "TAN" is for
Balochistan.

Initially, most Muslims did not support the idea of a separate nation, but events in the late 1930s made millions of
Muslims across India change their minds. The change began
with the 1937 elections to the provincial legislative assemblies held under the 1935 Government of India Act. Jinnah
had returned to India in 1934 to revive the Muslim League on
the invitation of Muslims in the minority provinces, the UP in
particular. The Muslim League had grown very weak and had
lost its sense of mission during Jinnah's absence. To legitimize
the representative role of the All India Muslim League and to
claim to be its sole spokesman, Jinnah needed support from
the Muslim-majority provinces. But the leaders and the elite
in Punjab and Bengal did not need Jinnah or the League as
yet. In Punjab, the Unionist Party, led by Sir Fazl-e-Husain
and his successor, Sir Sikandar Hayat Khan, was very powerful and the League barely existed. *Zamindar* (landlord) and
biraderi (clan) linkages with Jat peasants dominated the secular, intercommunal Unionist Party. They were also supported by the *pirs* or *Sajjada Nashins* (spiritual leaders)
whose interests were subtly intertwined with those of the
landlords in the Punjab. The party (and the landed elite) also
had the patronage of the colonial regime, to which they were
completely loyal (Alavi 2002, 9). On the other hand, in Bengal, landlords and *nawabs* dominated the Muslim League, but
the Krishak Praja Party (KPP), led by Fazlul Haq, was the pow-

The poet-philosopher Sir Muhammad Iqbal was the first to advocate an independent Muslim state on the Indian subcontinent. (Pakistan Mission to the UN)

erful party. It advocated the abolition of *zamindari* without compensation, which reflected the importance of small peasants and tenants in the Bengal economy.

The 1937 Elections. The League did poorly in the 1937 elections, particularly in the Muslim-majority provinces such

as Punjab and the North-West Frontier Province. In many
areas, it could not even put up a candidate, and across India,
it won only 21 percent of the seats allotted to Muslims (105
out of 499). The League did well in the Muslim-minority
provinces such as UP but won only one out of eighty-six seats
in the Punjab. In Sindh and the North-West Frontier Province,
the League did not win a single seat, losing to the Congress in
the NWFP. In Bengal, the League formed a coalition government with the KPP, with Fazlul Haq as the prime minister.
This was the least required to sustain the claim that the
League and Jinnah were the sole representatives of the Indian
Muslims. But the Congress, which gained large majorities in
seven of the eleven provinces, refused to share power and
form coalition governments with the Muslim League, even in
the UP. Jinnah had hoped that Congress would appoint several members of the League to cabinet posts, but it did not.
Moreover, some Congress governments influenced by the
Hindu Mahasabha imposed regulations that required school-
children to sing the Congress Party anthem or *Bande-
mataram,* a Hindu song offensive to Muslim sensibilities
because of being idolatrous; others gave tax money to Hindu
colleges; and one even closed several schools where the
medium of instruction was Urdu. Similarly the *Wardha*
scheme of education and the *Vidya Mandir* scheme in the
central provinces were allegedly hurtful to Muslim interests.

The Lahore Resolution.   The results of the 1937 elections
and the attitude of the Congress in not sharing power proved
the turning point for Muslims. They feared Hindu domination
in an independent India and wondered what their status would
be in a Congress dominated by the Hindu Mahasabha. They
rallied behind the leadership of Jinnah. Almost single-handedly he built the League into the broad-based political party
that in the 1940s unified India's 100 million Muslims behind
the demand for Pakistan. In 1940, just seven and a half years
before partition, the League formally demanded independent
Muslim states. At its annual session in Lahore on March 23,

1940, the League passed the Lahore Resolution, often referred to as the Pakistan Resolution, "Resolved . . . that the areas in which Muslims are numerically in a majority as in the North-Western and Eastern zones of India should be grouped to constitute Independent States" (Weston 1992, 80). The League demanded that India's six Muslim provinces—the Punjab, North-West Frontier Province, Balochistan, Sindh, Bengal, and Assam—be included in those two sovereign states. The demand was for an undivided Punjab and an undivided Bengal. The demand was based on Jinnah's Two-Nation Theory, which argued that Muslims were a nation different from Hindus. As Jinnah eloquently stated, "we are a nation with our own distinctive culture and civilization, language and literature, art and architecture, names and nomenclature, sense of values and proportion, legal laws and moral codes, customs and calendar, history and tradition, aptitude and ambitions. In short, we have our own distinctive outlook on life and of life. By all canons of international law, we are a nation" (Ziring 1999, 21).

The Pakistan Movement received its greatest support from the Muslim-minority provinces such as the UP, but less from the Muslim-majority provinces like Punjab and Bengal. In the Muslim-majority provinces, Muslims were "already well on top, and with a little forbearance could easily placate the minorities . . . they would gain little or nothing by Pakistan" (Noman 1990, 4). In fact, Sikander Hayat, leader of Punjab's Unionist Party, even denounced the Lahore Resolution and called for complete autonomy for the provinces. But Jinnah needed support from the Muslim-majority provinces, not to seek power, but to legitimize the representative role of the Muslim League. On the other hand, Muslims in the Muslim-minority provinces, like the UP, fearing domination by the numerically dominant Hindus, needed safeguards, which the League was fighting for. They strongly supported the League and Jinnah. Gandhi denounced the Pakistan Resolution as absurd. He and the Congress strongly objected to all proposals for partition.

World War II.   When World War II broke out, the Muslim League and Congress responded differently. The Congress refused to support Britain unless India was granted independence, while the League cooperated and contributed soldiers. In return, Britain made a pledge to the Muslims in 1940 that it would not transfer power to an independent India unless its constitution was first approved by Muslims, a promise it did not subsequently keep. To pressure the British, Gandhi launched the "Quit India movement" against the British in 1942. The League insisted that Britain should "Divide and then Quit." Negotiations between Gandhi and the viceroy failed, as did talks between Gandhi and Jinnah in 1944.

When World War II ended in 1945, both the Congress and the Muslim League intensified their political pressure on the British government to grant independence. Given the decline in British power and the spread of general unrest in India, the British finally realized that independence was the only alternative and the best way to keep some power over the Indian subcontinent. The British viceroy, Lord Wavell, ordered new elections to the central and provincial legislatures, and proposed that India be governed until its independence by an executive council composed of an equal number of Hindus and Muslims, with all but one of the Muslims appointed by the Muslim League. Jinnah claimed that only the League represented India's Muslims and that it alone had the right to appoint a Muslim to the executive council. Congress strongly objected to both these claims, as it always had. Jinnah challenged that new elections would prove his claim, and Congress accepted the challenge.

By 1945, Punjab's rural notables had realized that the Unionist Party was no longer the best security for their power and local interests as the Unionists were about to lose the backing of the British who were on their way out. They were the ones under the greatest threat from a Hindu-dominated Congress with a powerful center once the British left. They were afraid of restrictions on their freedom and a curtailment of their autonomy, which the Congress had indicated it would do. Many important families, including those of Shaukat Hayat of Wah, Mumtaz Daultana of Multan, Feroz Khan Noon of Sargodha, and others, switched their allegiance from the Unionists to the Muslim League between 1943 and 1945. Many of these new Muslim Leaguers contested the 1946 elections from their own constituencies. So did the landed magnates from Sindh. The *pirs* in Punjab and Sindh, landlords in their own right, also jumped on the Muslim League bandwagon. Moreover, because of their embattled provincialism and factionalism, leaders in Muslim-majority provinces needed to have a spokesman at the center, and Jinnah was the only Muslim leader with a national stature. Thus, by 1945, most leaders in the Muslim-majority provinces of Punjab and Bengal had come under the banner of the Muslim League, making Jinnah the sole spokesman for, and the undisputed leader of, the Indian Muslims.

The Elections of 1946.   In the elections of 1946, the Muslim League won 90 percent of the legislative seats reserved for Muslims. It was the power of the big *zamindars* in Punjab and Sindh behind the Muslim League candidates, and the powerful campaign among the poor peasants of Bengal on economic issues of rural indebtedness and *zamindari* abolition, that led to this massive landslide victory (Alavi 2002, 14). Even Congress, which had always denied the League's claim to be the only true representative of Indian Muslims, had to concede the truth of that claim. The 1946 election was, in effect, a plebiscite among Muslims on Pakistan. For the Muslim masses, the demand for Pakistan had become the symbol of a promised land that would be based on the principles of a just social order in the true spirit of Islam. The election results were a great triumph for Jinnah and the Muslim League. Jinnah was the undisputed leader of India's Muslims. He was the only Muslim leader who could balance the sometimes conflicting interests of the Muslim-majority and Muslim-minority provinces. The British had no choice but to take Jinnah's view into account as they made plans for India's independence.

Despite the League's victory in the elections, the British did not want the partition of India. As a last attempt to avoid it, Britain put forward the Cabinet Mission plan, according to which India would become a federation of three large, self-governing provinces and the central government would be limited to power over foreign policy and defense, implying a weak center. The three provinces were proposed to be northeastern Bengal and Assam with a slight Muslim majority; Punjab, Sindh, North-West Frontier Province, and Balochistan with a Muslim majority; and the remainder of the country with a Hindu majority. Initially, both parties seemed to accept the Cabinet Mission plan. The Muslim League accepted the plan for a confederate India, just a year before partition, demonstrating once again that all Jinnah wanted was a constitutional structure within a united India that could safeguard Muslim interests. But neither Nehru nor Gandhi was willing to accept a weak center for the sake of India's unity. Nehru announced that Congress would not be fettered by agreements with the British, implying that the Congress would write the constitution as it wished based on its majority standing.

Interim Government and Direct Action Day.   The formation of an interim government was also controversial. Congress insisted on the right to appoint some of its own Muslim members to positions in the government as ministers, while Jinnah claimed that only the Muslim League had the right to represent the Muslims of India. This might appear a small matter, but it was the essence of the League's case. Even the British viceroy, Lord Wavell, had concluded that "the objective of the majority of the Congress . . . [is] to establish themselves at the center and to suppress, cajole, or buy over the Muslims, and then impose a constitution at their leisure" (Jalal 1985, 224). Jinnah was willing to break the deadlock, but the Congress, once having tasted power, was not willing to share it. Jalal notes that Lord Wavell had, by now, "come to believe that there was a complete lack of greatness or generosity about Indian political leaders" (Jalal 1985, 213).

When the viceroy asked the Congress to form an interim government without the Muslim League, contrary to his wartime promise, Jinnah declared August 16, 1946, Direct Action Day to explain to the public why the interim proposals were not acceptable. Jinnah, a staunch constitutionalist, was pushed by events into mass politics, which he was wary of. Two days earlier, he urged Muslims to remain calm and to consider the day as a day of peaceful reflection. Although most of the demonstrations were peaceful, there was a major disaster in Calcutta when Hindus attempted to stop a Muslim march. More than 5,000 people lost their lives in a single afternoon. Communal rioting broke out at an unprecedented scale, particularly in Bengal and Bihar. The violence could not be controlled by secular constitutionalists like Jinnah or Nehru. The massacre of Muslims in Calcutta and the retaliatory killings subsided only when Mohandas Gandhi walked from village to village and threatened to fast unto death until the killing stopped. He worked with Hussain Shaheed Suhrawardy, the Muslim League provincial chief minister, and controlled the killings in Bengal somewhat. In October 1946, the Muslim League agreed to join the Congress government temporarily to cool down passions, but rioting quickly spread to the whole of northern India and continued until 1947, with Muslim masses demanding a country of their own, Pakistan.

The Muslim League had required a demonstration of popular Muslim support to improve its bargaining position vis-à-vis a strong, uncompromising Congress to get assurances of safeguards for Muslims and to bring the League into the interim government. But the rallying of mass support turned into mass hysteria, destroying the "India of Jinnah's dreams." As Jalal, in her exhaustive study of Jinnah and the Muslim League, writes about the Direct Action Day, "All that is certain is that Jinnah had no idea of what was coming. It is not just that the politics of violence . . . were anathema to him, alien to his political style and never to become a part of it, but the more powerful argument is that Jinnah did not expect, and certainly did not want, anything like this to happen. . . . Jinnah had his own priorities savaged tooth and claw by an unthinking mob, fired by blood lust, fear and greed" (Jalal 1985, 216). What had started as a constitutional struggle for protection of Muslim interests within an undivided India by Jinnah had ended in a mass movement for a separate state.

Creation of Pakistan and Partition

The communal rioting escalated, almost on the level of a civil war. Lord Mountbatten, the newly appointed viceroy with specific instructions to arrange for the independence of India by June 1948, was forced to revise the timescale. He reluctantly concluded that partition was preferable to continued violence and probable civil war. It has been alleged that on several occasions, Lord Mountbatten failed to observe protocol or the pretense of impartiality, often having negotiations with only one of two contending sides; sharing information only with Nehru and not Jinnah regarding important meetings, agendas, and even the partition plan; discussing the strategy for talking to Jinnah with the Congress leaders; and other similar occurrences. He believed that under the circumstances Jinnah would be willing to accept a smaller Pakistan than the one he demanded, meaning not all of Punjab and Bengal, Assam, Sindh, North-West Frontier Province, and Balochistan, but with a partitioned Punjab and Bengal, which is what the Congress wanted. Jinnah wanted neither a partition of Punjab and Bengal nor a truncated Pakistan. But this was all that he could now expect to get, and he accepted it. However, Gandhi opposed partition to the end and even suggested making Jinnah the prime minister to prevent partition. But Congress and Nehru ignored him and approved the partition plan by a 5–to–1 margin.

Independence came to India at last, after a century of British rule, in 1947. Pakistan came into existence as an independent Muslim state on August 14, 1947, with two parts sep-

Pakistan came into existence as an independent Muslim state on August 14, 1947. In the official ceremony, British viceroy Lord Louis Mountbatten (in uniform) officially hands power over to Mohammad Ali Jinnah (left), leader of the new nation of Pakistan. (Library of Congress)

arated by 1,000 miles of Indian territory. The eastern wing was called East Pakistan, presently the country of Bangladesh, and today's Pakistan was called West Pakistan. The geographic separation appeared to Pakistanis at that time to be of less consequence than the common bond of Islam. Muslims all over the subcontinent were in a state of euphoria. With 70 million people, Pakistan became the fifth most populous country in the world at that time (now the sixth). It also became the world's most populous Muslim country, a position that was lost to Indonesia in 1971 when the province of East Pakistan became the state of Bangladesh. Mohammad Ali Jinnah became the first governor general of Pakistan. He was and continues to be as highly honored in Pakistan as George Washington is in the United States. He is rightfully called the

Father of the Nation, Quaid-e-Azam Mohammad Ali Jinnah, without whose leadership Pakistan would never have been created as an independent Muslim state. (Pakistan Mission to the UN)

Father of the Nation. His people bestowed on him the title of Quaid-e-Azam (Great Leader) because Pakistan owes its very existence to his drive, tenacity, and judgment. To this day, Pakistanis honor him with this title. Jinnah's importance in the creation of Pakistan was monumental and immeasurable.

He united the subcontinent's 100 million Muslims behind his demand for a separate homeland for Muslims, and he won independence for Pakistan within seven years of the Lahore Resolution. It was a feat unprecedented in modern history: he created an entirely new state legally, without lifting a gun and without spending even a single day in prison.

The India Independence Act of July 14, 1947, created two independent states in the subcontinent, Pakistan and India. The 562 princely states were given the option to accede to either country. The immediate question was the drawing of the boundaries of Pakistan, which were not announced until three days after independence, and all the political parties agreed in advance to abide by it. The partition of India also included partitions of the Muslim-majority provinces of Punjab and Bengal. Under the guidelines of the partition plan, contiguous Muslim-majority districts in Punjab and Bengal were awarded to Pakistan. Muslims reluctantly agreed with Jinnah on this division of their homeland, where borders tore through power lines, railroads, irrigation canals, and fields. The legislatures in both Punjab and Bengal approved partition. Sindh's legislative assembly and Balochistan's *jirga* (council of tribal leaders) agreed to join Pakistan. A plebiscite was held in Assam's Sylhet district and in the North-West Frontier Province (boycotted by Congress), and the vote was for Pakistan. The princely states of Bahawalpur in Punjab, Khairpur in Sindh, and Dir, Chitral, Amb, and Hunza in the northwest acceded to Pakistan, with the frontier states retaining customary law and autonomy in internal administration.

With the exception of three states, all 562 princely states quickly acceded to India or Pakistan. The factors affecting the decision were geographic contiguity with Indian or Pakistani territory, religious identity of the majority population, and right of accession of the ruler, which was influenced to some extent by the religion of the ruler. The three that were problematic were the two largest princely states, Jammu and Kashmir (usually just called Kashmir) and Hyderabad, and one small state, Junagadh. Two of these states, Hyderabad and Junagadh, had Muslim rulers who wanted to accede to Pakistan but they had majority Hindu populations and were located in Indian territory. They tried to accede to Pakistan but were quickly incorporated by force into India. The third princely state of Jammu and Kashmir had borders with both India and Pakistan. It had the opposite situation of a Hindu ruler and majority Muslim population but was not absorbed in Pakistan, counter to the principle of consistency of criteria. Consequently, there was no peaceful resolution of its status, which has remained a source of armed conflict and tension between India and Pakistan to this day. Serious charges have been leveled against Mountbatten for improperly using his influence to steer the Maharaja away from acceding to Pakistan, about his alleged role in trying to influence the findings of the Boundary Commission, and about his part in creating the conditions for lasting conflict in Kashmir (Jones 2002, 59–60).

On August 17, three days after the creation of Pakistan, the boundaries were announced by a commission headed by Sir Cyril Radcliffe. No one was prepared for the holocaust that followed. In east Punjab, armed Sikhs and Hindus slaughtered thousands of Muslims with the purpose of driving all the Muslims into Pakistan, causing most of them to flee across the border. In west Punjab, Muslims took revenge and slaughtered thousands of Sikhs and Hindus, driving almost all the Sikhs and Hindus there across the border into India. Within less than a year, by conservative estimates, about seventeen million refugees moved between India and Pakistan (more than six million Hindus and Sikhs to India and more than eight million Muslims to Pakistan), the largest transfer of populations in recorded history. Almost one million people were murdered in the religious violence of 1947 and 1948, and countless women were raped on both sides. The violence fed on itself and could not be quelled by any attempt made by Jinnah, Nehru, and Gandhi. Gandhi tried to promote harmony in India, and Jinnah urged equal rights for all citizens including minorities. He repeatedly assured Pakistan's non-Muslims that "Pakistan is not going to be a theocratic state—to be ruled by priests with a divine mission. . . . Hindus, Christians and Parsis . . . will enjoy the same rights and privileges as any other citizen" (Weston 1992, 92). He also appointed A. R. Cornelius, a Christian, as the first chief justice of the Supreme Court.

Although Pakistan was born in bloodshed and turmoil, it survived in the initial and difficult months after partition only because of the tremendous sacrifices made by its people and the selfless efforts of its great leader. Jinnah traveled all over the country to build confidence and morale, although he was terminally ill and over seventy years old. In spite of the untold human suffering preceding and following partition, the burden of several million refugees, and the country's seeming economic nonviability, Pakistan and its people proved their resilience. In its first turbulent year, the Pakistan government struggled each day to prevent new violence, to set up refugee camps, to save crops that Hindus and Sikhs had abandoned, to feed eight million refugees, to set up schools and health facilities, and to man the jobs that needed to be done. Refugees and residents alike volunteered endless hours of work with missionary zeal in these early days. Although refugees flowed into East Pakistan, Punjab, and Sindh, the vast majority came to Karachi in Sindh. The Sindhis graciously welcomed millions of Muhajirs (refugees) into their land.

Communal violence and refugee rehabilitation were not the only concerns of the new state. There were other pressing problems, internal as well as external, and some immediate but others long-term. Pakistan's economy seemed on the brink of collapse because the major market for Pakistani commodities was India, an arrangement that was no longer viable. At partition, Pakistan had the capability to manufacture machine tools, diesel engines, and surgical instruments, as well as carding, ginning, rice hulling, and flour grinding machines. It also had many qualified engineers and artisans (Kibria 1999). But it did not have enough machinery and equipment or personnel for a new country. Although the League and Congress had negotiated the division of assets— weapons, military equipment, railroad cars, bank deposits, typewriters, and even paper—before partition, deliveries remained a problem. For example, none of the weapon production machinery ever left India. Division of the Indian Civil Service and Police Service was also very difficult. Only 101 out of 1,157 Indian officers were Muslim, 95 of whom opted for Pakistan, which was far lower than the requirement (Blood 1995, 37). Gandhi had earlier fasted until the Congress cabinet pledged to send Pakistan its rightful share of all of British India's assets and wealth (supposed to be in proportion to population at one-sixth of the total), but the pledge was never honored fully. Gandhi continued to insist even after partition, and this was one of the reasons for his assassination at the hands of a Hindu fanatic on January 30, 1948. His death was a great shock to Muslims also, who felt that the shield that he had provided to Muslims against Hindu violence was gone. Moreover, India posed a threat to Pakistan's sovereignty as many Indian leaders expressed the hope after independence that Pakistan would collapse and be reunited with India.

Other pressing problems pertained to the North-West Frontier Province, Afghanistan, and Kashmir. The continued popularity and grassroots support for a Congress government in the North-West Frontier Province posed an immediate problem. Its leader, Khan Abdul Ghaffar Khan, and his followers had boycotted the 1947 plebiscite and supported the Congress. Moreover, relations with Afghanistan were hostile as it periodically disputed, together with the Pakhtun tribes straddling the Pakistan-Afghanistan border, the legitimacy of the Durand line. This line was drawn by the British in 1893 as a boundary between the two countries. Afghanistan, claiming that the line had been imposed by the British, favored the creation of an independent state of *Pashtunistan* or *Pakhtunistan.* Pakistan insisted that the boundary was legal and permanent. Diplomatic ties with Afghanistan were severed, and it cast the only vote against Pakistan's admission to the United Nations in 1947.

Kashmir posed a special problem then as it does now. The overwhelming majority of Kashmiris are Muslims, but the Hindu Maharaja had been reluctant to decide on accession to either India or Pakistan. He was unpopular among his subjects, and there were widespread reports of oppression of Muslim farmers by Hindu landlords in western Kashmir. In October 1947, the farmers rebelled against the landlords and the Maharaja's government. They were supported by 5,000 armed, Pakhtun tribesmen from the North-West Frontier Province, who entered the Maharaja's territory and came within a few miles of Srinagar, the capital. Indian troops were deployed and dispatched to Kashmir on the Maharaja's request, and he had to sign documents acceding to India. The Indian Army drove the Pakhtuns back. Had the Pakhtuns taken the airport instead of engaging in plunder on the outskirts of Srinagar, it would have changed the course of war in Kashmir. Many Pakistanis believe that Kashmir may then have been a part of Pakistan. India and Pakistan agreed to a United Nations cease-fire line on August 13, 1948, thus ending the first Indo-Pakistan War. The cease-fire agreement formalized the military status quo, leaving about 30 percent of Kashmir under Pakistani control and the rest under Indian. The Indian-held eastern part of Kashmir includes the Muslim-dominated Vale of Kashmir and the Hindu-majority region of Jammu to the south. The Pakistani-held western part is drier and less populated, and includes the Northern Areas and Azad Kashmir.

Pakistan maintained that India had secured Kashmir through fraud. Moreover, under the terms of the UN cease-fire, India was supposed to hold an election to see whether the people of Kashmir wanted to join India or Pakistan or be independent. But India has never allowed such a vote, as a result of which Pakistanis regard the Indian presence in Kashmir as illegitimate and tyrannical. And India has never honored the UN resolutions and has never held elections for fear that Kashmiri Muslims would vote for Pakistan. Both India and Pakistan claim the whole of Kashmir. The Kashmir dispute has dominated India-Pakistan relations for over four decades. They have fought two major wars to maintain or seize control over this state: in 1947–1948 and in 1965. Kashmir's contested and indeterminate status continues to be a source of tension and conflict between India and Pakistan, causing each country to devote half or more of its budget to defense, thereby depriving its social sectors.

Two other important challenges faced Pakistan in both the short and long run. The first challenge concerned the distribution of power between the central and provincial governments. The second was about the role of Islam in the new nation: would Pakistan be a secular homeland for Muslims, or would it be an Islamic state governed by the *Sharia?* Both questions would continue to plague Pakistan for a long time after independence, even extending to the present. (These controversies are addressed more in Chapter 3.)

On September 11, 1948, Quaid-e-Azam Mohammad Ali Jinnah died of lung cancer at the age of seventy-one. The fourteen-hour workdays he had experienced for so many years had finally taken their toll. Only he and his physician had known for years, even before independence, that Jinnah was terminally ill. Many Pakistanis believe that had the British or the Congress known of his terminal illness, Pakistan would have never come into existence and the dreams of Indian Muslims would have never come true. The young nation lost its founding father just thirteen months after its creation. But it lost more than just its founding father. Jinnah's death deprived Pakistan of a leader who could have enhanced stability and democratic governance in the country. He was also perhaps the only one who could have brought about regional cohesion. Although India also lost Gandhi the same year, it was fortunate in having at least one of its two great leaders, Nehru, govern it for seventeen years. The rocky road to democracy in Pakistan and the relatively smooth one in India can in some measure be ascribed to Pakistan's tragedy of losing an incorruptible and highly revered leader so soon after independence. After the Quaid's death, his longtime associate and lieutenant, Liaquat Ali Khan, became the prime minister. The nation was also to lose him in the next three years.

Since its creation, Pakistan has gone through many crises, the most devastating being the civil war and separation of East Pakistan. The challenges have been both internal and external. Periods of brief democracy have been interspersed with military rule. It has also faced challenges stemming from its role in the fight against the Soviet occupation of Afghanistan, which has led to a massive social and economic burden of refugees, a *Kalashnikov* culture, increasing lawlessness, and proliferation of drugs. Being the frontline state and a critical ally of the United States in the war on terrorism has created its own problems, including a backlash by religious extremists. In the fifty-nine years since its creation, Pakistan has seen three wars with India, one civil war and dismemberment, four military coups, and excessive corruption of democratically elected governments. Yet the nation has weathered all these storms and has done reasonably well in terms of economic growth and fostering an overall climate of optimism and hope. That it has done so owes much to the spiritual and political legacy of leaders like Quaid-e-Azam, and to the resilience and fundamental value of the Pakistan ideal that they forged. The ideal of a just social order in the promised land still holds for many, but when and to what extent that ideal will become a reality remain to be seen.

References and Further Reading
Alavi, Hamza. 2002. "Misreading Partition Road Signs." *Economic and Political Weekly,* November 2–9.
Blood, Peter R. (ed.). 1995. *Pakistan: A Country Study* (Area Handbook Series). Washington, DC: Library of Congress.

Human Development Report 2003. 2003. New York: Oxford University Press.

The Human Rights Watch Report. 2002. *Closed Door Policy: Afghan Refugees in Pakistan and Iran.* http://hrw.org/reports/2002/pakistan/pakistan0202–01.htm.

Jalal, Ayesha. 1985. *The Sole Spokesman: Jinnah, the Muslim League and the Demand for Pakistan.* New York: Cambridge University Press.

Jones, Owen Bennett. 2002. *Pakistan: Eye of the Storm.* New Haven, CT: Yale University Press.

Kibria, Ghulam. 1999. *A Shattered Dream: Understanding Pakistan's Underdevelopment.* Karachi, Pakistan: Oxford University Press.

Malik, Sohail J., Safiya Aftab, and Nargis Sultana. 1994. *Pakistan's Economic Performance 1947–1993: A Descriptive Analysis.* Lahore, Pakistan: Sure Publishers.

Mumtaz, Khawar, and Yameema Mitha. 2003. *Pakistan: Tradition and Change. An Oxfam Country Profile.* Great Britain: Oxfam.

Noman, Omar. 1990. *Pakistan: A Political and Economic History since 1947.* New York: Routledge, Chapman and Hall.

Population Census Organization. 1998. Statistics Division, Ministry of Economic Affairs and Statistics, Government of Pakistan.

Sathar, Zeba, A. 1992. "Child Survival and Changing Fertility Patterns in Pakistan." *The Pakistan Development Review* 31(4), Part 2.

Siddiqui, Fakhari A. 2001. "Importance of a Population Policy in Pakistan." *The Pakistan Development Review* 40(1), Part 1.

Spear, Percival. 1972. *India: A Modern History.* Ann Arbor: University of Michigan Press.

"Study of Taxi Drivers Finds More Immigrants at Wheel." 2004, July 7. *New York Times.* http://www.nytimes.com/2004/07/07/nyregion/07taxi.html?ex=1142830800&en=073d2f1a502f3fae&ei=5070.

Tonchev, Plamen. 2003. *Pakistan at Fifty-five: From Jinnah to Musharraf.* European Institute for Asian Studies, BP 02/03, 8 EUR Series.

Weaver, Mary Anne. 2002. *Pakistan: In the Shadow of Jihad and Afghanistan.* New York: Farrar, Straus and Giroux.

Weston, Mark. 1992. *The Land and People of Pakistan.* New York: Harper Collins.

World Bank Data. 2005. http://devdata.worldbank.org/hnpstats/thematic Rpt.asp.

World Development Report 2005. 2004. Washington, DC: The World Bank.

Ziad, Zeenut (ed.). 2002. *The Magnificent Mughals.* Karachi, Pakistan: Oxford University Press.

Ziring, Lawrence. 1999. *Pakistan in the Twentieth Century: A Political History.* Karachi, Pakistan: Oxford University Press.

CHAPTER TWO
The Economy of Pakistan

Pakistan's economic performance over the past fifty-nine years since its independence has been impressive. This performance is reflected in a tripling of real per capita income over the period, increasing real wage rates and declining levels of poverty, and a structural transformation of the economy. In 2003, Pakistan's gross national income (GNI—formerly gross national product, or GNP), which is the broadest measure of the output of goods and services of an economy plus net receipts of primary income from foreign sources, was estimated to be US$69 billion. Since money buys more in Pakistan than it does in the United States, as in all countries where prices are low, the GNI is converted into international dollars by using purchasing power parity (PPP) conversion factors, which depend on Pakistani prices. At the PPP rate, one international dollar has the same purchasing power in Pakistan as it does in the United States. In 2003, the PPP-GNI (GNI adjusted for the lower Pakistani prices) was estimated to be US$306 billion, about five times the unadjusted GNI of US$69 billion, reflecting the fact that a dollar buys five times as much in Pakistan as it does in the United States. Given a population of 148.4 million in 2003, the per capita income was $470 (about $40 per month), and the PPP per capita income at $2,060 was a little over $170 per month (World Development Report 2004, 257).

The increase in Pakistan's income has been fairly steady since its creation as an independent nation at the partition of British India in 1947 under difficult circumstances, with a meager resource base. Table 2.1 indicates that GDP increased from US$3.8 billion in 1947 to US$67 billion in 2001; an increase of over 1,600 percent, implying a growth of 5.3 percent per year. During the same period, population increased from 33 million to 143 million, at a rate of 2.6 percent per annum. Despite this relatively high population growth rate, the high GDP growth rate allowed per capita incomes to grow at least 2.7 percent per year during the period (from US$85 in 1947 to US$414 in 2001). This upward trend in growth rates is all the more significant because of inconsistencies and several turnarounds in economic policies with every change in government over the years. The growth rate of per capita GDP from 2002 to 2003 is reported to be 3.3 percent.

Although the level of per capita income and its growth rate are higher in Pakistan than in some of its South Asian neighbors like Bangladesh and Nepal, it is still one of the poorest nations in the world outside of Africa. The purchasing power of a family in Pakistan is about the same as that of one in Cambodia, or about half that of a family in Guatemala.

Pakistan ranks 137 out of 175 countries in terms of GDP per capita (PPP US$). Its ranking on the Human Development Index (HDI), which measures achievements in health, education, and standard of living, is even worse. It ranks 144 out of 175 countries, which is lower than any of its South Asian neighbors. Average life expectancy at birth in Pakistan is sixty years, less than the average for all developing countries and for South Asia. The adult literacy rate, measured as the percentage of persons above age fifteen who are literate, is 44 percent, and the combined primary, secondary, and tertiary enrollment ratio is 36 percent. Both the education indicators—the enrollment ratio and the adult literacy rate—are lower than even the average for the least developed countries of the world. Pakistan's performance in the education and health sectors is much worse when compared to countries with the same level of income such as Vietnam and Mongolia. Moreover, countries like Korea, which were at the same level of development and growth in the 1960s as was Pakistan, have experienced much faster economic growth and social development. The per capita GDP (PPP US$) in Korea is nine times

Table 2.1   Long-Term Structural Change in the Pakistan Economy

	1947	1970	2001
Population (in million)	33	60	143
GDP (US$ billion)	3.8	10.8	67
Per Capita Income (US$)	85	170	414
Agricultural Production Index	100	219	514
Manufacturing Production Index	100	2,346	12,107
Literacy Rate	11	20	49
Primary Enrollment Rate	5	22	91

Source: Ishrat Hussain. 2003. *Economic Management in Pakistan 1999–2002*. Oxford: Oxford University Press, p. 222.

that of Pakistan today. Thus the potential for growth and development in Pakistan has not been fully realized (Human Development Report 2003, 239–240).

But there is reason for hope. More recently, liberalization of the economy through greater reliance on markets, privatization, and removal of subsidies and some trade restrictions has started to bear fruit, and integration with the world economy has begun. Pakistan's credibility with the international finance institutions has been restored, the erosion of institutions appears to have been halted, and corruption seems to be coming under control. The problem of deterioration in physical infrastructure has been recognized, and attempts to resolve it have begun. The growth rate of GDP has been impressive at 5.1 percent in 2002–2003 and 6.4 percent in 2003–2004, and that in manufacturing even more so. The growth rate in the manufacturing sector increased from 7.6 percent in 2000–2001 (and 1.5 percent in 1999–2000) to 13.4 percent in 2003–2004. In the external sector, exports as a percentage of GDP have been consistently increasing since 1998–1999, as has the surplus on current account balance, which shows the difference between export and import of goods and services, net investment income and remittances, debt-service repayments of principal and interest, and foreign aid. The growth rate of GDP in 2004–2005 was reported to be almost 8.5 percent, among the highest levels in the world and the fastest in Asia, excluding China (IMF 2005).

OVERVIEW OF ECONOMIC PERFORMANCE

Pakistan's fifty-nine years since independence in 1947 can be divided into six different periods or eras, which represent different economic policies, political systems, and planning choices, and roughly coincide with Pakistan's Five-Year Development Plans (Table 2.2). The first eleven years, between 1947 and 1958, were devoted to coping with the unprecedented scale of migration, the largest in history; in building an economic base through the public (government) sector; and particularly in embarking on an import-substituting industrialization (ISI) strategy in line with the prevailing economic ideology of the time. An ISI strategy aims to replace imports by promoting domestic industries through a set of policies designed to restrict imports on the one hand and encourage domestic production on the other. Imports are typically restricted by the imposition of a tariff, a fixed percentage tax on the value of an import, or of a quota, which is a physical limitation on the quantity of an item that can be imported. The period between 1947 and 1958 was also characterized by high political turnover and instability as seven different non-military governments succeeded each other—either appointed or nominated. The second period, 1958–1971, dominated until 1969 by the military rule of General Mohammed Ayub Khan, is often known as the golden era of economic development, which was characterized by greater attention to economic planning and witnessed unprecedented growth rates. Pakistan was then considered to be a model for other developing countries and one of the few that would achieve developed country status. However, serious disruptions were caused by the war with India in 1965 and by the separation of East Pakistan in 1971 to form the independent nation of Bangladesh. The third period, 1971–1977, under the elected government of Zulfiqar Ali Bhutto, witnessed the nationalization of large parts of the economy, accompanied by the oil crisis and bad weather. The fourth period, 1977–1988, under the military regime of General Ziaul Haq, was characterized by the Afghan War (with its consequences of large aid flows from the United States and a drug and arms culture in Pakistan), opening up of employment opportunities in the Middle East resulting in large remittances from Pakistani workers abroad, and the Islamization of the economy and society. The fifth period, 1988–1999, saw the restoration of democratically elected governments, adherence to the process of liberalization and privatization of the economy, and governance problems and fiscal imbalances. The current period, starting in 1999, under the military regime of General Pervez Musharraf, has been characterized by a consistency in policy continuing with liberalization of the economy and increasing credibility with international finance institutions, but slow progress in the social sectors, particularly education. This section briefly presents the main features, accomplishments, and challenges of the six eras since Pakistan's independence.

The growth pattern in Pakistan, as in Brazil, Mexico, Kenya, Nigeria, and the Philippines, conforms to an elitist growth model in which a small group of elites exercises both economic and political power. According to Hussain, "the market is rigged and the state is hijacked in order to deliver most of the benefits of economic growth to this small group" (1999, xii). The outcome is that both the market and the state are deprived of their strengths: markets lead to inefficient rather than efficient outcomes, and the state exacerbates the inequities in the system rather than ensuring equity. For the first fifty years, Pakistan followed this same model under different forms of governments and ideologies (nonmilitary governments of the early years, the secular military regime of Ayub Khan, the elected government of Zulfiqar Ali Bhutto, the Islamic military regime of Ziaul Haq, the liberal elected government of Benazir Bhutto, and the conservative elected government of Nawaz Sharif). Each time, "the same constellation of landlords, industrialists, traders, politicians, military and civil bureaucrats, and some co-opted members of the religious oligarchy, and professional and intellectual groups dominated the scene under every single government" (Hussain 1999, xiii).

The Early Years and the Import-Substituting Industrialization (ISI) Strategy: 1947–1958

Pakistan, born as a new nation in 1947, started its history with a predominantly agrarian economy dominated by a small number of large landowners, almost no industry or infrastructure, and a net outflow of human capital as Hindu entrepreneurs migrated to India. Ports, transportation, energy, and power were underdeveloped, as were services such as banking and government. The two wings, West Pakistan and East Pakistan, were separated by more than 1,000 miles of Indian territory.

The early years of economic planning focused on the Herculean task of rehabilitating about 6.5 million Muslim refugees from India and providing basic necessities to them. These refugees (Muhajirs) included skilled workers, experienced civil servants, and a mercantile class, who used the modest capital that they brought from India to start trading firms. The Korean War led to a boom in raw material prices between 1950 and 1952, and an increase in demand for Pakistani exports of raw cotton and raw jute. The windfall gains and export revenues accumulated by the Muhajir traders, and their shift to industry in the 1950s in response to government policy geared to channel merchant capital into the industrial sector, paved the way for the foundation of industry. Protected by severe controls on the import of consumer goods,

Table 2.2 GNP/GDP Annual Growth Rates under Different Plan Periods

Items	Pre-Plan	First Plan	Second Plan	Third Plan	Non-Plan PERIOD	Fifth Plan	Sixth Plan	Seventh Plan	Eighth Plan	Non-Plan	Ten Years Plan
	1950–55	1955–60	1960–65	1965–70	1970–78	1978–83	1983–88	1988–93	1993–98	1998–01	2001–11*
GNP (Factor Cost)	—	3.0	6.8	6.7	5.2	6.4	5.0	4.2	3.9	3.4	5.3
GDP (Factor Cost)	3.1	3.0	6.8	6.6	4.4	6.6	6.2	4.8	4.3	3.5	5.4
Sectors:											
Agriculture	1.2	2.0	3.8	6.3	1.8	4.5	3.5	4.0	5.9	1.8	3.8
Manufacturing	4.4	5.2	11.7	8.1	4.5	9.9	8.2	5.0	3.6	4.3	6.9
Others	3.9	3.5	8.3	6.5	6.2	6.9	7.0	5.2	3.8	4.1	5.9

* Projections

Source: Government of Pakistan, Federal Bureau of Statistics. 2003. *Statistical Pocketbook: Pakistan.* http://www.statpak.gov.pk/.

and aided by their Korean boom gains to import machinery, the erstwhile traders started producing consumer goods domestically.

Rapid industrialization was viewed as a vehicle for economic growth in consonance with the prevailing thinking in the development economics literature in favor of export pessimism and infant-industry protection, which argued that developing countries would be better off if they shifted from a policy of reliance on traditional primary-product exports to promoting new or infant domestic industries by imposing tariffs and quotas on imports that competed with these industries. Moreover, disillusionment with the market mechanism and with free-trade policies in many developing countries after the economic depression also caused a shift to protection of domestic industry by trade barriers such as tariffs. The emphasis was on establishment of import-substituting industries and heavy tariff protection was given to these infant industries. At the same time, the capital goods and machinery used by these industries were subsidized through credit at low interest rates and preferential access to foreign exchange allocation for imports of capital goods. Moreover, the official exchange rate (the price of one currency in terms of that of another, say, the rupee in terms of the dollar) was set at a level higher than its real or *shadow* value, for example, 5 Pakistani rupees per dollar instead of, say, 10 rupees per dollar. This overvalued exchange rate reduced the real cost of imported machinery for the industrial sector and increased the real cost of exports for the agricultural sector. Government policy also provided liberal fiscal incentives for the private sector as investment in approved projects was tax-free for a number of years. Moreover, public investment in infrastructure complemented private investment. While there was exclusive public ownership in the production and operation of military armaments, hydroelectric power, railways, telephone, and telegraph, the government also helped develop some industries to hand them over to the private sector.

The notable achievement of this era was the development of a consumer goods sector that produced textiles, processed foods, footwear, and other goods directly used by consumers under cover of protection. While manufacturing grew at 9.6 percent per year and construction at 6.8 percent during the period, the overall GNP growth rate was only 3.2 percent because of a stagnant agriculture with a growth rate of 2.8 percent per year. During this period, per capita rural incomes and wages of industrial workers declined in both East and West Pakistan. The stagnation of farmers' incomes in the major commodity-producing sector of the economy limited the market for the high-priced consumer goods produced domestically by the protected industrial sector, eventually limiting industrial growth. Moreover, agricultural stagnation increased food imports, creating a foreign exchange shortage and balance-of-payments problems. The agricultural sector stagnated both because of low public investment in agriculture and anti-agriculture pricing policies. The prices of domestically produced manufactured goods were kept high through tariffs on imports, while the prices of food and raw

materials were artificially kept low through compulsory pro-
curement prices (or ceiling prices, which are set below market prices), thus deliberately turning the terms of trade (ratio
of agricultural to industrial prices) against agriculture and
causing a resource transfer from agriculture to industry.
Moreover, the overvalued exchange rate meant that the
farmer, being the exporter of agricultural products, was paid
less than what he would have received under a free-market
exchange rate, which amounts to a tax on agriculture. Similarly, an importer of industrial machinery and raw materials
paid less than what he would have paid under a free-market
exchange rate, amounting to a subsidy to industry. It is estimated that the agricultural sector transferred 15 percent of its
gross output annually to the urban sector, of which only 15 to
37 percent was invested (Noman 1990, 18). According to Hussain, "the transfer of resources from East to West Pakistan,
and from agriculture to protected and inefficient industry,
were two of the worst legacies of the 1950s" (Hussain 1999,
14). The net transfer of resources is estimated to be 2 to 3 percent of West Pakistan's GDP during 1950–1960 (Islam 1981).
The transfer of foreign exchange revenues earned by jute
exports of the eastern wing to industrialists in West Pakistan
became a symbol of regional exploitation. Resentment against
the transfer ultimately led to the civil war and separation of
East Pakistan in 1971.

Also, economic policy did not tackle the problem of mass
poverty, and the pledge of economic reform was not fulfilled,
largely because of the the dominance of the landed elite in the
political structure. Moreover, allocations for education and
health were squeezed by military expenditures to safeguard
against Indian threat, thereby establishing a pattern of governmental neglect of social sectors. Only 4 percent of government expenditure was allocated annually for education,
health, and social services, whereas the expenditure on
defense was 193 percent of total development expenditure
and 64 percent of central government revenues in 1949–1950

(Noman 1990, 18–19). The continuing coexistence of large allocations for defense and low allocations for the social sectors has its unfortunate roots in the 1950s.

The ISI regime created a climate in which access to cheap credit, import licenses, and fiscal incentives depended more on political connections and patronage than on efficiency. Since profitability and managerial rewards depended more on securing government support than on long-term planning, time spent on lobbying politicians or government officials yielded a higher return than time spent on economic management. This led to a public-private sector relationship in which patronage predominated, opening the door to both inefficiency and corruption.

The two groups that benefited from the economic policies of the 1950s were the mercantile class, whose profit margins were high because of the high prices of consumer goods and the low prices of capital goods, as explained earlier, and large landowners, who were able to obstruct land reform proposals.

Ayub Khan's Decade of Development: 1958–1969

The Ayub Khan era is most remembered for its impressive growth rates, which have been unprecedented in Pakistani history, for its strong macroeconomic performance, and for its sound economic management in formulating and implementing economic plans, policies, and programs. But this period was also characterized by regional inequity, which hampered the process of national unification and ultimately led to the breakup of Pakistan, as well as by class inequities and the concentration of economic power. Nonetheless, the Ayub government was successful in its objective of creating a substantial class of large industrialists, most of whom were Muhajirs from Karachi and from a different ethnic group than Ayub Khan.

The Ayub era was marked by substantial development of both the agricultural and industrial sectors of the economy.

GNP grew annually at more than 6 percent throughout the decade (Table 2.2), and per capita GNP growth was 3.5 percent in the first half of the decade (1959–1960 to 1964–1965) and 3.7 percent in the second half (1964–1965 to 1969–1970).

Large-scale manufacturing grew at a phenomenal rate of around 17 percent during the first half of the decade. In fact, all sectors grew faster than the targets set in the Second Five-Year Plan (1960–1965). In the second half of Ayub Khan's rule, as Table 2.2 shows, agriculture grew by 6.3 percent per year, while manufacturing grew by 8.1 percent (and large-scale manufacturing by 10 percent). Accordingly, Pakistan was considered to be a model capitalist economy in the 1960s. Figure 2.1 shows the growth rates of key sectors in the economy in the 1960s.

Reversing the neglect in agriculture that had happened in the fifties and early sixties was one of the successes of the Ayub era. This period was marked by an increase in infra-structure investment in agriculture, including irrigation and drainage works, construction of Mangla Dam, and investment

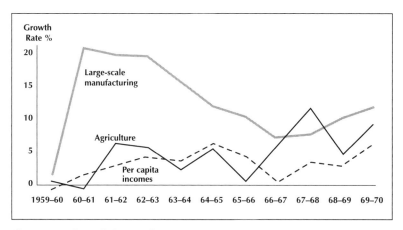

Figure 2.1: Growth Rates of Key Sectors, 1959–1969

Source: Omar Noman. 1990. *Pakistan: A Political and Economic History since 1947*. London: Kegan Paul International, p. 38.

in research, which led to the development of high-yield variety (HYV) seeds of wheat and rice. These seeds could absorb much more fertilizer and water, and consequently their use increased yields per acre significantly. Thus production of wheat and rice increased by more than twofold in the latter half of the 1960s, particularly in Punjab, and agricultural terms of trade also improved. This ushered in the *green revolution,* which was centered on the fertilizer-responsive HYV seeds of wheat and rice, and was accompanied by the increased use of tubewells and tractors. Between 1959 and 1968, usage of tubewells increased sixteenfold, fertilizers thirteenfold, and tractors tenfold, from 2,000 to 19,000. This increase occurred partly because irrigation, fertilizers, and pesticides were heavily subsidized; the subsidy was 100 percent on pesticides and 35 percent on fertilizers. Tractors were implicitly subsidized through remission of import duties, low interest rates, and an overvalued exchange rate, as explained earlier.

Although the biological-chemical technology required by the green revolution (HYV seeds, fertilizers, pesticides, etc.) was scale-neutral, in that it was unaffected by size and could increase yields on both small and large farms, the supporting techniques required to obtain maximum benefits from the new technology had a scale bias in favor of large farms (Mohi-uddin 1983, 46). For instance, HYVs require not merely irrigation, but also sophisticated water management because they are more sensitive to both too much and too little water. Thus higher yields from the new seeds depended on a tubewell for a controlled water supply, which was beyond the means of a small farmer. Moreover, government policies were biased systematically in favor of large farmers. Subsidies to mechanization through low, or even negative, real rates of interest (equal to nominal interest rate minus inflation rate), remission of import duties, and overvaluation of currency combined with import quotas and foreign exchange licensing gave special advantages to the larger farmers. For instance, in

1964–1965, over a third of all loans granted by the Agricultural Development Bank of Pakistan (ADBP) were for purchases of tractors and other mechanical equipment. These policies were supported by foreign aid institutions such as the World Bank and the United States Agency for International Development (USAID). The results to mechanization were reinforced by support prices that were well above world prices, the major beneficiaries being the large farmers who invariably had larger marketable surpluses than smaller farmers.

The green revolution, embodied in high-yield, seed-fertilizer technology, initially increased the demand for labor because the associated cultivation practices regarding the amount, frequency, timing, and method of use of inputs directly increased the level of farming activity and hence labor use. It increased the labor requirements in almost all the individual operations involved in crop production, such as land preparation; sowing; fertilizing; irrigation; weed, pest, and disease control; and harvesting, threshing, and winnowing. For example, HYV seeds required more careful seedbed preparation and planting practices, including precise plant spacing and exact depth of planting, to gain optimum yields. The number and timing of irrigations were also crucial, and two more irrigations were recommended for HYV wheat than for local varieties. Similarly, chemical fertilizers could be applied in dosages of up to three times those for traditional seeds before yield increases leveled off. But heavy application of fertilizer resulted in greater weed and pest infestation, which required more frequent and intensive weeding and at least four sprayings and two dustings of fungicides during the crop cycle. All of these factors increased labor input. Moreover, HYV wheat had to be harvested more quickly than traditional wheat, and HYV rice required quick drying after harvest to avoid deterioration. Finally, HYV technology was associated with higher yields requiring higher labor input in harvesting, threshing, and winnowing operations. The net result was that HYV technology in itself was labor-intensive.

But the combination of HYV technology with mechanization reduced the employment-enhancing effects of the green revolution. Mechanization also had a displacement effect and tenants were evicted as owners resumed land for self-cultivation (Mohiuddin 1983, 122–124).

The growth of the industrial sector was largely due to the gradual liberalization of the economy, combined with profit incentives created by government distortions. In contrast to the 1950s, bureaucratic controls on industrial investment were replaced by a greater reliance on markets and prices. Similarly, restrictions on exports and imports were relaxed. There was greater access to import licenses, and several imports were placed on the "free list," not requiring official licenses at all. Thus imports of industrial raw materials and spare parts became relatively easier. Moreover, controls on profit margins and prices were removed. By 1968, 90 percent of imports had been freed from administrative controls but subjected to tariffs. However, the government protected domestic industry from foreign competition, which inhibited the development of an efficient, competitive industrial sector. Both the tariff protection and an overvalued exchange rate led to the establishment of several inefficient industries. Several studies have shown (Noman 1990, 39) that the value added was negative for almost half of the sampled industrial units. This meant that, at world prices, the value of goods produced by these units was less than the cost of the inputs. Alternatively, the effective rate of protection (on value added) was much higher than the nominal rate (on price of import).

The overvalued exchange rate was favorable to importers and unfavorable to exporters. To promote exports without hurting industrialists who imported capital goods and raw materials, the Export Bonus Scheme (EBS) was introduced in 1959. This scheme introduced multiple exchange rates and gave a premium to exporters of manufactured goods and raw materials. Under its provisions, certain exporters received import permits equal to 10–40 percent of the value of exported goods, which could be sold at one-and-a-half times their value, enabling exporters to receive additional income (Noman 1990, 38). Exporters were also given preferential access to credit. This led to an increase in exports by about 7 percent per year and by 20 percent per year for manufactured exports (Hussain 1999, 17). It led to a diversification of exports in favor of jute and cotton textiles rather than raw jute and cotton. The outcome was that several industries, including cotton textiles, footwear, and leather, became competitive enough to export at the overvalued exchange rate.

Income inequalities increased significantly in the 1960s. There was increasing disparity across regions and classes. Economic prosperity was concentrated in both the agricultural and industrial sectors in central Punjab and in industry in Karachi. Sensitive regional equity issues were utterly neglected, and an ever-increasing gap developed between incomes in East and West Pakistan. Thus, the difference in per capita incomes between East and West Pakistan increased from 30 percent in 1958 to 45 percent in 1965 and 61 percent in 1969 (Noman 1990, 41). Similarly, personal income inequality increased during the period, as shown by a worsening of the Gini coefficient (a measure of aggregate income inequality that ranges from 0—perfect equality—to 1—perfect inequality). Moreover, the percentage of people living below the poverty line increased both in number and as a percentage of the total population. Ayub's industrial and trade policies were accompanied by a deliberate repression of wages. Real wages declined by about a third during the sixties. It is ironic that workers' wages fell during the boom years of Pakistan's industrial expansion. Social sectors such as education and health were also neglected, while population growth rates remained high in spite of a family planning program, which ran into implementation difficulties because of resistance from religious leaders. In fact, the population growth rate increased from 2.3 to 2.8 percent during the sixties. During the Ayub era, Pakistan's performance in education was the worst in Asia in terms of the percentage of national expenditure allocated to education.

The Ayub administration believed in the prevailing wisdom that benefits of economic growth would trickle down to the poor. In fact, the economic development model adopted during the Ayub era under the chief economist of the Planning Commission, Mahbub-ul-Haq, and the Harvard Advisory Group led by Gustav Papanek promoted "functional inequality" as a necessary precondition for high economic growth. It was believed that increasing the incomes of the wealthy, who are high savers, would increase savings and investment in the economy, leading to a larger pie that would benefit everyone. But a few years later, it was Mahbub-ul-Haq's speech that twenty-two families owned 66 percent of industry, 97 percent of insurance, and 80 percent of banking (Noman 1990, 41) that stirred resentment against Ayub and led to a call for economic reform. But while the concentration of industrial wealth was pinpointed, the concentration of wealth and landownership in the agricultural sector was downplayed, partly because the critics were from a different ethnic background than the industrialists and partly because of the power of the landlords.

The three groups that were the beneficiaries of Ayub Khan's development decade were the rural elite and large, wealthy farmers of West Pakistan, particularly Punjab; the extremely wealthy urban groups, including industry and finance moguls; and urban middle-class groups, including white-collar workers and senior civil and military officials.

The industrialization policy, the regional inequities, and particularly the articulation of the concentration of industrial wealth led to a wave of resentment against the income inequalities of the Ayub era and a demand for social and economic reform. Bhutto was instrumental in articulating these demands and in capitalizing on them by promising *roti, kapra,* and *makan* (food, clothing, and shelter) in his election campaign. Promise of social and economic reform and the radical rhetoric of Bhutto and his political party, the Pakistan Peoples Party (PPP), got mass support—from the peasantry, labor unions, urban lower middle class, and students—which propelled the party into prominence in Punjab and Sindh. Surprisingly, support for reform and for Bhutto also came from the landlords from Bhutto's province, Sindh, despite the PPP's avowed objective for land reforms. The interests of the rural elite in Sindh were in conflict with those of the Muhajir traders and industrialists of Karachi; hence the Sindhi land-lords gave full support to the PPP and were well represented in it from the start, because of, and not in spite of, the avowed objective of the PPP for reducing wealth concentration and power of industrialists. Mass demonstrations by students and labor unions led to Ayub's downfall. He resigned in 1969, transferring power to another general, Yahya Khan. It was under Yahya Khan that the first general elections were held in Pakistan, where one party, the Awami League (AL), won virtually all the seats allotted to the east wing, which ensured a majority in the national legislature, and the Pakistan Peoples Party won an absolute majority in West Pakistan. The West Pakistani politicians and the army did not want to transfer power to the majority, which ultimately led to a bitter civil war, a military crackdown, and the loss of East Pakistan. East Pakistan became the independent nation of Bangladesh, and the new Pakistan consisted only of the former West Pakistan, where the majority party, PPP, came to power led by Bhutto in 1971.

Nationalization and Authoritarian Populism under Bhutto: 1971–1977

In 1971, Zulfiqar Ali Bhutto, the leader of the Pakistan Peoples Party (PPP) and former foreign minister in the government of Ayub Khan, became the first leader of a truncated Pakistan after the cessation of East Pakistan following a brutal civil war and the surrender of the Pakistan Army in the war with India. The performance of the economy in both the agricultural and manufacturing sectors during the Bhutto years was worse when compared to the previous two eras or the era following Bhutto. The average annual growth rate in agriculture during 1970–1978 was 1.8 percent, and in manufacturing 4.5 percent, compared to about 10 percent during the Ayub era (Table 2.2). In fact, per capita agricultural output declined during the period. The GNP growth rate of 5.3 percent was largely due to a 6.2 percent growth rate in other sectors (about 8.9 percent in construction and 4.4 percent in the trade sector) (Hussain 1999, 22). The fastest growing sector in the economy was defense and public administration. In addition to the loss of East Pakistan, which had provided a market for 50 percent of West Pakistani goods and 20 percent of its imports, the PPP administration had to contend with other exogenous shocks. The quadrupling of oil prices following the 1973 OPEC (Organization for Petroleum Exporting Countries) price increases, and the consequent stagflation (the 1970s phenomenon of falling or stagnating output and rising prices), increased Pakistan's import bill and reduced export earnings because of the worldwide recession that followed, leading to a deterioration in the balance of payments. The recurrent domestic cotton crop failures, pest attacks, bad weather, and floods in 1973, 1974, and 1976 adversely affected agriculture. But the policy impact of nationalization and the resulting stifling of private investment, the ad hoc decision making, and political and economic patronage in public enterprises also played a significant role in the overall performance of the economy. Moreover, the promised, more equitable development strategy and social and economic reforms fell far short of expectations, in both formulation and implementation. Thus income inequality increased between 1970 and 1980, and social sectors remained neglected. Nonetheless, Bhutto's popularity remained high among the masses, because, as Noman (1990) points out, his government at least acknowledged the economic rights of the poor, and its attempt at economic reforms, regardless of the degree of success, was enough to sustain popular support for PPP.

The cornerstone of economic policy during the Bhutto era was the nationalization (transfer of ownership and operation from individuals and private groups to the government) of large private manufacturing and financial institutions, which was done in two phases. In 1972, the government nationalized thirty-two large manufacturing plants in eight major industries, including iron and steel, heavy engineering, basic metals, motor vehicle and tractor assembly and manufacture, petrochemicals, cement, chemicals, and public utilities. In spite of the rhetoric, only 20 percent of the value added of the large-scale manufacturing sector came under public ownership because the takeover was confined to the intermediate goods industries, producing raw materials like cement, fertilizer, and chemicals, and capital goods industries, producing capital goods like iron and steel. This first phase, motivated by distributional concerns, was in line with PPP's avowed objective of reducing concentration of wealth in the twenty-two families that had been so important in articulating the inequities of the Ayub era. Support for this nationalization was particularly strong among the rural Sindhi elite for reasons outlined earlier and among the left-wing PPP leadership. By and large, it was generally perceived as an attempt to curb the growth of monopoly capital. But by 1974 the left wing within the PPP had been purged or marginalized, and distributional concerns were no longer important.

The second phase of nationalization began in 1973–1976, and the motivation was different. This second phase was the outcome of ad hoc political responses to different crises and a way to hijack the state for private gains. In 1973 after the devastating floods, when vegetable oil producers hoarded their product leading to a tripling of prices, the government nationalized the vegetable oil industry. This caused a panic in the private sector because the vegetable oil industry was owned not by the top twenty-two families, but by small and medium-sized capitalists. In 1974, all domestically owned private banks and insurance companies were taken over by the state. However, this was anticipated. But industrial confidence was totally eroded, and a fatal blow was struck to private-sector investment when, unexpectedly, in 1976, despite assurances of no further nationalizations, the Bhutto government nationalized the grain milling, cotton-ginning, and rice-husking mills—all owned by small entrepreneurs. By 1976, the state had been hijacked by groups and individuals in command to extend their power and wealth, and access to the state had become "a primary avenue of accumulating a private fortune." Resources were redistributed arbitrarily from public enterprises to private individuals who had access to the state's patronage, through corruption. Public enterprises "became a device to extend political patronage to those whom the regime favored, to pay political debts, or to accumulate power" (Noman 1990, 77–79).

The inevitable outcome of these waves of nationalization and the new industrial strategy was a flight of capital out of the country or into small-scale manufacturing and real estate, stifling of private investment, and a dramatic reversal in the mix of private and public investment. Private investment fell to a quarter of its value between 1971 and 1975 (from Rs. 700 million to Rs. 183 million), while public investment increased by about 19 times during the period (from Rs. 58 million to Rs. 1,085 million). The share of private investment in total decreased from 51.3 percent during the Ayub era to 33.8 percent in the Bhutto era (Hussain 1999, 24).

Figure 2.2 shows the change in private- and public-sector investments between 1970 and 1977. The fall in private investment and the mistrust in the minds of private investors regarding the intentions of elected governments are one of the worst legacies of the Bhutto era, a malaise from which the economy never fully recovered, at least for the next two decades.

The impact of nationalization on the efficiency and growth of the manufacturing sector was not favorable. The share of

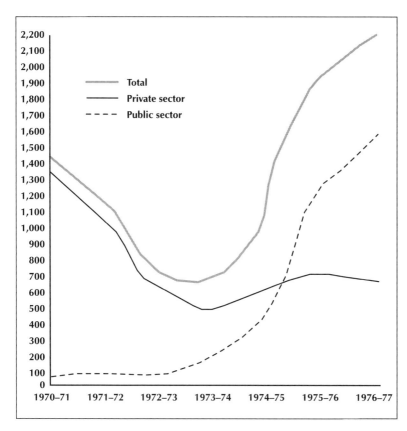

Figure 2.2: Industrial Investment 1970–1977 (constant 1969–1970 prices)
Source: Omar Noman. 1990. *Pakistan: A Political and Economic History since 1947.* London: Kegan Paul International, p. 85.

large-scale manufacturing in GDP declined from 12.6 to 10.7 percent in the period 1971–1977. However, as private investment got diverted to small-scale enterprises, their share in GDP rose from 3.8 to 4.5 percent during the period (Hussain 1999, 25). Inefficiencies abounded because managers were recruited on the basis of loyalty rather than ability or experience. Even clerical jobs were distributed as a reward mechanism to extend political patronage. On the whole, centralized economic planning and the accompanying technical and institutional competence were replaced by a highly personalized and ad hoc approach to planning. In fact, the Planning Commission was bypassed, and economic decision making became more politicized. Moreover, some of the large industrial units that were taken over by the public sector were the most inefficient in the industry sector, with accumulated losses of Rs. 254 million. They also had to employ surplus workers for political reasons, which led to decline in productivity and increase in losses. While some public-sector industries made profits, like cement, petroleum and fertilizer, and automotives, many incurred heavy losses, particularly those that were located in remote areas such as Larkana, Bhutto's hometown. The combination of overstaffing, inefficient management appointees, and inappropriate and political location choices affected financial performance. The inevitable outcome was huge losses; fall in growth rates; high budget deficits, showing an excess of government expenditures over revenues; and inflation.

The biggest contradiction in policy, and the largest gap between expectations and outcomes, was in the regime's record on income distribution. Bhutto had gained popularity on the platform of social justice and equality, but income distribution worsened during his years in office. The Gini coefficient, a measure of personal income inequality, increased by nearly 22 percent for rural areas, 10 percent for urban areas, and about 14 percent for all areas during this period. More specifically, the Gini coefficient increased from 0.291 in 1972 to 0.355 in 1980 for rural areas, from 0.363 in 1970 to 0.400 in 1979 for urban areas, and from 0.231 in 1972 to 0.263 in 1980 for all areas (Hussain 1999, 22). The inflation rate was 16 percent during the period compared to 5 percent in the 1960s. The petite bourgeoisie, consisting of small industrialists, traders, and shopkeepers (who had resented Bhutto's second phase of nationalization), joined hands with politicians (who resented Bhutto's authoritarian populism) in the opposition movement that toppled the PPP government in 1977. General Ziaul Haq, whom Bhutto had patronized and appointed commander-in-chief of the army, superseding several other generals, led a coup against Bhutto. Subsequently, Bhutto was executed and Ziaul Haq continued in power.

The winners and losers during the Bhutto era were some-what different from those of earlier eras. As in the previous two decades, the rural elite and large landowners were the beneficiaries from the policies of the 1970s, with a caveat. It was only the landlords of Punjab and Sindh, particularly old and new members of PPP, who were the real beneficiaries, as they could subvert resumption of their landholdings under Bhutto's land reforms (discussed in a later section). On the other hand, large landowners in the NWFP and Balochistan, who were Bhutto's political opponents, did not benefit, as land reforms were used to punish them and to resume some of their lands. But in contrast to the early years and the Ayub era, the erstwhile merchants and industrialists, mostly from Karachi and Muhajirs, lost under Bhutto's government, which met its declared objective of "clipping the wings of the large industrial families." Again, in contrast to the sixties, the urban middle class lost ground as it was hit by a reduction of subsidies on consumption goods and nationalization of pri-vate schools, which adversely affected the quality of educa-tion. At the same time, people in all classes, rich or poor, rural or urban, benefited greatly if they had access to state patron-age, which was true mostly for Sindhis. Low-income indus-trial workers also made significant gains due to an increase in their wages (which was also true for low-income government employees) and an improvement in their benefits package under the new labor laws passed by the government. In fact, the government's pro-poor attitude, whether real or per-ceived, reflecting policy or rhetoric, was instrumental in Bhutto's unparalleled popularity among working classes and the poor, in life as well as in death.

Islamization and Liberalization of the Economy under the Military Government of Ziaul Haq: 1977–1988

The two cornerstones of Mohammad Ziaul Haq's economic policy were the liberalization and the Islamization of the economy. The Zia era was also marked by a second economic revolution after Ayub's, fueled by unprecedented remittances from Pakistanis working in the Middle East, and U.S. aid in support of Mujahideen and for being the frontline state against Soviet expansionism in the region. The economy performed very well during the period, with an average annual growth rate of more than 6 percent in GDP, 4 percent in agriculture, and about 9 percent in manufacturing during the Fifth and Sixth Plan periods, 1978–1988 (Table 2.2). The Planning Commission was revived, but economic policy did not occupy center stage under the Zia regime as it did in the Ayub era. The worst legacy of the Zia era was the development of a *Kalashnikov* and drug culture, increasing ethnic violence and religious intolerance, and a deterioration in the status of women. The period was also marked by current account deficits and a widening gap in the balance of payments.

The economic policy of the Zia years was characterized by greater reliance on private enterprise. The Zia regime set out to reverse the nationalization policies and the public-sector-led growth strategy of the Bhutto era and to liberalize the economy. In fact, the economic policies under Zia were more liberal than those of any of his predecessors. Both his industrial and trade policies were framed to restore private-sector confidence in the government's decision not to nationalize and to encourage private investment. Several public-sector industries were denationalized, but not banks. Regulatory controls were liberalized, and investment-licensing procedures were streamlined. Fiscal incentives in the form of tax holidays were also extended to the private sector, and price distortions were also corrected. Initially, the response of the private sector was very cautious, particularly in large-scale manufacturing. Although the big industrial families remained cautious, smaller entrepreneurs responded very favorably to these incentives. Spurred by the capital infusion in the 1970s in the wake of nationalization of large-scale industry, the small-scale manufacturing sector got another boost by these incentives and performed very well during the Zia era. These small-scale industries included leather products, sporting goods, and surgical goods. The intermediate and capital goods sector, including steel, automobile, chemicals, and light engineering, had a modest growth. On the whole, private investment increased from 33 percent of total investment in 1980 to 46 percent in 1989 (Hussain 1999, 32). Moreover, the industrial sector was more diversified than before, and the share of real estate in private investment was higher than before.

Pakistan's performance in the agricultural sector in the Zia era was very good, with growth rates averaging 4 percent per year, the highest in any decade, because of both favorable weather and appropriate policies. The production of major crops (wheat, rice, cotton, and sugarcane) reached record levels in 1981 and 1982. Sugar rationing and controls by government were removed in response to the increase in sugarcane production. The agricultural sector was liberalized too. The sugar, fertilizer, and pesticides industries were deregulated, and subsidies on pesticides and fertilizers were removed. The ban on private-sector import of oils was lifted, and the monopoly power of rice and cotton export corporations loosened. The access to credit increased through the Agricultural Development Bank of Pakistan (ADBP), with lending almost doubling between 1980 and 1983, although access remained limited or nonexistent for small farmers. On the whole, agriculture still had negative protection, as in the fifties, and industry had protection of over 25 percent. Export taxes on agriculture were imposed. While cotton production doubled during the 1980s largely because of the increase in yields per acre with the use of new and improved varieties of seeds, wheat production stagnated, requiring increased imports. Agriculture's share of total development expenditure fell from 20 to 13 percent during the decade (Hussain 1999, 34), with the decline occurring mostly in rural infrastructure such as roads, irrigation systems, and extension services. The Zia government also repealed the land reforms announced by the PPP in 1977.

The Islamization of the economy has been considered a policy innovation of the Zia government, which was initiated partly to improve the tarnished image of the army after the humiliating surrender in 1971. In 1977, a group of Islamic scholars was asked to recommend measures for an Islamic economic system. The Zakat and Ushr Ordinances were promulgated in 1980 on the recommendations of Islamic scholars. Zakat, levied at 2.5 percent annually on savings (wealth) to help the needy, is one of the five pillars of Islam, and every eligible Muslim is required to fulfill the obligation. *Ushr,* levied at 5 percent on agricultural produce, is to be paid in cash by the landowner or leaseholder, and its proceeds go to Zakat committees to help the needy. Ushr replaced the former land tax (revenue) levied by the provincial governments.

The Zia years were the golden years of remittance inflows from overseas Pakistani workers. The dramatic rise in remittances coincided with the first year of the Zia government, and is considered to be the most significant economic development during his era. These remittances, totaling $3.2 billion per year for most of the 1980s, were substantial, particularly in relation to the size of the economy. They accounted for 10 percent of GDP, 45 percent of current account receipts, and 40 percent of total foreign exchange earnings (Hussain 1999, 30).

By 1984, remittances were the largest single source of foreign exchange earnings for Pakistan. They financed about 86 percent of the trade deficit and closed the 6 percent gap

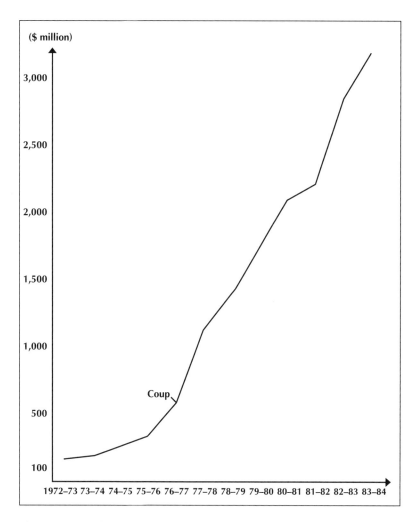

Figure 2.3: Remittances by Pakistani Migrants

Source: Omar Noman. 1990. *Pakistan: A Political and Economic History since 1947.* London: Kegan Paul International, p. 162.

between savings and investment. They were four times greater than the net aid inflow to Pakistan. With capital flight estimated at $1 billion from 1981 to 1987, remittances compensated for that loss. Figure 2.3 shows the growth in remittances during the twelve-year period from 1972 to 1984. They also increased household incomes and the living standards of the poor since most of the migrants came from low-income households. Their incomes increased about eightfold, having an egalitarian impact in both rural and urban areas. The distributional impact has been very wide, with 10 million people (11 percent of the total population) benefiting directly from these remittances, leading to improvement in income distribution and Gini coefficients, and temporarily serving as a substitute for an asset redistribution (land reform) program. However, the pattern of expenditure of families benefiting from remittances did not increase the national savings rate or enhance the long-term growth of the economy. About 63 percent of remittances were spent on consumption goods (primarily imported luxury goods such as video-recorders, cars, TVs), and 22 percent on real estate, and only 12 percent went to savings. As a consequence, the domestic savings rate fell from 7.8 percent of GDP in 1977–1978 to 5.4 percent by 1982–1983, less than a quarter of the ratio in India and about one-eighth of the ratio in Singapore (Hussain 1999, 162).

Nonetheless, the manpower migration to the Middle East also partially solved the unemployment problem created by a combination of high population growth rates of about 3.1 percent during the 1980s, mechanization of agriculture, and the capital-intensive nature of Pakistan's second phase of ISI policies followed under Bhutto. Thus, 33 percent of the increase in the labor force during the Fifth Plan period (1978–1983) was absorbed by manpower export. However, the migration has not solved the problem of regional imbalances in growth, since most of the migrants come from the Punjab, particularly the urban areas of Lahore, Faisalabad, Rawalpindi, Sialkot, Gujranwala, and Jhelum, as well as from NWFP, but very few from Sindh, excluding Karachi. Punjab's share of the migrant population is 70 percent, 14 percent higher than its share of total population. The worker remittances, combined with substantial inflow of foreign aid and war-related assistance for the Mujahideen, provided a safety valve for the Pakistani economy. The average annual remittances amounted to $3 billion per year, and the aid inflows amounted to $2 billion per year by the mid-1980s. Exports also grew at about 10 percent per year during the period, partly in response to the government's decision to put the Pakistani rupee on the managed float system, where the exchange rate of the rupee with other currencies was not fixed as before, but was flexible and floated (adjusted) in response to demand and supply of foreign exchange, with the government also buying and selling it to manage the exchange rate. The reliance on the market forces of demand and supply led to a depreciation of the overvalued rupee, that is, a fall in the value of the rupee in terms of the dollar, thereby increasing exports.

One of the worst legacies of the Zia years and his support of the Afghan War was the mushrooming of the "parallel," or the "underground," or the "subterranean" economy, estimated to be about 20 to 30 percent of GDP. This economy includes a thriving black market, smuggling, a large illicit drug industry, weapon and arms sales, and bribes to politicians and government officials to ensure state contracts. The annual value of the drug trade alone is estimated to be about 8 percent of GDP. The expansion of the underground economy resulted from Pakistan becoming a "frontline" state in the Afghan War against Soviet occupation of Afghanistan supported by the United States, and the resulting massive infusion of U.S. aid to Pakistan. Some aid went to the Pakistan government to enhance its military capability and to support millions of refugees that kept pouring into Pakistan across the border, but large amounts also went to Afghan resistance movements based in Pakistan and supported by the United States and Pakistan—to the Mujahideen. Some of this money was reportedly invested in weapons and the drug business, which played havoc with the Pakistani society by creating a *Kalashnikov* culture—high crime rates, ethnic and religious violence, breakdown of law and order at times, drug addiction, and corruption.

One of the key macroeconomic problems of the Zia years was current account deficits and balance-of-payments problems. Fiscal deficits increased during the Zia era, being about 8 percent of GDP in the second half of the 1980s. The deficit was not financed by printing money (which would have led to inflation) or by external financing (which would have led to a debt crisis). Instead, it was financed partly by domestic borrowing, which had an adverse effect on macroeconomic stability later in the 1990s. Financing of the deficit by attracting private savings at higher than market interest rates through different sorts of savings schemes crowded out private investment because of the negative effects of high interest rates on private investment, straining the financial system. Moreover, the social sectors were neglected, as in the sixties, and expenditure on education decreased from 2.1 percent of GDP in 1976–1977 to 1.5 percent in 1982–1983. This squeeze on the education sector was partly due to the high allocations to defense, which accounted for about 30 percent of central government expenditures (highest in the world except for Israel), and about 7 percent of GNP (higher than that of any country in South Asia and double that of India) (Noman 1990, 177–179).

The prime beneficiaries during the Zia years were the rural rich, who escaped taxation on their incomes and were successful in getting the land reform legislation repealed, while the rural and urban poor suffered most. Another beneficiary group was the skilled workers from the lower middle class—both those who migrated to the Middle East for work and their families, who received their remittances, and those who stayed behind but received higher wages because of shortages created by the migration. Most from this group were from Punjab (but also from NWFP and Karachi). This is the group that came to believe in upward mobility and could not be mobilized for a mass movement against the military by the forces that were in opposition to the Zia regime. Other beneficiaries of the regime were members of the religious political parties and a small select group of army officers, who bene-fited both because of increases in the military budget and increasing opportunities for lucrative civilian appointments after retirement. On the whole, between 1979 and 1985, aver-age incomes increased by about 80 percent for the lowest 40 percent of income recipients and by 94 percent for the top 20 percent (and by 100 percent for the top 10 percent) of income recipients. This led to a simultaneous reduction in poverty and an increase in income inequality during the period. The rural poor suffered the greatest relative decline. The middle class also lost ground. Only government employees did not experience any wage increases. They were also among the ones to suffer more than other groups, owing to the decline in education and health facilities, the worsening of the law-and-order situation, and the extension of the corruption, arms, and drug culture. Another group whose status declined was women, who found that several of the gains made earlier were reversed during the Zia regime (discussed in Chapter 3).

Structural Adjustment, Return to Democracy, Corruption, and Mismanagement: 1988–1999

Following Ziaul Haq's death in a plane crash in 1988, the period from 1988 to 1999 witnessed Pakistan's return to democracy. During this period, five elections were held, with both Benazir Bhutto and Nawaz Sharif being returned to power twice. There were also as many as four caretaker gov-ernments in between because neither of the elected govern-ments could complete its full term. Benazir was elected prime minister and remained so from 1988 until 1990 when her gov-ernment fell. This was followed, after a brief caretaker period, by the government of Prime Minister Mian Nawaz Sharif (1990–1993), which was eventually dismissed by former pres-ident Ghulam Ishaq Khan and accused of corruption, partic-ularly in connection with the privatization program. The caretaker government of Moeen Qureshi in 1993 was followed by the return of Benazir Bhutto in the 1993 elections. This was followed by the caretaker government of Meraj Khalid and then the elected government of Nawaz Sharif until 1999.

The GDP growth rate during these years fell from 6 percent or higher in the previous decade to 4 percent, with agriculture growing at 4 percent per year during the Seventh Plan period (1988–1993) and at 5.9 percent during the Eighth Plan period (1993–1998), and manufacturing growing at 5 percent per annum in the first phase and 3.6 percent in the second phase (Table 2.2). This declining trend in GDP growth and reversal from the trend of the previous four decades was due to structural and institutional problems, as well as to poor governance and the short, two- to three-year life spans of different political regimes. Moreover, inflation peaked, fiscal deficits increased to 7 percent of GDP, the current account deficit widened, and external debt servicing rose to almost 40 percent of export earnings as total external debt became 47.6 percent of GDP, up from $20 billion in 1990 to $43 billion in 1998 (Hussain 2003, 2). Moreover, income distribution worsened, and the incidence of poverty almost doubled.

There was a fundamental consensus on basic economic policies between Benazir Bhutto and Nawaz Sharif, the leaders of the two major political parties in Pakistan, the Pakistan Peoples Party and the Muslim League. However, there was a lack of continuity of programs, administrative ad hoc decisions, and policy reversals. The economic policy with the greatest impact under the first Sharif government was his privatization, deregulation, and economic reform policy. By 1995, ninety units had been denationalized and were sold to private investors, and plans were under way to begin denationalizing several utilities. Proposals to end state monopolies in insurance, shipping, telecommunications, airlines, power generation, port operations, and road construction were in different stages of implementation. The first Sharif government instituted investment reforms, which eliminated government authorization and sanction requirements, and authorized foreign banks to issue shares in Pakistani enterprises. A package of policies was introduced to encourage private investment, including tax holidays, reduction of tariffs on capital goods, and simplification of investment procedures. Despite liberalization, the government continued to have chronically high budget deficits, which led to inflation and balance-of-payments problems and adversely affected capital formation and overall financial stability of the economy. This, in turn, led to a loss of confidence in the government among foreign aid donors, paving the way for the caretaker government to take over after Nawaz Sharif was dismissed by the former president in 1993.

The caretaker government of 1993 was led by Moeen Qureshi, a former World Bank senior vice-president, who asserted that Pakistan was on the brink of insolvency. Accordingly, to impose fiscal discipline, his government increased utility prices, imposed new taxes (and stiffer enforcement), and reduced government spending. Known as "Mr. Clean," Qureshi, during his three-month tenure, also published lists of unpaid debts and prevented politicians under debt from running for office. He also devalued the currency and cut farm subsidies. The boldest action of the interim government was to institute an agricultural income tax for the first time in the history of the country, despite opposition by the rural elite, partly because it was temporary and not much constrained by the pressures of vested interests.

The Bhutto government that got elected in 1993 declared its intention to continue the deregulation, denationalization, and liberalization policy of the Nawaz Sharif government, as well as the tighter fiscal policies of the Qureshi government. She also promised higher allocations for health and education, particularly for women. The government agreed to a three-year structural adjustment program of fiscal austerity and deficit cutting in order to receive the badly needed preferential credit of US$1.4 billion from the International Monetary Fund (IMF). The main focus of the structural adjustment program imposed on Pakistan as a conditionality of loan by the IMF was the fiscal deficit. The conditionality of agreements with the IMF required that the deficit be lowered to 4 percent of GDP. This was done through reducing government spending and increasing tax revenues. Between 1994 and 1997, additional taxes of Rs. 140 billion were imposed, but these were mostly sales and other indirect taxes, which did not increase the number of new direct taxpayers. As always, agricultural income tax could not be considered because of the opposition of large landlords. Moreover, the largest cuts in public expenditure occurred in development expenditures, which decreased from 9.3 percent of GDP in 1981 to only 3 percent in 1996–1997. In addition, the administered prices of utilities such as electricity, gas, and petroleum products were raised. The burden of all these reforms fell disproportionately on the poor and the salaried groups, since the structural adjustment program did not have built-in safety nets to avoid these consequences of the adjustment.

The structural adjustment package also involved privatization of state-owned enterprises (public corporations owned and operated by the government). Several public-sector enterprises, utilities, and financial institutions were privatized, and state monopolies in banking, insurance, shipping, telecommunications, airlines, and power generation were eliminated. The opening up of the economy to foreign competition and privatization led to closure of some industrial units and worker layoffs, thus increasing unemployment. The privatization process was criticized for not being fully transparent. Investment and foreign exchange regulations were also liberalized. Exchange controls were eliminated to reverse the capital flight that had occurred in the Zia era, when deposits of Pakistani residents in foreign banks had increased from $700 million to $1.7 billion between 1981 and 1987 (Hussain 1999, 3).

The 1988–1999 period was also marked by allegations of corruption against politicians. Asif Ali Zardari, husband of Benazir Bhutto, was accused of corruption by the president after her government fell in 1990. Nawaz Sharif was also accused of corruption by the president, and then Bhutto and Sharif accused each other. Corruption was so pervasive that industrialists and businessmen considered bribery to government officials to be a routine cost of production, a processing fee to get any contract. It permeated all levels, from the lowest-level employees to top management, in almost all official institutions, including the police, judiciary, tax collection and revenue departments, passport office, customs and excise offices, and electricity and gas boards. It has been estimated that even in the mid-1980s, illegal payments to government officials were equal to 60 percent of total taxes collected by the government. But in 1996, the Transparency International survey ranked Pakistan as the second most corrupt country in the world (Hussain 2003, 5).

The 1990s have been characterized as a lost decade because of the "growing burden of debt, fiscal and current account imbalances, lowering of growth rates, poor social indicators, increase in incidence of poverty and higher rate of inflation" (Hussain 2003, 3). Although there was a basic consensus between the two major political parties regarding the appropriate policies for economic reform, such as denationalization, opening up of the economy, reliance on the market system, and higher investment in social sectors, the implementation of policies, programs, and projects was very poor. External shocks such as imposition of economic sanctions following the nuclear testing in 1998 may partly explain the poor performance of the 1990s. But the root causes were internal. The sequence of events was that economic mismanagement or corruption by the majority political party of the time led to the dismissal of the elected government (of the Nawaz Sharif government in 1993 and of the Benazir Bhutto government in 1996), which created political instability and the politicization of the bureaucracy. All of these factors adversely affected the investment climate in the country and posed serious external liquidity problems. Pakistan had no access to private capital markets, foreign economic assistance had been withdrawn, workers' remittances had been reduced by $500 million, and foreign investment had fallen by $600 million (Hussain 2003, 6). It is estimated that the entire Pakistani reserve could only buy three weeks of imports and not even meet its short-term debt service obligations. To tide over these problems, the Pakistan government entered into eight different agreements with the IMF during 1988–1999, but none was fully implemented, and hence half of the agreed loan amount could not be drawn, and the external liquidity problem remained unsolved.

Liberalization and IMF Conditionality under Pervez Musharraf: 1999–Present

The period since 1999 has been characterized by a consistency in economic policy focusing on market-led economic growth, macroeconomic stability, structural reforms, and control of corruption. Although the military regime of General Pervez Musharraf faced political legitimacy issues when it took over, as well as economic isolation following Pakistan's first nuclear test in May 1998, it was able to meet commitments with international financial institutions and close the credibility gap among donors that had led to withdrawal of assistance earlier. To overcome the credibility gap and receive loans from the IMF, the Musharraf government had to fulfill thirty performance criteria and structural benchmarks in a short period of time, and undertake wide-ranging and deep-rooted reforms. These included removal of subsidies, exemptions, and privileges; market-based pricing of outputs, inputs, and public utilities; privatization of state-owned banks, energy companies, and other large units; widening of the tax base; reliance on markets rather than administrative discretion; and reduction of government expenditure and indebtedness. Since these economic reforms were likely to hurt the poor (for example, the removal of subsidies),

Table 2.3   Pakistan's Macroeconomic Indicators

	1997–1998	1998–1999	1999–2000	2000–2001	2001–2002	2002–2003	2003–2004
GDP, Sectoral Income & Prices (growth rates–%)							
GDP at Factor Cost	4.3	4.2	3.9	2.5	3.6	5.1	6.4
Agriculture	3.5	1.9	6.1	–2.6	1.4	4.1	2.6
Manufacturing	6.9	4.1	1.5	7.6	4.4	6.9	13.4
Consumer Price Index	7.8	5.7	3.6	4.4	5	3.1	3.9
External Sector (% of GDP)							
Exports	13.9	12.8	13.3	15	15.2	15.5	15.8
Import	16.3	16.4	15.6	17.1	17.4	16	16.5
Current Account Balance	–2.7	–3.8	–0.4	0.6	4.8	4.8	6.1

Source: For Columns 1–5: Ishrat Hussain. 2003. *Economic Management in Pakistan 1999–2002.* Oxford: Oxford University Press, p. 51. For Columns 6 and 7: Federal Bureau of Statistics, Government of Pakistan. http://www.statpak.gov.pk/depts/fbs/statistics/economic_indicators/economic_indicators.html.

poverty-targeted interventions and social safety nets became an integral part of the reforms. The economy performed very well during the period, with an average annual growth rate of more than 4 percent in GNP since 1999 and as high as 6.4 percent in 2003–2004. The growth rate in manufacturing has been particularly impressive since 2000 and reached 13.4 percent in 2003–2004. On the other hand, agriculture did not perform so well during this period (Table 2.3). The results were impressive in the external sector also: exports increased as a percentage of GDP and imports were somewhat stable, the current account balance became positive during the period, the debt burden fell, foreign exchange reserves increased significantly, and the exchange rate remained stable. The fiscal deficit was reduced from 7 percent of GDP to 5.2 percent as early as 2000–2001, and tax revenues grew by more than 28 percent during the period; both indicators reflect a decline in the level of corruption. Although the record of GDP and sectoral growth was somewhat mixed until 2002, the results of economic policies started bearing fruit, and GDP grew at more than 5 percent annually during the last two years (Table 2.3). The country achieved food self-sufficiency and became a net exporter of grains owing both to increased agricultural productivity and provision of incentives for the agricultural sector during the period. The manufacturing sector also performed very well, with its growth rate jumping up to more than 13 percent in 2003–2004. However, the manufacturing sector has not yet been able to diversify much beyond textiles, food and beverages, and other consumer goods. Also, the incidence of poverty rose, at least until 2002, and unemployment rates have been high. But inflation decreased from 10 percent during 1990–1998 to less than 5 percent during the early period of the Musharraf era. Nonetheless, the achievements of the Musharraf era are commendable in view of the fact that the economy was subject to serious external shocks, including a severe drought for three years, global recession, the September 11 tragedy, the war in Afghanistan and the war against terrorism, and a volatile relationship with India.

The key reforms in this period focused on governance issues in different sectors of the economy, and on privatization and liberalization of the economy. The outcome was that governance improved, as reflected in a curtailment of discretionary powers, greater freedom of the press, devolution of power to the local governments, and setting up of an accountability process for stemming corruption. Hussain notes that the "most dramatic shift introduced by the military government is in promoting good economic governance. Transparency, consistency, predictability and rule-based decision making have begun to take roots" (Hussain 2003, xiv). The response of the private sector has been positive as privatization procedures are more transparent and do not favor specific groups or individuals, contrary to the experience of past privatizations. The Musharraf government plans to sell assets to domestic and foreign investors in the oil and gas industry and in the banking, telecommunications, and energy sectors. To that end, the foreign exchange regime has been liberalized, and restrictions on remittance of profits and dividends have been removed. Similarly, the trade regime has been liberalized; the maximum tariff rate declined from 225 percent in 1990–1991 to 25 percent in 2002–2003, and the average tariff decreased from 65 to 11 percent. Moreover, quantitative import restrictions, such as quotas, have been largely eliminated. Similarly, all restrictions on the import and export of agricultural products have been removed. In the financial sector, the interest rates are no longer regulated, and private banks, domestic and foreign, have a 40 percent share of the market in loans and deposits. The nationalized commercial banks have also become more competitive by closing down their unprofitable branches and reducing their surplus staff by 50 percent. Along with encouragement of the private sector, the interests of consumers have been protected by setting up independent regulatory agencies in the area of public utilities and public services.

As regards anticorruption measures, an agency was set up known as the National Accountability Bureau. During the Musharraf era, many government officials, businessmen, and politicians have been fined, sentenced to prison, and disqualified from holding public office for twenty-one years. Moreover, loan and tax defaulters have also been fined and sentenced, and overdue loans have been recovered from them. On the whole, the Musharraf government has been successful in meeting most of its objectives, such as achieving macroeconomic stability, establishing credibility with international financial institutions, improving economic governance, and curbing corruption. According to a recent IMF statement at a donors' meeting (IMF 2005), the Musharraf government's implementation of sound economic policies and broad-based structural reforms (financial-sector reform, privatization, trade liberalization, and deregulation) increased GDP growth rates to almost 8.5 percent in 2004–2005, improved private-sector confidence, increased remittances and foreign investment, and reduced Pakistan's debt burden significantly. But structural reforms to remove distortions, such as removal of subsidies and deregulation of petroleum, gas, and energy prices, have led to higher prices that have particularly hit the middle class and the poor. The poverty-alleviation strategies and the safety net provisions have not been very successful yet, and social sectors have not improved significantly, although literacy rates and school enrollment have begun to improve significantly.

SOME KEY ECONOMIC SECTORS

Despite formidable problems, the Pakistan economy has performed respectably well during the last fifty-nine years. Rates of growth averaged about 3.1 percent in the 1950s when agriculture stagnated, rose to 6.8 percent in the 1960s when performance in both agriculture and industry was strong, and again fell to 3.8 percent between 1971 and 1977. Strong performance in the 1980s, with growth averaging 6.4 percent, was followed by slower growth in the 1990s. Overall growth rates consistently increased from 2.5 in 2000–2001 to 6.4 percent in 2003–2004. Rapid growth altered the share of the key economic sectors in the economy. Agriculture's share (including forestry and fishing) of GDP declined from slightly more than 50 percent at the time of independence to about 25 percent currently. The share of industry (including mining, manufacturing, and utilities) rose from about 8 percent at the time of independence to about 25 percent in 2003–2004. The share of services (including construction, trade, transportation and communications, etc.) remained more or less stable during this time period.

Agriculture

Farming is Pakistan's largest economic activity. In FY 2004, the agricultural sector employed about 50 percent of the labor force, a figure comparable to that of America in the 1890s. It contributed about 23.6 percent of GDP and was the source, directly or indirectly, of about 75 to 80 percent of exports. Cotton alone provides 60 percent of Pakistan's exports such as raw cotton, cotton yarn, fabric, garments, towels, stockings, and canvas. Moreover, the sector provides a market for industrial goods since about 70 percent of the population lives in the rural areas and is dependent on agriculture, directly or indirectly.

The agricultural sector stagnated in the 1950s because industrialization was considered the key to economic development; as a result, government policies were biased against agriculture, leading to a transfer of resources from agriculture to industry. Agricultural growth rates were very impressive in the 1960s, particularly after 1967 when the fertilizer-responsive HYV (high-yield variety) seeds of wheat and rice were widely used by farmers, and the green revolution resulted in a more than doubling of yields. In the 1970s, a combination of natural disasters and interventionist government policies severely restricted the growth of agriculture. The performance of the sector was very impressive in the 1980s and to a certain extent also in the 1990s. The performance since 2000 has been mixed, with high growth rates alternating with low rates. Although agricultural production increased more than fivefold from 1947 to 2001 as the index of agricultural production increased from 100 in 1947 to 514 in 2001 (Table 2.1), the full potential has not been realized yet. Yields of most crops are low by international standards and lower than the potential.

Land Use and Irrigation.   The agricultural sector in Pakistan is characterized by a relative abundance of land in comparison with other Asian countries. It is located in the arid

Farmers harvest wheat in a field in Punjab, and load it on a wooden cart pulled by an ox. (Ric Ergenbright/Corbis)

and semiarid zones, which makes increased agricultural production crucially dependent on the availability of irrigation water. These physical factors, combined with the existence of large ownership holdings and widespread prevalence of share tenancy, make for extensive farming as the main mode of production. Accordingly, cropping intensities and land-use intensities are rather low in the whole region.

Pakistan's total land area is about 80 million hectares, out of which 60 percent (48.4 million hectares) is not available for cultivation as it consists mostly of deserts, mountain slopes, and urban settlements. About 22.2 million hectares were cultivated in 2001–2002, and another 9 million hectares were cultivable waste. The cultivated land consists of the net sown area plus the area that is currently left fallow (uncultivated for one season so as to replenish the soil). The 22.2 million hectares of cultivated land consisted of 6.5 million hectares of current fallow and 15.7 million hectares of net sown area. The cropped area, defined as the net sown area plus the area sown more than once, was 22 million hectares, reflecting a cropping intensity (defined as cropped area times 100/cultivated area) of 140 percent. In other words, farmers produced two crops per year on 40 percent of cultivated land.

Out of a total cultivated area of 22.2 million hectares in the four provinces of Pakistan (Punjab, Sindh, North-West Frontier Province, and Balochistan), about a fourth consists of rain-fed *(barani)* lands, which rely on summer rainfall to establish winter-sown crops. In these areas, heavy reliance is placed on fallowed land. The fallows are plowed a number of times to conserve moisture and to improve soil fertility. For the same purpose, a cropping sequence of alternating legume crops (peas, beans, and lentils) with grains, or mixed cropping of the two, is followed. The *barani* lands have a wide variation in rainfall. The main *barani* areas of Punjab and NWFP have a rainfall of above 20 inches, with some parts receiving 12 to 20 inches. The southwestern areas of Punjab and NWFP and the *barani* lands of Sindh and Balochistan get 6 to 12 inches of rainfall. In the low-rainfall areas, rainfall is supplemented by periodic flooding from streams or rivers (riverine-s*ailaba* areas). In irrigated areas, water is provided either by canals, wells, tubewells, or a combination of the three. The canals are massive in scale. They can be classified as perennial, which supply water to fields all year round, as those in southeast Sindh or as nonperennial, which supply water only for six months, as those in north or southwest Sindh. In Punjab, districts in the central zone are mostly canal-colony districts, while others are partly irrigated by canals and partly by tubewells. The cropping and land-use intensities are high in this region. The use of tubewells is also extensive in the NWFP.

Landownership and Farm Size. The agrarian system of Pakistan is characterized by the coexistence of fairly small and very large farms. At the top, large farms (equal to or more than 50 acres), which are only 1 percent of all farms, occupy 21 percent of the total farmland and 16 percent of the cultivated land. At the bottom, small farms (less than 5 acres), which comprise 58 percent of all farms, occupy 16 percent of the total farmland and 18 percent of the cultivated land. The middle-sized farms (5 acres to less than 50 acres), which constitute 41 percent of all farms, occupy 63 percent of farmland and 65 percent of cultivated land.

Landownership is highly skewed in Pakistan. Moreover, landed wealth is often accompanied by political influence and social status, and these can be and have been used to ensure privileged access to scarce means of production, especially land, capital, and externally purchased inputs. Land is the most important means of production in rural areas, and often the only way to ensure access to it is to own it or rent it. Yet the majority of people have restricted access to land. For instance, the largest 1 percent of farms occupy 21 percent of the total farm area, and the largest 27 percent of farms occupy as much as 73 percent of the total farm area (Pakistan Census of Agriculture 2000). Moreover, this land is generally the most fertile and the most advantageously located with respect to irrigation, transport, and marketing facilities and similar inputs. The small peasants are almost excluded from the land market because of imperfections in the market for land. Such purchase has become even more unlikely after the green revolution, either because landlords want to self-cultivate and capture the higher returns themselves or because a new class of farmers—moneylenders, bureaucrats, military officers, and city-based speculators—is competing for land.

The small farmers also have only restricted access to credit, particularly in the organized capital market (Mohiuddin 1983, 42). For instance, subsidized credit available for purchase of tubewells went to large farmers because of strict standards of creditworthiness imposed by lending agencies, the greater familiarity of the larger farmers with the procedures for getting credit, and their influence in obtaining permission for electricity connections. Moreover, they were able to use their political influence so that government credit institutions cater to their needs. Consequently, the small farmers turn to the informal money market—the village moneylender, local shopkeeper, or large landowner—where the rates of interest are high, to some extent because of monopoly elements and to a greater extent because of the high risk of default, the lack of collateral, and the large overhead costs of small loans. The interest rates charged by the informal lenders are about two and a half to three times as high as institutional sources. Even credit programs aimed expressly at improving the capital markets faced by small farmers have left the majority of small farmers untouched, and cooperatives set up for small farmers have ended up discriminating against them in practice.

The unequal access to land and capital by small farmers is accentuated by unequal access to technology. Empirical evidence shows that small farmers had limited access to inputs such as fertilizer, water, seeds, tractors, and tubewells. In the 1970s, at the height of the green revolution, when fertilizers were subsidized, farmers complained of the nonavailability of fertilizers at the controlled prices, while large landlords had bought fertilizer at the previous year's actual price and stored it. Moreover, the real price of fertilizer to small farmers was often substantially above its official price. For a small farmer, purchase of fertilizer on credit required a payment to the revenue official to secure landownership or a tenancy affidavit, a payment to the bank official to obtain the loan, and the payment of the so-called black market prices to the fertilizer vendors (Mohiuddin 1983, 45–46). Large farmers also have greater access to government agricultural extension agents and instruction literature. In some cases, the large landlords hired government agricultural and pest control experts to solve their technical problems.

Pakistan's agricultural landscape is composed of four different groups: large landowners, peasant proprietors, tenants, and landless agricultural laborers. The large landowners may be absentee landlords living in urban areas or even abroad who lease out their land to tenants, or they may be involved in self-cultivation with the use of hired labor. The peasant proprietors cultivate their land themselves with the use of family labor, particularly of women. They may occasionally use hired labor for short periods of time and for specific tasks, such as harvesting. They may also hire themselves out if there is a need and an opportunity. The tenants, or sharecroppers, lease land from landowners, and share the crop with the landlord on a 50:50 or a 40:60 basis. They do not have much security of tenure. A large number of the landless rural population, both men and women, work as agricultural laborers.

Tenants have traditionally been of two types, namely occupancy tenants and tenants-at-will. The occupancy tenants are those who have a more or less permanent and transferable right to land as long as they continue to pay the fixed rent (in cash, kind, or a share in the produce) to their landlords. It has been observed in Punjab and NWFP that they enjoyed most of the privileges that the owner-operators had. The tenants-at-will have their tenancies fixed from year to year. Their share and rent are usually determined by custom or more often the dictates of the landlords. These tenants can be ejected, as their name implies, by the landlord at his will. Most tenants in Sindh have been in this category.

Although there is concentration of landownership in Pakistan, most large ownership holdings are not operated as large holdings. Rather, large landowners lease out their land in small parcels to a number of small peasants, often dictating the rental terms to their advantage. They can exploit the tenants by limiting the amount of land rented to a single tenant, by continuously changing tenants, or by refusing to share inputs other than land. In most cases, landowners change their sharecroppers every year so that they may not acquire occupancy right under the provision of the 1950 tenancy legislation. In such an insecure situation, the sharecropper may not have the incentive to improve the land that he rents, to invest in modern inputs, or to expend more of his labor. Since he shares the total output with the landlord but only some expenses like land revenue and water rate (and fertilizer-seed cost in some cases), it is likely that the tenant may particularly economize on the cost that he has to bear alone, such as hired labor costs. Tenancy thus has a negative effect on employment. Also, sharing the product but not costs reduces tenant incentives to work, and less output is produced. Thus cropping intensities, land-use intensities, and productivity are lower on tenant- than on owner-operated farms. It has been found that tenants use less labor than owner-cultivators and prefer to spend a part of their time in off-farm work because it brings income exclusively to them.

Major Crops and Other Subsectors. The agricultural sector has five subsectors: major crops, minor crops, livestock, fishing, and forestry. The major crops include wheat, cotton, rice, and sugarcane. The minor crops include maize (corn), barley, pulses (lentils), oilseeds, tobacco, fruits, and vegetables. The shares of the major crops and livestock in the agricultural value added have remained relatively stable over the years, at about 55 and 33 percent, respectively, while the share of minor crops has decreased and those of forestry and fishing have increased.

There are two basic crop-rotation systems in irrigated agriculture in Pakistan—wheat-cotton and wheat-rice—although a number of minor crops, especially fodder, are also grown in both seasons. Sugarcane is grown as a full-year crop. Wheat is a *rabi* (winter) crop, which is planted in winter (October or early November) and harvested in late winter (April) or during early summer (May). The other important *rabi* crops are

Typical rice fields of Punjab or Sindh. (Robert Holmes/Corbis)

gram, rapeseed, barley, and mustard. Cotton and rice are *kharif* (summer) crops, which are sown in summer and harvested in late summer or early winter. The other important kharif crops are maize (corn), jowar, and bajra.

The four major crops, namely, wheat, cotton, rice, and sugarcane, accounted for about 65 percent of cropped area in Pakistan in 2002–2003. Among the major crops, wheat is the most important in terms of acreage. Pakistan currently grows about 19 million metric tons of wheat per year, more than the output of Kansas and Nebraska combined, on an area of 8.2 million hectares, which is about 37 percent of the total cropland. Wheat is grown in all four provinces and in both *barani* and irrigated areas. The second most important crop is cotton, grown on an area of about 3 million hectares. Pakistan is the fifth largest producer of cotton in the world and grows more cotton than all of the southern United States east of Texas. Cotton is planted in May, just after the wheat harvest, and harvested in October or November. Most cotton is picked by hand,

and by women. Cotton is largely grown in canal-irrigated areas of the Indus Plain like southern Punjab and southern Sindh. Rice is grown on about 2 million hectares, and one of the varieties, *Basmati* rice, is a major export crop known for its very fine quality. Rice is grown in the river-flooded and canal-inundated areas of Sindh like northern Sindh, and in canal-irrigated areas of Punjab like parts of central and southern Punjab.

Land Reforms.   One highly contentious issue that has been discussed since independence is the question of land reforms. The first land reforms, introduced by Ayub Khan in 1959, imposed a ceiling of about 200 hectares (500 acres) of irrigated land and 400 hectares (1,000 acres) of nonirrigated land on landownership and allowed compensation to landowners for land surrendered. About 1 million hectares (2.5 million acres) of land were surrendered, of which about 956,000 hectares (2.3 million acres) were sold to about 187,000 tenants (Zaidi 1999, 31). The reforms affected only 5 percent of the landholdings, partly because the reforms gave very generous exemptions, including title transfers to family members, and partly because *zamindars* (landlords) colluded with the local revenue officials to alter the records. These reforms did not lessen the power of the landed elite, although they did increase security for tenants in that they could not be evicted without sufficient reason. But it has been pointed out that such provisions were little respected at the village level.

The second land reforms were introduced in 1972 by the Bhutto government, which imposed a ceiling of about 60 hectares (150 acres) of irrigated land and 120 hectares (300 acres) of nonirrigated land. Exemptions were given to owners having tractors and tubewells to the extent of 20 percent of land, and the ceiling was also extended for poor-quality land. In contrast to the Ayub reforms, no compensation was given to landowners for land surrendered, and beneficiaries were not charged for land distributed. Only about 481,000 hectares of land were surrendered, of which about 296,000 hectares (0.7

million acres) were redistributed to about 71,000 farmers. The landlords deeded excess land to relatives. Nonetheless, under the Bhutto reforms, security of tenure improved for the tenants, as eviction of tenants was prohibited as long as they cultivated the land. Rents were also lowered, and landlords were required to pay all taxes, water charges, seed costs, and one-half of the cost of fertilizer and other inputs. In 1977, under the Finance Act, the Bhutto government abolished land revenue and replaced it with an agricultural income tax on large landowners, although small farmers owning 10 hectares (25 acres) or less were exempted. The act also reduced the ceiling on landholdings to 100 acres of irrigated and 200 acres of non-irrigated land. After the overthrow of Bhutto by the military regime of Ziaul Haq, the 1977 Finance Act was suspended. Most successive governments have avoided land reform measures, perhaps because of the power of the landed elite.

Industry

The industrial sector includes manufacturing, mining, construction, and electricity and gas. It currently contributes 25 percent to GDP (2002–2003) and employs 11 percent of the total labor force. The structure and magnitude of the industrial sector have changed significantly since Pakistan's independence. The index of agricultural production increased by a factor of 60 (from 22.5 to 1,347) between 1951 and 1994. The share of the industrial sector in value added increased from 9.6 percent in 1949–1950 to 26.5 percent in 1995–1996. During the same period, the share of manufacturing in value added increased from 7.8 to 18 percent (Hussain 1999, 112).

Manufacturing is the largest subsector within the industrial sector. Its growth has been stable, around 7 to 8 percent per year, but growth rates were particularly impressive in 1960–1965 at 11.7 percent, and more recently in 2003–2004 at 13.4 percent. In fact, in only three time periods was growth of the manufacturing sector less than 5 percent. The first was the preplan period of 1950–1955, soon after partition, when an industrial base had not yet been established and the growth rate was 4.4 percent per year. The second was the nonplan period of 1970–1978, during the Bhutto era, when the annual growth rate was only 4.5 percent, partly because of the exogenous shocks and partly because of the ill-guided nationalization policies. The third period was 1993–2001, when the growth rate was between 3.6 and 4.3 percent, partly owing to the stop-go policies of the more than half dozen successive governments (Table 2.2).

The manufacturing sector includes both large- and small-scale enterprises. Small-scale manufacturing has constituted only about 20 to 30 percent of industrial value added on average from the 1950s until now. Thus, while the share of large-scale manufacturing in value added increased from 2.2 in 1949–1950 to 12.1 percent in 1995–1996, the share of small-scale manufacturing increased only from 5.6 to 5.9 percent during the same period. Similarly, less than 3 percent of the nation's labor force works in large factories, where many have unionized jobs that give them higher wages, longer vacations, and better working conditions. But many factories hire temporary workers for less than a year, and sometimes rehire them, in order to avoid paying union-scale wages and benefits, which they can do because labor laws do not cover temporary workers. Most workers in the industrial sector are employed in small-scale industry. They work in small workshops, making carpets, knives, furniture, garments, sports goods, leather goods, and the like. Carpets alone account for more than 5 percent of Pakistan's exports and are made by children between the ages of nine and sixteen years because they have the most nimble fingers. They are paid very poorly—about one-quarter to one-half the rate for adult males and no more than 50 cents a day. Similarly, women often work at home making garments, handicrafts, gloves, sports goods, baskets, cigarettes, lace, and embroidery on a piece-rate basis. The work is done along the lines

Pakistani carpets are known all over the world for their high quality.
This photograph shows carpet-weaving on a hand-operated loom in
Peshawar. (Ric Ergenbright/Corbis)

of the putting-out system, where the middleman supplies the home-based producers with the raw materials and later collects the finished product and captures most of the profits. The women barely make 25 to 50 cents a day (Mohiuddin 1985, 50).

It is the large-scale manufacturing sector that has always been the focus of industrial strategy in Pakistan. In the 1950s, heavy protection was given to infant industries in the sector through tariffs. Import licensing was introduced to allocate imports to large industrial establishments and ease their access to inputs. The rupee was not devalued, so that an overvalued exchange rate could make machinery imports artificially cheap for large-scale manufacturing. In the 1960s, the pro-industrial growth strategy was continued by also suppressing exports of agricultural raw materials and tax incentives for industry. In the second half of the 1960s, however,

Smoke spills from the chimneys of the ZealPak cement factory in Hyderabad, Sindh. (Corbis)

the government pursued a more balanced growth strategy, as it was realized that high GDP growth rates are not sustainable if the agricultural sector is neglected. Then, in the 1970s, there was a reversal of the pro-industrialization strategy, and both large and small industrial enterprises, and those producing consumer goods as well as capital goods, were nationalized in two different phases. This was accompanied by massive increases in public investment in large-scale manufacturing and a corresponding decline in private investment. From 1978 until now, the growth strategy by successive governments, military and civilian, elected or not, has been pro-industrial, with increasing privatization, denationalization, and liberalization of the economy.

The large-scale manufacturing sector is dominated by the consumer goods industries, producing textiles, garments, leather goods, processed foods, beverages, sugar, cigarettes, and so on. The share of consumer goods industries in large-

Fishing boats crowded at the dock in Karachi. (Kapoor Baldev/Sygma/Corbis)

scale manufacturing value added decreased from 84.4 percent in 1954 to 59.3 percent in 1995, but it is still very high. The corresponding shares of the intermediate goods industries, producing fertilizers, cement, paints and varnishes, dyes, insecticides, chemicals, glass, paper, and surgical instruments, increased from 12.3 percent in 1954 to 31 percent in 1995; and the share of capital goods industries, producing steel, automobiles, and engineering goods, increased from 3.2 to 9.2 percent in the same period. Since the intermediate goods and capital goods industries are more capital-intensive and employ less labor, growth in the share of these industries over the years has meant that industrial employment has not kept pace with industrial output. In fact, the share of these industries in industrial employment remained almost constant at 10 percent for the period between 1960 and 1995.

The leading sector in Pakistan's industrialization has been the cotton textile industry. It is the largest industry in terms of output, employment, and exports. One-fourth of Pakistan's industrial workers are in the cotton textile industry, and two-fifths of Pakistani exports originate from this industry. Its output increased from 114 million kilograms of yarn in 1955 to 1,300 million kilograms in 1995, an increase of about 1,000 percent, or elevenfold. But the lack of diversification of the industrial base, where just two industry groups, textiles and food processing, account for 50 percent of value added, is, in fact, the greatest weakness of the industrial sector.

Services

The services sector is the largest sector in the Pakistan economy, contributing about 50.7 percent of GDP in 2002–2003. It includes wholesale and retail sales, transportation and com-

The rickshaw is a common form of transportation for the middle class. In the background, a vendor is selling vegetables in an open-air stall. (Mehryn Ahmad)

A typical truck in Pakistan, decorated with paint, metal, tinsel, and plastic ornaments. (Mehryn Ahmad)

A fruit vendor in Lahore. (Mehryn Ahmad)

munications, telecommunications, tourism, and personal services. The domestic transportation system includes road, air, and rail networks. In the 1970s and 1980s, road and air networks grew faster than the railroads. In 2002–2003, there were 252,000 kilometers of roads in the country and 3.5 million motor vehicles on roads. The number of vehicles per 1,000 persons increased from 1 in 1947 to 30 in 2001. Road transport (buses, minivans, taxis, rickshaws, and trucks) is mostly in the private sector, the railroad system is government-owned, and air transport has also been opened to private investors in the last decade. In 1994, the government-owned Pakistan International Airlines (PIA) was the major airline, serving five domestic airports at Karachi, Islamabad, Lahore, Peshawar, and Quetta, and international airports. In 1993, several small private airlines began operating on domestic routes. There are also 4.8 million telephones, and their number per 10,000 persons increased from 4 in 1947 to 286 in 2001. The telecommunications network is based on radio and television, which are dominated by government corporations. Until 1992, there was only one TV channel, a second was added in November 1992, and now other channels have been added in the private sector. The number of TV sets per 10,000 persons increased from 0 in 1947 to 15 in 1970 and 263 in 2001 (Hussain 2003, 222).

A large part of the services sector is personal services, which range from maid service by *masees* (female domestics) to hawkers, street vendors, travel agents, and teachers. The proliferation of these services is partly in response to the outflow of workers to the Middle East, which has created a big demand for services such as air and road transport, travel agencies, hotels, banks, health clinics, secretarial services, and recruiting agencies. The remittances sent home by these workers have increased the demand for services such as tailoring, hairdressing, maid service, and personal attendants. The deterioration in the law-and-order situation in cities like Karachi since the 1980s has also increased the demand for security services of all types. Finally, the mushrooming of nongovernmental organizations (NGOs) and donor aid has increased the demand for secretaries and low-level managers. The deterioration in public education has led to provision of teaching and tutoring services by the private sector and a proliferation of schools, coaching and tutoring centers, and the like.

CONCLUSION: CHALLENGES AND FUTURE PROSPECTS

The Pakistan economy still faces some very serious challenges, the foremost being reduction of absolute poverty and improvement in income distribution. The second challenge is to undo all the years of neglect of social sectors and to invest in human capital (education and health); otherwise Pakistan will not be able to compete in the new global economy. No less important are investment in physical infrastructure and the further strengthening of institutions of good governance, accountability, and sharing of growth.

On the whole, the productivity growth in agriculture has been modest in terms of output per hectare, total factor productivity, and significant yield gaps between average and best farmer yields. The reasons are many: weak irrigation networks; lack of quality control and inefficient distribution systems for seeds, pesticides, and fertilizers; inadequate investment in agricultural research and extension and in rural infrastructure; and inconsistent and poorly planned governmental policies. Although the Indus irrigation system is the world's largest, problems of water management, waterlogging, and salinity continue to plague the agricultural sector. Moreover, the influence of the feudal system has spread to the industrial and bureaucratic culture, and the middle class has emulated some of the feudal values and behavior patterns instead of resisting them. The industrial sector, on the other hand, is not diversified at all, and the dependence on textiles and food processing is very high. Moreover, many industries have developed under high tariff walls and high effective rates of protection, creating an inefficient sector that is not fully capable of competing in world markets. Moreover, the worst legacy of nationalization of industry has been that industrialists mistrust the government and are still cautious in their investment decisions. At the same time, the potential of the small-scale sector has not been fully realized.

Although the economy of Pakistan faces significant challenges, there is also sufficient reason for hope. Both the agricultural and manufacturing growth rates have been very high in recent years. The current trend indicates that the economy of Pakistan is growing at a rate comparable to or better than that of other developing countries. The economic reform process is well under way. The current account deficit and budget deficits are under control. The population growth rates have started to come down, and the incidence of poverty is declining. The problem of low investments in social sectors is being addressed. Above all, corruption has reduced significantly, and the law-and-order situation has improved. All these factors bode well for the future.

References and Further Reading

Blood, Peter R. (ed.). 1995. *Pakistan: A Country Study* (Area Handbook Series). Washington, DC: Library of Congress.

Development Planning Pakistan. 2003. Islamabad, Pakistan: Planning and Development Division, Government of Pakistan.

Economic Indicators Pakistan. 2003. Islamabad (FBS), Government of Pakistan. http://www.statpak.gov.pk/depts/fbs/statistics/economic_indicators/economic_indicators.html.

Human Development Report 2003. 2003. New York: Oxford University Press.

Hussain, Ishrat. 1999. *Pakistan: The Economy of an Elitist State.* Karachi, Pakistan: Oxford University Press.

———. 2003. *Economic Management in Pakistan 1999–2002.* Oxford: Oxford University Press.

International Monetary Fund (IMF). 2005. IMF Statements at Donor Meetings. Pakistan International Donors' Conference, Islamabad, November 19, 2005. http://www.imf.org/external/np/dm/2005/111905.htm.

Islam, Nurul. 1981. *Foreign Trade and Economic Controls in Development: The Case of United Pakistan.* New Haven, CT: Yale University Press.

Kibria, Ghulam. 1999. *A Shattered Dream: Understanding Pakistan's Underdevelopment.* Karachi, Pakistan: Oxford University Press.

Malik, Sohail J., Safiya Aftab, and Nargis Sultana. 1994. *Pakistan's Economic Performance 1947–1993: A Descriptive Analysis.* Lahore, Pakistan: Sure Publishers.

Mohiuddin, Yasmeen. 1983. An Investigation into the Determinants of Farm Employment in Pakistan. Unpublished Ph.D. dissertation, Vanderbilt University.

———. 1985. *Women's Employment in the Putting-Out System in Sindh.* Karachi, Pakistan: Applied Economics Research Center Report prepared for the International Labor Organization.

Noman, Omar. 1990. *Pakistan: A Political and Economic History since 1947.* London: Kegan Paul International.

Pakistan Census of Agriculture. 2000. Lahore, Pakistan: Agriculture Census Organization, Government of Pakistan. http://www.statpak.gov.pk/depts/aco/publications/agricultural_census2000/table01a.pdf.

Statistical Pocketbook: Pakistan. 2003. Islamabad, Pakistan: Federal Bureau of Statistics (FBS), Government of Pakistan. http://www.statpak.gov.pk/.

World Development Report 2005. 2004. Washington, DC: The World Bank.

Zaidi, S. Akbar. 1999. *Issues in Pakistan's Economy.* Karachi, Pakistan: Oxford University Press.

CHAPTER THREE
Political Development since 1947

Since achieving independence in 1947, Pakistan has faced unusual sociopolitical challenges, including resettlement in the early years of about 7 million Muslims fleeing from the horrifying communal violence in India following partition; a civil war, and dismemberment of the country in 1971; an influx in the 1980s of more than 3 million Afghani refugees resulting from Pakistan's support of the United States against the Soviet occupation of Afghanistan; and the demands of being the frontline state in the war against terrorism following the 9/11 tragedy. It has seen five martial laws since 1958, three wars with India, and innumerable ethnic and religious riots that have claimed many lives. Yet it survived these traumatic experiences and continues to adapt to changing circumstances. The process of nation building continues.

Pakistan, in its short history, has experimented with a variety of political systems and governments. The six different economic eras in Pakistan since independence in 1947 (discussed in Chapter 2) coincide roughly with the same number of distinct political regimes, although the number of governments was more than six. There have been three periods of civilian rule in Pakistan, interrupted each time by military takeovers. The first period, from independence in 1947 until 1958, saw seven prime ministers in ten years. It ended with the martial law imposed by General Ayub Khan, who had been asked twice before by civilians to step in. Ayub Khan's secular, military government remained in power for nearly the next eleven years, until 1969, followed for a short period by the military government of Yahya Khan. The second period, from 1971 to 1977, began with Zulfiqar Ali Bhutto (whose party won the second highest number of votes in the

1971 elections) at the helm of affairs in a truncated Pakistan after the loss of East Pakistan and came to an end with the martial law imposed by General Ziaul Haq, who later ordered Bhutto to be hanged in 1979. Zia's Islamic military government remained in power for the next eleven years, from 1977 until his death in a plane crash in 1988. The third period, from 1988 to 1999, was dominated by the elected governments of Benazir Bhutto and Nawaz Sharif but saw a frequent change of hands, with Bhutto and Sharif both being returned twice and four caretaker governments in the interim periods. This era also ended with a military coup by the army, while the army chief, Pervez Musharraf, was on a plane on his way to Pakistan from Sri Lanka that Nawaz Sharif was not allowing to land. There are promising signs that the military government of Musharraf will be a modernizing regime despite pressures from religious forces inside and outside Pakistan.

The political process and events in Pakistan have been shaped by five main trends cutting across the history of independent Pakistan, namely, the synthesis of Islamic principles with the needs of a modern state, the role of the military and the bureaucracy in governance, overriding regional and ethnic loyalties, the central role of the landed aristocracy, and the threat of neighboring India.

The role that Islam should play in Pakistan has been a crucial and perplexing question in Pakistan from the beginning, and remains so today. The Pakistan movement was rooted in the Islamic concept of society as well as in secular notions. Jinnah envisioned Pakistan to be a democratic state informed by Islamic values of social justice. The framers of the first constitution avoided constructing an Islamic state, but they did form an Islamic republic, which is how each of Pakistan's constitutions has defined it. What this implies in practice has been left for decision by successive governments and peoples. The traditionalist *ulema* (Islamic scholars) and the less learned *mullahs* (Muslim clerics) who exercise influence over the masses have demanded that Pakistan be an Islamic state.

They have asserted that the *Quran, Sunnah,* and *Sharia* provide the general principles for all aspects of life if correctly interpreted, and that it is they who have the power of legal interpretation. It would not be until the regime of Ziaul Haq that the *ulema* would get such powers.

Both the bureaucracy and the military have played a vital role in the politics of Pakistan. The Civil Service of Pakistan (CSP) cadre originated in the pre-partition Indian Civil Service and played a key role in the early years after independence. It prided itself on being the backbone of the nation, the "steel frame," and became one of the most elite and privileged bureaucracies in the world. While the bureaucracy has been a continuing source of stability and leadership in the face of political upheaval and government instability in Pakistan, it has also to some extent hindered the development of democratic institutions.

The military is perhaps the strongest and most cohesive national institution. It has been a major source of power since independence, assuming direct control for thirty-one of the fifty-nine years of Pakistan's existence, from 1947 to 2006. Successive military regimes in Pakistan have provided alternative leadership in times of political crisis and deadlock that threatened the state, legitimizing their actions and prolonged rule by the doctrine of necessity. Over the course of Pakistan's history, several factors opened the door for the military to step in: the failure of civilian political rule, the abuse of power by the bureaucrats, lack of ethnic cohesion, and continuing confrontation with India over Kashmir and the fear of India's further expansionist designs. It is also true that each time the army has taken over, ordinary people have been happy to see their country relieved of power-hungry, autocratic, or corrupt politicians. But army takeovers and martial laws typically have a devastating effect on democratic institutions and the nurture of democracy.

Ethnic and religious identities are strong in Pakistan. Religious rivalries between the Shi'a and Sunni and between ethnic groups have impeded the progress of national integration. It is also ethnic tensions that lie at the root of separatist movements in Pakistan from time to time, most importantly in the former East Pakistan (now Bangladesh), but also in all provinces except the majority province of Punjab. More recently, particularly since the Ziaul Haq regime, these tensions have often taken the form of violent clashes leading to civil unrest, significant loss of life and property, and general lawlessness.

In periods of both military and civilian rule in Pakistan, the major landowners of Sindh and Punjab, or "feudals" as they are known, and tribal leaders of Balochistan and NWFP have wielded tremendous power. Having been given land and power by the British in India in exchange for their loyalty and supply of troops, the feudals have maintained their position in Pakistan by supporting the different regimes that have come to power and exacting favors in exchange in the form of ministerial positions, loans, and property allocations. They command extraordinary loyalty in their own localities, partly because they carry a number of functions that are the responsibility of the courts, police, or administration (e.g., resolving legal issues). Although it has been argued (Zaidi 1999) that the mode of Pakistani agriculture is now capitalist and not feudal, it is still true that feudals can and do ignore state institutions, and can use religion, their landownership, and the tribal system to wield absolute power, thus impeding social and economic development in their areas.

The threat of India and the fight over Kashmir have also affected Pakistani politics very significantly and remain a recurring theme in discussions of social and economic issues. In October 1947, the Kashmir *maharaja* Hari Singh decided to join India, even though the majority of his subjects were Muslims. Pakistan and India engaged in a military conflict in 1947–1948, the first of a long series of clashes to come in the future. Since then, the Kashmir issue has been a source of continuous conflict between India and Pakistan, and has affected political development through different regimes.

The main features of the six different political eras in Pakistan since independence in 1947, and the impact of the military, bureaucracy, religious leaders, landlords, and tribal chiefs during these periods, are briefly presented in the following section.

POLITICAL INSTABILITY OF THE EARLY YEARS: 1947–1958

When the new nation gained independence on August 14, 1947, it was a geographic oddity, with its western and eastern wings separated by 1,000 miles of hostile Indian territory. Moreover, the two regions had little in common but Islam. The terrain was entirely different: the irrigated desert of the west wing and the rain-soaked delta of the east wing were as different as Egypt and Vietnam. The ethnic and linguistic diversity of the western wing was in sharp contrast to the homogeneity of East Pakistan, which was almost exclusively Bengali. The western wing, on the other hand, had five major ethnic groups—Punjabis, Sindhis, Pathans, Baluchis, and Muhajirs (refugees from India, mostly from the United Provinces [UP] and Bombay). Building national consensus and achieving national integration in the face of provincialism and ethnic rivalries were a serious challenge to national stability.

In addition to being confronted by fundamental national issues such as the demand for provincial rights, the role of Islam in the new state, and the status of the Urdu language, the first generation of politicians faced the daunting task of rehabilitating millions of refugees in a new nation with severe shortages of material assets and administrative personnel (physical and human capital). It is estimated that between 5.5 and 7.5 million Muslim refugees reportedly fled to both parts of Pakistan from India, and between 5.5 and 10 million Hindus left Pakistan for India. In 1947, Pakistan had hardly any industry, almost no electric power plants, only 17 cotton mills (India had 380), and not a single jute mill (though it was producing the bulk of raw jute). Pakistan had been dealt a bad hand at partition, and India did not even transfer assets as promised.

The Government of India Act of 1935 (as amended by the India Independence Act of 1947), which governed Pakistan at independence, provided for a governor general as head of state to replace the British viceroy, and a Constituent Assembly. The Constituent Assembly was charged with the dual responsibility to draft a constitution and to enact legislation until the constitution came into effect. Jinnah became the first governor general, the chief executive, and chief of his party. Since his ultimate authority came not from the support of the military or the bureaucracy, but from the political support of the people, it has been argued that he chose to unite in himself the three functions to preserve national unity. He accumulated power at the center to bind diverse elements into a national framework and to facilitate the work of the new government. Jinnah's towering personality, which had dominated the Pakistan movement, undoubtedly lifted the nation after independence. Ziring notes that, "after partition, it was his [Jinnah's] presence alone that prevented the country from imploding on itself. But only his use of extraordinary viceregal powers, combined with the power of his persona, kept the foxes from devouring the fledgling state" (1999, 97). The Quaid lived long enough to nurture it during its most critical, crisis-driven first year. It is a testament to the enterprising spirit of the Pakistanis and their loyalty to the memory of Jinnah that they could and did rise to the challenge of sustaining the country and working tirelessly during the very early years despite the lack of political cohesion, an empty treasury, a nonexistent economy, the arrival of millions of desperate refugees who were holocaust survivors, and a war in Kashmir.

The death of Mohammad Ali Jinnah, the revered Quaid-e-Azam, in 1948, just thirteen months after independence, was a severe blow and a setback in the country's economic and

Pakistan's prime minister Liaquat Ali Khan during a visit to New York City in 1950. (Bettmann/Corbis)

political development. It deprived Pakistan of more than just its founding father. Tonchev writes that "the new nation lost its most charismatic leader who could have enhanced common sense and stability in the country" (2003, 6). No one else had the vision, the formidable negotiation skills, and political acumen of the Quaid, qualities that had won independence for Pakistan within seven years of the Lahore Resolution. No one except Liaquat Ali Khan, Jinnah's right-hand man, and to a limited extent Shaheed Suhrawardy, had popular support. Few had the personal integrity, the ability to go beyond pursuit of personal gain, and the commitment to the nation rather than to provincial, ethnic, or religious interests that Quaid had.

When Jinnah died, Khwaja Nazimuddin became the new governor general. But Jinnah was irreplaceable, and no successor could command the respect that was reserved for Jinnah alone. Nazimuddin acquired a more traditional, nonpolitical role as head of state, and Liaquat Ali Khan, Jinnah's chief lieutenant and the prime minister, assumed more power. But there were many challenges that threatened their leadership and the constitution making: the struggle between the center and the provinces, and between the provinces of western Pakistan and East Bengal. The first major step in framing a constitution was taken when the Constituent Assembly of Pakistan (CAP) adopted the historic Objectives Resolution on March 12, 1949, as a set of guiding principles for the future constitution. It proclaimed that the state of Pakistan would not follow the European pattern, but would be a state "wherein the principles of democracy, freedom, equality, tolerance and social justice, as enunciated by Islam, shall be fully observed; wherein the Muslims shall be enabled to order their lives in the individual and collective spheres in accordance with the teachings and requirements of Islam as set out in the *Holy Quran* and *Sunnah;* [and] wherein adequate provision shall be made for the minorities freely to progress and practice their religions and develop their cultures" (Blood 1995, 204). The same year saw a cease-fire agreed upon by both India and Pakistan, as well as a temporary demarcation line partitioning the disputed state of Kashmir. The new nation appeared to progress well on the road to statehood.

The Constituent Assembly created the prestigious Basic Principles Committee (BPC) of twenty-five members, charged with framing the constitution and reconciling differences on constitutional issues. The BPC produced an Interim Report in September 1950, which made only peripheral reference to the Islamic nature of the state, upheld the goal of establishing Urdu as Pakistan's official language, and appeared to deny Bengalis, though not explicitly, the appropriate representation in the National Assembly in accordance with their greater numbers. It drew immediate and significant criticism from both the religious clerics and the Bengalis. This delayed constitution making. Liaquat was confronted with the difficult task of accommodating different provinces in the distribution of seats in the National Assembly, given that East Bengal had 54 percent of the country's total population. Some Bengalis boycotted the meetings of the BPC, staged protests, defected from the Muslim League, and organized opposition parties. Hussain Shaheed Suhrawardy quit the Muslim League to form the Awami League. In the western wing, the 1951 provincial elections in Punjab returned the Muslim League with an overwhelming majority of seats in the legislature, establishing Mumtaz Daultana, the largest landlord in Punjab, as its leader.

Serious differences erupted between Punjab's chief minister, Daultana, and the prime minister, Liaquat Ali Khan. During his visit to East Bengal, Liaquat had hammered out a formula that would give parity to East Bengal with the combined provinces of western Pakistan in the allocation of seats in the National Assembly. Daultana opposed this scheme of the central government on the grounds that this formula would relegate his province to a secondary status vis-à-vis East Bengal. Daultana was supported in his opposition to parity by many other Punjabi leaders, most notably Mushtaq Ahmad Gurmani, the minister of interior in Liaquat's cabinet. This further delayed constitution making.

Liaquat announced a five-day tour of Punjab, and as he was about to deliver a public address in Rawalpindi on October 16, 1951, he was shot at close range: his assassin was killed on the spot by a police inspector, who was also shot nine years later, leaving no direct witnesses or proof of conspiracy. It is widely believed that a conspiracy had taken the life of Quaid-i-Millat (Leader of the Nation), Liaquat Ali Khan. Some believe that Daultana and Gurmani had lured the prime minister to give a public speech in Punjab to sell the parity formula to the Punjabis himself, as they would not do it, and were in some way involved with the assassination. Ghulam Mohammad and Gurmani were both in Rawalpindi on the day of the assassination, thus feeding the rumor mill about their likely complicity. The Bengalis "could not dispel a fear that Liaquat had been killed because he leaned toward the east, and that in silencing the prime Minister, their voices too had been muted. . . . Bengalis were convinced that high members of the central and Punjab governments were implicated in Liaquat's death" (Ziring 1999, 120–121). Another speculation is that Liaquat was planning to remove Ghulam Mohammad from his cabinet post, thereby providing a motive for him. Some people believe that since Liaquat was less hostile to India than some officers wished and was apparently willing to find a compromise arrangement with India, as indicated by the 1950s "No-War Pact" with India, his life was taken by army officers or disgruntled Kashmiri Mujahideen. But no evidence supporting a conspiracy thesis was ever found.

Liaquat's assassination before his government could draft a constitution plunged Pakistan into seven years of political chaos and led to a collapse of the parliamentary system. After his assassination, there were six prime ministers in seven years. Liaquat's successor, Khwaja Nazimuddin (seventeen months); Mohammed Ali Bogra (tweny-nine months); Chaudri Mohammed Ali (thirteen months); Shaheed Suhrawardy (thirteen months); I. I. Chundrigar (two months); and Firoz Khan Noon (eleven months) all became victims of intrigues. During this period, two bureaucrats, Ghulam Mohammad and Iskander Mirza, brazenly abused their powers as head of state to make or break governments. As politicians and bureaucrats bickered and quarreled and were unable to govern, the military became increasingly involved and finally took over. The period from Liaquat's death to the first military takeover is very significant in the political history of Pakistan because it set the stage for recurring themes in Pakistani politics: lack of religious tolerance, tense relations between center and provinces, the dominating role of military and the bureaucrats, precedence of administrative over legislative and judicial power, and squabbling of politicians. Many of the unresolved issues in Pakistan today have their roots in events that happened and choices that were made during this period of Pakistan's history, between 1949 (after Jinnah's but before Liaquat's death) and 1958.

After Liaquat's death in 1951, Governor General Khwaja Nazimuddin naively agreed to resign as governor general and step down to take over as the country's second prime minister, believing that he was needed to save the nation at a difficult time. But he inherited an impossible legacy of reconciling opposite views on constitution making. To fill the post left vacant by Nazimuddin, Gurmani proposed the name of Ghulam Mohammad, the finance minister, on the grounds that because of his failing health he would be a ceremonial head of state and would not threaten the prerogatives of the prime minister. Nothing could have been further from the truth, as events would prove in the next few years. Ghulam Mohammad's promotion to governor general was a strategic maneuver by Chaudhri Mohammad Ali and Gurmani, encouraged by many civil and military officials, including General Ayub Khan, as well as some Punjabi politicians, to bypass Nazimuddin and in time to discredit and finally drive him from office. But Nazimuddin was not "privy to the machinations of clever politicians, both east and west, who were intent on destroying his provincial power base. . . . Nazimuddin had become a target of the power-brokers" (Ziring 1999, 126).

The governor general and the prime minister made a very odd couple. Ghulam Mohammad, an aggressive and self-confident Punjabi bureaucrat, detested politicians and wanted to rely more on the civil bureaucracy. Nazimuddin, like Jinnah, believed in a single, unified Pakistan, and in Urdu as a unifying language, even though it was not his mother tongue, thereby putting national interests above personal and provincial interests. None of the constitutional issues were resolved: instead a series of events took place that eventually led to the collapse of the parliamentary system. Ghulam Mohammad centralized authority in his person, dominating Nazimuddin and making a shambles of the office, causing great harm to the nation. In January 1952, when Nazimuddin delivered a speech at *Paltan Maidan* in Dhaka and cited the need for Urdu to be the national language, his comments evoked an explosive response. The Bengali language movement was reconstituted, and on February 21, 1952, Sheikh Mujibur Rahman of the Awami League led the demonstrations calling for a general strike. The demonstrations degenerated into a riot involving thousands, leading to opening fire on the demonstrators, which killed four students. From then on, this day would be known as *Shaheed* Day (day of martyrs), and Sheikh Mujib and *Shaheed* Day would both become the symbols of Bengali nationalism and, then, secession. The Muslim League government of Nurul Amin had to call the military in to restore order, which destroyed the party's provincial base forever. And Nazimuddin was renounced in his own province and in Dhaka, the very city that formed his power base.

At this point, a major confrontation occurred between the governor general and the prime minister over the "Ahmedi" problem. In February 1953, the army was called and martial law was imposed due to the civil unrest that developed following the demand of religion-based parties that *Ahmedis (Mirzais or Qadianis)* be declared non-Muslims since their beliefs violate the central tenet of Islam that the Prophet Mohammad (peace be upon him) is the last prophet. The Ahmedis are the contemporary followers of Mirza Ghulam Ahmad who believe that he received a revelation from God. The Punjab riots targeting the Ahmedis were sparked by the Majlis-i-Ahrar-i-Islam, a political party opposed to the Muslim League and founded in 1931 by Muslim Punjabis, presumably supported by the Jamaat-i-Islami and its leader, Maulana Maudoodi. The riots tore the Punjab apart, but the chief minister of Punjab, Mumtaz Daultana, took few preventive measures, despite the warning by police intelligence reports of the impending disaster of the anti-Ahmedi campaign. Ziring reports that "a later court of inquiry would single him [Daultana] out for condemnation, citing his duplicity, his perfidy, as well as his dishonesty" (1999,

143). Nazimuddin ordered martial law throughout Punjab and obtained the resignation of Daultana, arrested the perpetrators, and banned some religious parties, including the Ahrars. But the action was late in coming.

In April 1953, Ghulam Mohammad dismissed Nazimuddin, citing the government's failure to resolve the difficulties facing the country. He was supported by the military and civil high command, as well as strong landed interests in Punjab. In 1954, he appointed his own "cabinet of talents," giving the military a direct role in politics and doing away with the facade of parliamentary government. His cabinet included Mohammad Ali as the minister of finance, General Ayub Khan as the minister of defense, and Major-General Iskander Mirza as the minister of home affairs. Ghulam Mohammad tried to minimize the role of politicians and isolate the clerics. However, the Civil Service dominated the decision-making process, and both the governor general and the new prime minister, Mohammed Ali Bogra, Pakistan's ambassador in Washington, were bureaucrats.

But Nazimuddin's ouster was totally undemocratic since he still had the support of a majority in the assembly. Ghulam Mohammad did this by cleverly using a constitutional clause, which was originally constituted to give the British viceroy discretionary powers and which provided that the prime minister held office during the pleasure of the governor general. This dismissal was unfortunate, both because it set a precedent of a bureaucrat dismissing an elected head of government, which would haunt Pakistan later, and because the dismissal was preceded by a civilian government undermining its own authority by asking the army to manage a political crisis. Years later, the same pattern would be repeated when President Ghulam Ishaq Khan would dismiss the elected governments of Benazir Bhutto and Nawaz Sharif.

The dismissal of Nazimuddin has also been identified by some as the display of the power of the feudals, or the landed aristocracy, in Pakistan politics. Kibria (1999) argues that the

West Pakistani feudals felt threatened by Nazimuddin because of his leading role in the abolition of *zamindari* without compensation in East Pakistan, a promise made by the Muslim League in the 1946 elections that was fulfilled in 1951. Accordingly, the agitation against the Ahmedis by *maulvis* was instigated by feudals like Daultana and encouraged by the bureaucracy to destabilize and oust Nazimuddin. This had the tacit approval of the army chief, General Ayub Khan, who had his own agenda. Qutbuddin Aziz points out that Ayub approved because Nazimuddin, faced with a budget deficit and an acute shortage of food grains, wanted to streamline the army and was planning a reduction in the army budget. Kibria adds that Ayub also had a personal grudge against Nazimuddin as he had rejected Ayub's requests for extension of his service tenure and for funds to renovate and refurnish his official residence. Ghulam Mohammad also dismissed several provincial governments and nominated his own chief ministers. Eventually, he proclaimed a state of emergency in 1954 and dismissed the Constituent Assembly. This supremacy of the governor general over the legislature has been referred to as the viceregal tradition in Pakistan's politics. The dismissal was declared illegal by the Sindh Chief Court, but its decision was overturned by Pakistan's Federal (Supreme) Court. It was widely believed to be a political, not a judicial, decision, and a deal between the governor general and Chief Justice Munir of the Federal Court. At the least, it showed the power of the executive over the judiciary.

From 1954 to 1958, Pakistan's parliamentary system was a facade. The Civil Service, assisted by the military, dominated the decision-making process, and the League became dependent on, and smothered by, the civil servants. The Muslim League did not seek a popular mandate and did not form a national government through parliamentary elections, which could have curbed the growth of bureaucratic power, because of the reluctance of western wing bureaucrats and politicians to share power with those in the eastern wing. If an election were called, majority rule would have shifted power from the western to the eastern wing, which contained 54 percent of the total Pakistani population, and from the Muhajir-Punjabi elite to the Bengalis. This reluctance to share power was also the primary cause of delay in constitution making. The Constituent Assembly met only sixteen days a year, between 1948 and 1954, to frame a constitution, with an average attendance of forty-six members.

The political elite spent several years devising arrangements that would reduce the voting power of the Bengalis and guarantee parity of the western wing with the eastern. A plan was devised whereby the Bengali majority was reduced by creating two provinces, East Pakistan and West Pakistan, with equal representational power. The four provinces of West Pakistan as well as the federally administered areas and princely states were merged into one unit, a single province, West Pakistan. The Bengali majority of 54 percent in East Pakistan was to elect the same number of members for the National Assembly as the minority of 46 percent in West Pakistan. Kibria notes that "this was against the basic democratic principle of one-man one vote and was a grossly dishonest formula, robbing the Bengalis of their legitimate majority by calling it parity" (1999, 116). But some politicians such as Daultana and Gurmani were even against parity for East Pakistan, let alone giving them representation in accordance with their population share, because it would give Bengalis more seats in the National Assembly than those held by the Punjab. Kardar goes further and notes that "a decision must have been taken to keep East Pakistan out of decision-making. To begin with, parity was introduced so that as a majority province East Pakistan should not impose such radical measures as Land Reforms for the benefit of the landless peasants of West Pakistan. This tacit understanding among the feudal class by Kalabaghs, Gardezis, Gilanis and Qureshis was to sow the seeds of the eventual separation between the two wings of the country" (Kibria 1999, 110).

There was resentment in the eastern wing against the one-unit scheme, as in the three smaller provinces of the western wing. But the primary source of conflict was the center and the province relationship. Politicians could not agree on whether the central government should be strong, as West Pakistanis preferred, or weak, as East Pakistanis wanted. Anti–Muslim League parties joined in a coalition to form the United Front to contest the 1954 provincial elections in East Pakistan, the first ever in the province. The manifesto of the party was based on demand for a weak center, in charge of defense, currency, and foreign affairs, in conformity with the 1940 Pakistan Resolution that had won Bengali support in favor of partition in pre-partition India. The Muslim League was badly defeated, winning only 10 out of a total of 309 seats, while the United Front won 233 seats. The 1954 election results and the earlier language riots in East Pakistan against Urdu being imposed as the national language were warning signs to accommodate Bengalis in nation building. But instead the United Front government was dismissed on May 30, 1954, governor's rule (administrative rule, not by the leading political party) was imposed throughout the province, and all political activity was suspended.

In 1955, Iskander Mirza, governor of East Pakistan, forced Ghulam Mohammad to resign as head of state, in consultation with other politician-bureaucrats, both because of his failing health and his increasing obsession for power. The one-unit plan was expedited. The executive controlled political parties. Even the once-powerful Muslim League disintegrated into small factions dominated by conservative landlords. A series of short-lived governments were formed, and four prime ministers served in three years, 1955–1958. Three months after the creation of West Pakistan as a single provincial unit, the draft bill of the 1956 constitution was brought before the Constituent Assembly despite considerable dissatisfaction in East Pakistan and minority provinces of West Pakistan. The constitution was adopted in March 1956, nine years after independence.

In March 1956, Pakistan acquired its first full-fledged constitution, and Pakistan became an Islamic republic. The governor general was replaced by a president, and the revived Constituent Assembly was reconstituted as the Legislative Assembly, the national legislature. But the constitution did not represent legislative dominance but rather the dominance of civil servants who were the true architects of the document. The parliamentary system outlined in the 1956 constitution required disciplined political parties, which were not there. The Muslim League had lost support. Moreover, societal violence and ethnic separatist sentiments further complicated the parliamentary process. In West Pakistan, the chief minister, Khan Sahib, was assassinated, and his brother, Khan Abdul Ghaffar Khan of the National Awami Party (NAP), declared his intention to work to attain a separate homeland for the Pakhtoons or Pathans (the ethnic group living in the North-West Frontier Province of Pakistan and in Afghanistan). In Balochistan, the khan of Kalat again declared his independence, but the Pakistan Army restored control. Under the constitution, national elections were to be held for the first time in February 1959, which would have shifted power to a Bengali-dominated legislative government. To circumvent the transfer of power, President Iskander Mirza canceled the elections, disbanded the Legislative Assembly on October 7, 1958, and declared martial law. Ayub Khan assisted Mirza in abrogating the constitution and removed the politicians he believed were bringing Pakistan to collapse. Then another coup by Ayub Khan in October 1958 ousted Mirza, who was sent into lifetime exile in London, and Ayub Khan became the president of Pakistan. Few were surprised, and many were relieved that the political instability had come to an end.

AYUB KHAN: FIRST MILITARY RULE, DECADE OF DEVELOPMENT, AND CIVIL WAR: 1958–1969

The consistent failure of the civilian politicians and the bureaucrats to provide effective government and to manage

164 PAKISTAN: A Global Studies Handbook

political crises in the early years, 1948–1958, eventually led to the military coup in October 1958 when General Ayub Khan ousted the "inefficient and rascally" politicians. Ayub Khan invoked martial law, army rule unchecked by civilian courts or legislatures, and made himself president of Pakistan. His coup ended eleven years of unstable democracy and began a new era of military rule in Pakistan. Generals were to rule Pakistan for thirty-one of the next forty-eight years. Few were surprised, and many relieved, hoping that at last Pakistan would have a leader who would make decisions in the national interest rather than for personal gain. Although Ayub Khan viewed himself as a reformer, he followed the Mughal and viceregal traditions of benevolent authoritarianism. The Ayub era is often known as the golden era of economic development in Pakistan. But his policies also led to sharp interregional and interpersonal inequities in income distribution and in concentration of wealth and power, paving the way for the 1971 dismemberment of Pakistan. Though delayed and imperfect, the 1956 constitution did provide a framework for incorporating Bengalis within a national political system. "There were signs of Bengali frustration, but not of despair" (Noman 1990, 30). The 1959 elections would have provided them acceptable representation in the central government. Ayub's coup undermined this process, reinforcing the dominance of the bureaucracy and the military, both institutions where Bengali representation was minimal, particularly in the army.

The Ayub era can be divided roughly into two periods: the first from 1958 to 1962 characterized by martial law, and the second from 1962 to 1969 following the 1962 constitution. During the first four years, Ayub banned political parties and political activity. The martial law of 1958 targeted "antisocial" practices such as abducting women and children, smuggling, and black marketing. Many civil servants were punished for corruption, misconduct, inefficiency, or subversive activities. He also put corrupt politicians in jail. About 7,000 individu-

Mohammad Ayub Khan, president of Pakistan (1958–1969). (Corbis)

als, mostly former politicians, were tried for "misconduct" by special tribunals under the Elective Bodies Disqualification Order (EBDO). The EBDO politicians could avoid prosecution if they agreed not to be candidates for any elective body for a period of seven years.

Perhaps one of the worst charges against the martial law regime of Ayub Khan was that the independence of the press, judiciary, and academics was severely curtailed. Journalists were curbed by press laws, lawyers and judges by law reforms, and academics by control over publishing—all of which had grave implications for cultural and social development. Trade unions, labor organizations, student groups, and even mosque *imams* were cautioned to avoid political activity. The 1959 Martial Law Ordinance that empowered the government to take over the largest and most influential English and Urdu daily newspapers like the *Pakistan Times* and *Imroz* "suffocated all forms of social, political, and cultural expression. Pakistan has yet to dismantle the structures of regimentation and control imposed by the Ayub regime" (Noman 1990, 29).

At the same time, many also believed that, "on the whole, the martial law years were not severe" (Blood 1995, 46). Most Pakistanis today believe that as military dictators go, Ayub Khan was a fairly good ruler. His government was efficient, and the economy grew. He did not execute political prisoners, as Ziaul Haq would later do. He did not embezzle millions of dollars, as Benazir Bhutto and Nawaz Sharif would later be allegedly charged of doing in their terms of office. Ayub Khan has generally been credited with introducing some significant reforms in Pakistan during the martial law years and later. Some have gone so far as to say that "more than any other political leader in a modernizing country after World War Two, Ayub Khan came close to filling the role of a Solon or Lycurgus or great legislator on the Platonic or Rousseauien model" (Huntington 1968, 251). Or, as Ayub's own minister, Zulfiqar Ali Bhutto, had said, "This man of history is more than a Lincoln to us, . . . more than a Lenin . . . . He is our Ata

Turk, . . . and above all a Salahuddin" (Kibria 1999, 118). Although these depictions of Ayub Khan may be an over-statement in the case of Huntington's statement and outright flattery in the case of Bhutto's, it cannot be denied that the Ayub era brought stability and economic development to Pakistan, though at the cost of equity and regional tensions.

Among Ayub's contributions are his program of agricultural and industrial development, his advocacy for women's rights, and his successful foreign policy, particularly with respect to the United States and China. He introduced the Muslim Family Laws Ordinance of 1961, which provided legal protection to a woman against divorce by a husband without cause and without the permission of a local arbitration council, and generally reduced polygamy to cases in which a couple had been unable to have a son. This legislation is the strongest legal protection for women to date in Pakistan. The late sixties also witnessed the green revolution due to the widespread use of HYV (high-yield variety) seeds of wheat and rice by farmers, along with biological-chemical inputs like fertilizers and pesticides, as well as tubewells and tractors. This was also accompanied by rural credit and work programs, agricultural support prices, and higher budget allocations for agriculture. Accordingly, wheat and rice production more than doubled in Pakistan during the late 1960s. Ayub Khan also initiated land reforms, and the government imposed a ceiling of 200 hectares of irrigated and 400 hectares of unirrigated land in West Pakistan for individual holdings. But the government resumed only about 4 million hectares of land, which was sold mainly to civil and military officers. In the industrial sector, policies of tax incentives, import substitution, and the export bonus scheme boosted industrial production. (For details, see Chapter 2.)

Ayub Khan was the architect of Pakistan's policy of close alliance with the United States. He signed bilateral economic and military agreements with the United States in 1959 and was responsible for seeking and securing military and economic assistance from the United States. He also sought to improve relations with Pakistan's neighbors, including India, China, and the Soviet Union. He also moved the capital of Pakistan from the port city of Karachi to a newly constructed city called Islamabad, which means home of Islam, to reduce Pakistan's vulnerability to a naval attack by India.

Recognizing early on the need to relinquish some military control, Ayub introduced his unique governmental system of "Basic Democracies," becoming the "civilian" head of a military government. This system allowed for controlled and indirect participation of the electorate and was supposed to suit what Ayub called the particular "genius" of Pakistan, with its largely illiterate population unsuitable for sophisticated parliamentary democracy. The Basic Democracies system consisted of a multitiered pyramidal system of institutions from the village to the provincial level. The lowest but most important tier consisted of the union councils that were responsible for local government, including agricultural and community development, and maintaining law and order. The successively higher tiers consisted of the *tehsil* (subdistrict) councils performing coordination functions, the *zilla* (district) councils, the divisional advisory councils, and the highest tier of provincial development advisory councils. The union councils, one each for groups of villages having a population of about 10,000 people, consisted of ten directly elected members and five appointed members, all called Basic Democrats. The Basic Democrats formed an electoral college for the election of the president and members of the national and provincial assemblies. In 1960, the Basic Democrats were asked to endorse Ayub Khan's presidency and to give him a mandate to frame a new constitution. The electoral college elected the president by a 95.6 percent vote, based on a referendum question, "Have you confidence in President Ayub Khan?"

A constitution was framed in 1962, which ended martial law and established a presidential form of government, giving vast executive, legislative, and financial powers to the president, but with a weak legislature. Heavy reliance was placed on the bureaucracy in much the same way as that of previous governments. Routine matters and day-to-day functioning were left to the bureaucrats, and the army was not involved much in administration. The civilian bureaucrats formed the majority of Ayub's advisors and cabinet ministers. The legislature was weak, with members of the National Assembly chosen on personal merit, since the 1962 constitution did not recognize political parties. Adult franchise was limited to the election of Basic Democrats.

Not only did the Basic Democracy system provide a safe electoral college for the election of the president, but it also extended bureaucratic control over the political process since civil servants selected the Basic Democrats. It also created a network of allies for the government by developing a direct relationship between the bureaucracy and the rural elite who were given access to the state's resources. But the system was top-down, and this "democracy from above" was criticized as a form of "representational dictatorship." It did not provide access to certain groups; it included only those who benefited from state patronage. So instead of neutralizing political tensions, these institutions became a symbol of mass alienation. Since it had no mechanism for accommodating opposition, it forced groups with political grievances into mobilizing for violent confrontation.

Ayub's policies also led to the ultimate split of Pakistan. Dissatisfaction with Ayub's government was strongest in East Pakistan, though West Pakistan soon followed suit. The East Pakistanis, who had strongly supported Mohammad Ali Jinnah's dream of a separate Muslim state, found that, despite being the majority, they were poorly represented in positions of economic and political power. In a government where military and bureaucracy were very important, the East Pakistanis fared poorly since only 5 percent of army officers and less than a third of civil servants were East Pakistanis. Moreover, budgetary decisions also discriminated against them. East

Pakistan contributed more than 50 percent to Pakistan's foreign exchange earnings through its export of jute, but received less than a third of the nation's imported goods. About 90 percent of the defense budget and most foreign aid were spent in West Pakistan. Not surprisingly, economic indicators were much better in West Pakistan than in East Pakistan: per capita income was 50 percent higher, the rate of economic growth was twice as high, and access to hospital beds and electricity in homes four times as high. Moreover, Pakistan's 1965 war with India, following India's announcement in 1964 that its acquisition of Kashmir was final, added to the alienation of East Pakistanis from the central government. The East Pakistanis, surrounded by India on three sides, felt that a war for Kashmir had jeopardized their military and economic security.

East Pakistan's resentment of the Ayub government was crystallized in the Six Point program put forward in February 1966 by Sheikh Mujibur Rahman, the leader of the Awami (Peoples) League, the largest political party in East Pakistan. These demands had emerged from a climate of violent protests in East Pakistan against the Ayub regime. There were an estimated 4,946 riots a year, on average, in East Pakistan between 1958 and 1966. The six points later amended and incorporated in the 1970 election manifesto of the Awami League are listed below.

1. The character of the government shall be federal and parliamentary.
2. The federal government shall be responsible for only defense and foreign affairs.
3. There shall be two separate currencies mutually or freely convertible in each wing.
4. Fiscal policy shall be the responsibility of the federating unit.
5. Separate accounts shall be maintained of the foreign exchange earnings of each of the federating units.
6. Federating units shall be empowered to maintain a militia or paramilitary force.

Mujibur Rahman was arrested two years later in the Agartala Conspiracy case on charges of conspiring with Indian spies for secession, but the charges were subsequently dismissed. The arrest made him a hero to East Pakistanis. The trial was "one of those treason trials which makes martyrs of the accused" (Noman 1990, 31).

East Pakistanis were soon joined by West Pakistanis in their opposition to the Ayub government, although the revolt in East Pakistan was different from the agitation in West Pakistan. In West Pakistan, the smaller provinces had the same grievances as East Pakistan against the dominance of the Punjabi-Muhajir elite. In Punjab and Sindh, class tensions bred by Ayub's economic policies and Bhutto's fiery speeches led to class-based demands by urban groups, who were mobilized by the Pakistan Peoples Party. In addition, intellectuals objected to the lack of democracy, farmers to their lower relative incomes vis-à-vis urban dwellers, and factory workers to their stagnating wages and worsening income inequalities. Although the government tried to improve equity by enacting some piecemeal measures between 1968 and 1971 regarding minimum wages, collective bargaining for labor, and tax reform, implementation was very weak. Moreover, Bhutto gained support in the Punjab for his strong nationalist views against India, while Ayub Khan lost support even within the army for the cease-fire agreement following the war with India in 1965, signed at Tashkent, through Soviet mediation. An impression was created, though unfair and incorrect, that Ayub had lost on the negotiating table at Tashkent what the army had won on the battlefield.

Mass demonstrations by students and labor unions finally led to Ayub's downfall. In October 1968, students poured into the streets across West Pakistan, mobilized by the fiery speeches of Zulfiqar Ali Bhutto, who broke with Ayub Khan and formed his own political party, the Pakistan Peoples Party (PPP). By February 1969, factory workers all over Pakistan joined in the protests, bringing industry to a standstill through strikes. The rioting reflected protests of the population not only against interregional and interpersonal inequities, but also against the regime's perceived corruption, particularly of Ayub's sons, and responsibility for Pakistan's defeat in the 1965 Indo-Pakistani war over Kashmir. Finally, Ayub Khan resigned as president in March 1969 and, forever contemptuous of lawyer-politicians, handed over power to his fellow army officer, General Agha Mohammad Yahya Khan. Yahya Khan became the president and chief martial law administrator.

Yahya Khan declared martial law but promised to hold nationwide elections in 1970, Pakistan's first since independence. He also promised that the seats in the National Assembly would be apportioned on a one-person, one-vote basis. This meant that for the first time East Pakistan would have a majority of the seats. It was thus under Yahya Khan that the first general elections were held in Pakistan on December 7, 1970. Yahya adhered to his promise of impartiality and honesty, earning the respect of all participants. East Pakistanis voted overwhelmingly for one party, the Awami League (AL), which demanded autonomy for East Pakistan. The Awami League won 167 of East Pakistan's 169 legislative seats, and the Pakistan Peoples Party of Bhutto won 88 of West Pakistan's 144 seats, which ensured a majority for the Awami League in the 313-seat National Assembly, which, in turn, would make Mujibur Rahman the prime minister of Pakistan. But the results of Pakistan's first nationwide elections were not honored.

The nature and size of the Awami League's victory were a shock to West Pakistanis. While willing to decentralize many government functions, the West Pakistani politicians and the army regarded Mujib's demand for complete autonomy as equivalent to secession and, as such, unacceptable. They did not want to transfer power to the majority. It is speculated that Yahya may have believed that competition among too many political parties would prevent any one party from coming to power, thus perpetuating the role of the army. Another view is that instead of rigging elections, Yahya wanted to make a deal with Mujib, allowing him to share power as the president, failing which, he struck a deal with Bhutto instead. Nonetheless, Yahya tried to persuade Bhutto and Mujib to come to some sort of accommodation, but Mujib insisted on his right as leader of the majority to form the government and Bhutto claimed that there were "two majorities" in Pakistan. Bhutto declared that the Pakistan Peoples Party would boycott the National Assembly unless Mujibur Rahman scaled back his demand for autonomy. He threatened to "break the legs" of any party member who dared to attend the inaugural session of the National Assembly. Led by Bhutto and supported by senior army officers, the West Pakistani politicians pressured President Yahya Khan to indefinitely postpone the convening of the National Assembly just two days before it was scheduled to meet. On Mujib's call, a general strike to protest against this turn of events spread across the whole of East Pakistan.

When negotiations among Bhutto, Mujib, and Yahya failed, Yahya sent 75,000 West Pakistani troops to East Pakistan in March 1971 for a military crackdown. The Awami League was outlawed, and Mujib was arrested for treason. Before his arrest, he proclaimed East Pakistan to be the independent nation of Bangladesh. Major Ziaur Rahman (who would become president of Bangladesh in 1977) and others organized Bengali troops to form the *Mukti Bahini* (guerrilla liberation force) to resist the Pakistan Army. The savage civil war that followed and the massive military crackdown mark one of the darkest spots in the history of independent Pakistan. The army bombed the city of Dhaka, burned villages and crops, and raped Bengali women, killing tens of thousands of Bengalis and causing an estimated 10 million refugees to cross the border to India. Because of press censorship, people in West Pakistan remained uninformed about the crackdown in East Pakistan and discounted reports in the international press as an Indian conspiracy. War broke out between Pakistan and India when Indian troops invaded East Pakistan in

December 1971; snow in the Himalayas made it impossible for the Chinese, Pakistan's strong ally and India's enemy, to intervene. The East Pakistanis greeted the Indian Army with joy, and within two weeks the Indian Army had captured all of East Pakistan. The Pakistan Army surrendered, and East Pakistan was lost, becoming the independent nation of Bangladesh on December 16, 1971. A majority had broken away to form a new country. Yahya Khan resigned in disgrace on December 20, 1971. He had presided over the two most traumatic events in Pakistan's history: the humiliating defeat of Pakistan's army to India and the secession of East Pakistan. Moreover, 90,000 Pakistanis had been taken as prisoners of war; hundreds of *Biharis,* the minority ethnic group in East Pakistan that had collaborated with the Pakistan Army, were killed and tortured by the Bengali *Mukti Bahini;* and thousands of *Biharis* were put in refugee camps with limitations on mobility where most of them remain stranded to this day. They have been denied citizenship by the Bangladesh government because they supported Pakistan, but the Pakistan government has failed to repatriate them. To most Pakistanis, the news of Pakistan's defeat came as a numbing shock. As Blood remarks, "literally overnight, the country had lost its status as the largest Muslim nation in the world. Gone, too, were any illusions of military parity with India" (1994, xxxiv). Three weeks later, Mujibur Rahman was freed and allowed to return in triumph to Bangladesh. The new Pakistan consisted only of the former West Pakistan, where the majority party, PPP, came to power led by Bhutto.

NATIONALIZATION AND AUTHORITARIAN POPULISM UNDER BHUTTO: 1971–1977

In 1971, Zulfiqar Ali Bhutto, the leader of the Pakistan Peoples Party (PPP) and former foreign minister in the government of Ayub Khan, became the first president and the chief martial law administrator of a truncated Pakistan with "a disgraced military, a shattered government, and a demoralized population" (Blood 1995, 58), but Pakistan soon recovered under his charismatic leadership. He lifted martial law within several months, and a new constitution took effect in 1973. Bhutto's party had won a majority of the vote in West Pakistan in 1970 on the radical election pledge of *roti, kapra, aur makan* (food, clothing, and shelter) and had symbolized an alternative vision of a progressive, democratic, and participatory government. But the voters' optimism soon gave way to despair and a feeling of betrayal as Bhutto's regime became increasingly authoritarian and corrupt. Moreover, economic problems following nationalization were accompanied by the OPEC oil crisis and bad weather. The PPP's rigging of the 1977 parliamentary elections was the final blow, galvanizing nine opposition parties into forming a united front to lead a popular movement against Bhutto, causing the downfall of the PPP government.

Despite being a product of an aristocratic feudal background and educated at Berkeley and Oxford, Bhutto had campaigned in 1970 on the simple promise of "food, clothing, and shelter." The populist theme, Bhutto's charisma and oratory, and the PPP's outreach to the poorest slums and the most remote villages in the Punjab and Sindh had led to a landslide victory for the PPP in these two provinces. Bhutto's slogan, "Islam our Faith, Democracy our Polity, Socialism our economy," attracted the left in Punjab and Sindh to PPP, both radicals and reformists. It was these reformists who were the architects of Bhutto's agricultural and industrial reforms. But another group that swarmed to the PPP, some at the outset and others later, were Sindhi landlords—both those who supported reform and those who sought favors as fellow Sindhis or to avoid land reforms on that basis. A third group that supported Bhutto were some factions within the army who had grievances with Ayub for his handling of the 1965 war, particularly the Tashkent Treaty. It was the same group of generals that were on the same side as Bhutto in the reluctance to transfer power to the majority party of Mujibur Rahman earlier. The contradictions inherent in the combination of these three divergent sources of Bhutto's support in the election campaign—traditional feudal forces in Sindh, disadvantaged urban groups in Punjab and Sindh, and factions within the army—played out later in the policies that were followed and the greater importance given to one rather than the other group in later years. Nonetheless, Bhutto's policies rewarded these groups directly or indirectly, some to a larger extent than others.

In contrast to these three support groups, Bhutto's relationship with the industrialists and civil servants was adversarial from the beginning when he had broken off from Ayub Khan and criticized Ayub's policies that concentrated wealth in the hands of the proverbial "twenty-two industrial families." (For details, see Chapter 2.) Accordingly, his policies and reforms were directed at these two groups: the industrialists through nationalization of industries and the civil servants through reforms of the Civil Service. The following paragraphs discuss his policies and relationship with these groups: industrialists, civil servants, military, and landlords.

In January 1972, Bhutto issued the Economic Reform Order nationalizing thirty-two large manufacturing plants in eight industries, including iron and steel, basic metals, motor vehicles and tractors, heavy engineering, petrochemicals, cement, chemicals, and public utilities. Then, in the second round, domestic private banks, insurance companies, shipping as well as oil processing, grain milling, and cotton ginning were nationalized. This "clipped the wings" and broke the power of the twenty-two elite families, who had first been brought into public discussion (and criticism) by economist Mahbubul Haq. Like Bhutto, Haq had once been part of the Ayub administration whose policies had led to this concentration of wealth. Also, like Bhutto, Haq had broken away

Zulfiqar Ali Bhutto at press conference at the United Nations, 1965.
(Library of Congress)

from the Ayub administration during the later years. As a consequence of nationalization, private investment in large-scale manufacturing declined by about 50 percent from 1970 to 1973, and by 1976, public-sector investment was higher than private investment. There was considerable capital flight, both out of the country and into small-scale manufacturing and real estate. Profits in public-sector enterprises fell, partly because of minimum-wage legislation and partly because cautious civil servants, who became managers of nationalized industries, were not used to making quick business decisions. Many newly nationalized industries came to a standstill, and the industrial growth rate declined between 1970 and 1977. Even today, a lingering fear of nationalization restrains many domestic and foreign investors from investing in Pakistan.

Bhutto particularly targeted the powerful and privileged Civil Service of Pakistan, which had been considered the "steel frame" since the time of the British. The PPP government introduced several reforms to curtail the power of the civil servants, beginning with the dismissal of 1,300 civil servants in 1972. Moreover, the elite Civil Service of Pakistan (CSP) cadre was abolished in 1973 and replaced by the All Pakistan Unified Grades structure, consisting of twenty-two pay scales. These reforms reduced the role of the Civil Service from formulator to executioner of policy. A system of lateral entry was introduced to bring technocrats or technical specialists from different professions into the Civil Service. But a large number of senior-level recruits were relatives or close friends of cabinet members. The nepotism and partisan bias in official appointments, and the inefficiency as well as widespread corruption, shook confidence in public institutions under the Bhutto government.

The PPP adopted a three-pronged strategy to contain the military: constitutional safeguards to prevent a military takeover, creation of a paramilitary alternative, and appeasement. The constitutional safeguard was provided under Article 271 of the 1973 constitution, under which subversion of the constitution by a military coup was punishable by death. It has been argued that it was this feature of the constitution and Ziaul Haq's fear of the death penalty for his coup that played a major part in the execution of Bhutto in 1979. Then, the Federal Security Force (FSF), answerable only to Bhutto, was set up to serve as a reserve force to quell riots during civil disturbances, obviating the need to call upon the military to intervene and thus avoiding the likelihood of army takeovers. The army refused to offer technical assistance to FSF, either for training or providing equipment. Consequently, instead of becoming a reserve force and partial substitute for the military, the FSF became an additional coercive force and degenerated into a "group of official thugs," creating resentment and anger initially and mass protests subsequently. The PPP also tried to appease the military high command through increases in military expenditures, in absolute amounts and as a percentage of GNP, exemption of landholdings of military officers from land reforms, and a ban on public discussion of the military's role in East Pakistan. Accordingly, the Hamood-ur-Rahman Commission report, which had investigated the debacle and was very critical of the army's role, was never made public. It is believed that had it been made public, it may have tarnished the army's image and paved the way for civilian supremacy. Bhutto's protection of the army has also been ascribed to his role in the East Pakistan crisis and his need to support the military just as the military had supported him in his refusal to agree to a transfer of power to the East Pakistanis after the 1971 elections. On the whole, Bhutto failed to dominate the military, as later events would prove.

The Bhutto government also carried out extensive reforms in the agricultural sector, the most important being the Land Reforms of 1972. The Bhutto government reduced the ceiling on landholdings from 500 acres of irrigated and 1,000 acres of unirrigated land under Ayub Khan's government to 150 acres of irrigated and 300 acres of unirrigated land. Since land reforms were an integral part of Bhutto's election manifesto, it is alleged that big landlords made backdated transfers as soon as Bhutto assumed power. Not much land was resumed after land reforms by the government because the owners did not relinquish much land, and there was little to redistribute to poor tenants or the landless. Moreover, to cultivate the landed aristocracy, particularly of Punjab and Sindh, Bhutto reneged on his earlier promises of distributing land to the landless on the scale that he had promised. Nonetheless, the reforms were successful in giving tenants greater security of tenure. On the whole, however, Bhutto's agricultural policies helped the larger farmers. The devaluation of the Pakistani rupee in 1972 also helped the large farmers who had marketable surpluses. Farm laborers and tenants, on the other hand, were displaced by mechanization and many migrated to cities.

Although Bhutto had promised a more equitable development strategy and his populist rhetoric had radicalized the urban masses in the late 1960s, the PPP leadership was purged of its "reformist" left-wing members who were committed to the creation of a more egalitarian system within three years of forming a government. This included four ministers in Bhutto's first cabinet, including J. A. Rahim and Mubasshir Hasan. They were the architects of the land reform and nationalization policies of the Bhutto government. The removal of the radical left from the PPP, including Mukhtar Rana and Mairaj Mohammad Khan, within months of the party coming to power was expected since their objective of smashing "feudalism and capitalism" was inconsistent with that of Bhutto's reforms, but the ouster of the reformist left "marked a crucial turning point in the direction toward which the PPP was headed" (Noman 1990, 103). The marginalization of the reformist left was a signal to the landed aristocracy of Punjab, who had not joined the PPP at its inception, and whom Bhutto wanted to cultivate now that the party's reform program was not in control of the left-wing senior members, but in control of Bhutto, himself a member of the landed aristocracy of Sindh and not in favor of radical redistribution of wealth. Consequently, the Punjabi landlords joined the PPP, both to minimize the resumption of their lands under the PPP land reforms and to get access to resources through political patronage. Thus, by 1976, twenty-eight out of the thirty-three leading aristocratic families of Punjab had representatives in the PPP, and 66 percent of the PPP's top leadership were members of the landed elite (Noman 1990, 104).

Given that Bhutto's power derived mainly from his charismatic and ideological appeal to the masses, it may appear that the purge of the left and the large-scale entry of landlords transformed a radical left-wing party into a conservative one. But the PPP only used populist rhetoric and highlighted class-consciousness to get mass support, for which radical left-wing groups were cultivated in Punjab and Sindh. The prominence of the left-wing groups in mobilizing the masses and organizing mass rallies gave the PPP the appearance of a radical party, and covered its true profile of a moderately reformist party dominated by powerful conservative forces, particularly the landed rural elite of Punjab and *waderas* (landlords) of Sindh. The resolution of the internal power struggle within PPP in favor of the landed aristocracy led to the revival of factional feudal politics, political and bureaucratic corruption, and rising political violence.

Nonetheless, Bhutto remained popular with the poor. For the rural poor, he redistributed some land and guaranteed security of tenure. For the urban poor, he gave greater freedom to trade unions and required employers to raise the minimum wage. Thus trade unions were strengthened, and welfare measures for labor were announced. Similarly, the salary scales of low-paid government employees were revised. Bhutto also made the government officials and civil servants more responsive to common people by placing the Civil Service under the supervision of political appointees. Above all, he gave the poor self-confidence to stand up for their rights. They had the comfort that they could access the highest office in the land through his "open kutcheries" (county courts open to everyone) and lay their grievances. It was not uncommon to hear complaints from the middle and upper classes that Bhutto had emboldened the poor (domestics, wage labor, landless tenants) who, instead of bowing their heads before the powerful, began to stand up for their rights, demanding more humane treatment and even arguing with their employers, which was inconceivable earlier. It is no wonder that Bhutto is still loved and remembered by millions of common Pakistanis nearly three decades after his death.

Perhaps Bhutto's greatest contribution was his role in drafting a democratic constitution in 1973, about one year after taking office. Most Pakistanis continue to regard this constitution as the proper governing document for their country, despite the fact that it was modified in 1985 by General Ziaul Haq. The new constitution, with a modified parliamentary and federal system, was promulgated and came into effect in 1973. Bhutto stepped down as president and became prime minister. The constitution guaranteed freedom of speech and a judicial system with due process. The constitution addressed the standing controversies about the role of Islam; the sharing of power between the federal government and the provinces; and the division of responsibility between the president and prime minister, with a greatly strengthened position of the prime minister.

According to the constitution, the president, as the head of the state, was elected by the National Assembly, the Senate, and the four provincial assemblies. The prime minister, elected by the National Assembly, was the leader of the majority party or a majority coalition. The bicameral parliament consisted of the 217-member lower house or National Assembly (ten representing non-Muslim candidates) and the 87-member Senate, or upper house. The members of the National Assembly, serving five-year terms, were elected directly by voters, whereas members of the Senate, serving six-year terms, were elected indirectly by provincial assemblies.

The smaller provinces were protected from domination by the Punjab by establishing a bicameral legislature, with the Senate having equal provincial representation and the National Assembly having representation according to population. Bhutto also accommodated the opposition leaders from the other two major political parties, the National

Awami Party (NAP) and the Jamiat-ul-Ulama-i-Islam (JUI), both based in the North-West Frontier Province (NWFP) and Balochistan, on the matter of the constitution by agreeing that gubernatorial appointments would be made with their wishes. The 1973 constitution also contained provisions that made it almost impossible for the National Assembly to remove the prime minister. Also, army intervention through a military coup constituted subversion of the constitution and was punishable by death. It is somewhat ironic that the PPP itself failed to abide by the framework of legitimate civilian rule spelled out in the constitution and thereby "underwrote its own demise" (Noman 1990, 58).

But within just a month after the National Assembly had passed the new constitution, military operations began in Balochistan to put down an insurgency following the dismissal of the Balochi provincial government. Most leaders of the NAP were arrested just two days after the 1973 constitution had become legally operational. This intervention undermined the basis of a democratic structure, thereby facilitating the return of military rule in 1977. Bhutto's alliance with the army against a representative provincial government and his accusation of treason in relation to NAP led to a perception in the army that its intervention was needed to preserve the nation. The dismissal of the NAP-JUI governments, combined with a series of repressive measures to curb civil liberties, alienated the opposition, eventually leading to the nine-party mass movement against Bhutto.

Another of Bhutto's contributions was his repairing of Pakistan's tarnished image abroad. In fact, his greatest success was in the international arena. He successfully negotiated a peace settlement with India after the 1971 war through the Simla Agreement of 1972 and brought all of the 90,000 prisoners of war home without allowing any of them to come to trial in Bangladesh for war crimes. Bhutto reacted strongly to the nuclear tests conducted by India in 1974 and pledged that Pakistan would match that development even if Pakistanis had to "eat grass" to meet the costs. He also built new links with the oil-exporting Muslim countries and claimed that he had increased Pakistan's prestige in the Islamic world. It was during his tenure that the foundation was laid for massive export of Pakistani labor to the Middle East. Again it was Bhutto who played the lead role in building and sustaining relations with China, which led to collaborations on several fronts, including the joint project of the Karakorum Highway. Bhutto also claimed success for his economic policies since both GDP and the growth rate increased, while inflation declined from 25 percent in 1972 to 6 percent in 1976.

Perhaps Bhutto's worst trait was his autocratic tendencies, which started seriously interfering with his ability to govern by the mid-1970s. He acted more like an autocratic Sindhi land-lord than a democratically elected public servant, getting the reputation of "an elected dictator." By the mid-1970s, "Bhutto's . . . determination to crush any and all potential opposition had become obsessive. Bhutto purged his party of real or imagined opponents, . . .brought the prestigious civil service under his personal control, and sacked military officers who possessed what he described as 'Bonapartist' tendencies" (Blood 1995, xxxv). The PPP abused the Federal Security Force (FSF) to intimidate parliamentary opposition. It was ruthlessly used to imprison and beat up hundreds of opponents, with none more appalling than the treatment of J. A. Rahim, a founding member of PPP in his advanced years, and his son. Bhutto was also notorious for ridiculing his opponents mercilessly in public speeches. The poor loved Bhutto's insults of the powerful, but the many politicians, generals, and clerics whom he mocked became his enemies for life. More importantly, democratic institutions could not take root because of Bhutto's near-monopoly over the national decision-making process.

To give his party total control of the National Assembly by catching the opposition unprepared, he abruptly called national elections in March 1977. Nine political parties from across the ideological spectrum responded by forming   a united front, the Pakistan National Alliance (PNA). The official results indicated that the PPP won 68 percent of the popular vote and 77 percent of the seats in the National Assembly (PPP winning 155 seats and PNA 36). Although victory was expected, the margin of PPP victory was so overwhelming that the opposition made allegations that the elections had been rigged, leading to demands for new elections. When Bhutto refused, the opposition parties launched mass protests against him, and violent riots broke out throughout the country. Bhutto then tried to meet the major demands of his opponents and agreed to new elections in October 1977. To appease Muslim clerics, who were his strongest critics, he also outlawed gambling, imposed prohibitions on the consumption of alcoholic beverages, and changed the official holiday from Sunday to Friday, the Muslim holy day. By late June 1977, the number of demonstrations throughout the country was dwindling, but it was too late. On July 5, General Mohammad Ziaul Haq, army chief of staff chosen by Bhutto over ten more senior generals in 1976, led a military coup and declared martial law, beginning the longest period of rule by a single leader in Pakistan's history. He suspended the constitution and declared that he had taken over only to create an environment for holding free elections for national and provincial assemblies within ninety days, in October. It was a promise he never kept. Soon he brought criminal charges against Bhutto and postponed the elections. Bhutto was arrested on September 3, 1977, on dubious charges of conspiracy to murder a political opponent. General Zia kept Bhutto in a small, dark, unheated, damp jail cell for a year and a half until a court convicted Bhutto of complicity in the murder of a political opponent, by a 4-to-3 vote. The Supreme Court upheld the sentence, and Bhutto was hanged on April 4, 1979, by Zia's order. Zia canceled the promised elections (a few days after Bhutto's hanging) and kept the country under martial law until 1985. Fearing that Bhutto's daughter, Benazir, might lead an opposition movement, General Zia placed her under house arrest for four years, until she was allowed to leave the country to get treatment for an ear infection. The memory of Bhutto and his tragic death became a rallying cry for Benazir, who sought revenge. She finally succeeded Zia in 1988 after he died in a mysterious plane crash.

THE MILITARY GOVERNMENT OF ZIAUL HAQ: SELF-PRESERVATION, THE AFGHAN WAR, AND ISLAMIZATION: 1977–1988

This was the fourth time in Pakistan's short history that martial law had been imposed, the first two being in 1958, one by Iskander Mirza and the other by General Ayub Khan, and the third in 1969 by General Yahya Khan. There were several similarities as well as differences between the martial laws of Ayub Khan and of Ziaul Haq. Like Ayub Khan, Ziaul Haq had been appointed as chief of army staff, superseding several senior generals, because he was known to have no political ambition and had no strong power base. Like Ayub Khan, he had ousted his benefactor in a military coup with support from some opposition leaders who believed that military intervention would be better for the country at a time when the democracy experiment had failed. Thus, Asghar Khan of PNA had pleaded to the chiefs of armed forces for a coup "on the naive expectation that the military would take over, hold elections, transfer, and return to the barracks" (Noman 1990, 118). But while Ayub Khan had sent the then governor general and president, Iskander Mirza, to a lifelong exile in London, Ziaul Haq had Prime Minister Bhutto executed. There were other differences between Ayub Khan and Ziaul Haq too. While Ayub Khan had a modernizing impact on society and introduced various forward-looking reforms, such as the Muslim Family Laws Ordinance, Ziaul Haq was known as an ardent advocate of a more stringent version of Islamic orthodoxy, and introduction of an Islamic order was his top priority. Moreover, Ayub Khan relied heavily on his steel frame of senior civil servants and did not

Mohammad Ziaul Haq, president of Pakistan (1977-1988).
(Reuters/Corbis)

involve the army much in the day-to-day administration and the governmental decision-making process. Zia, on the other hand, relied on a small number of powerful army officers and involved the army significantly in the administration of the country. Ayub came at a time when the army commanded public prestige, and Zia, when it had been disgraced, both morally because of its actions in the military crackdown in East Pakistan and militarily because of its surrender with 90,000 troops to the Indian Army. Above all, Ayub had ousted a weak, incompetent, and unrepresentative government, but Zia had deposed an elected civilian government, which was an act of treason under the 1973 constitution.

The period between 1977 and 1988, under the military regime of General Ziaul Haq, was characterized by the Soviet occupation of Afghanistan and the resistance by Afghans (with its consequences of large aid flows from the United States and a drug and arms culture in Pakistan); the opening up of employment opportunities in the Middle East, resulting in large remittances from Pakistani workers abroad; and the Islamization of the economy and society. Zia's eleven years of rule left a profound, and controversial, legacy for Pakistani society. It can be divided into three periods: the first from 1977 to 1979, when the regime "deceived and outmaneuvered the civilian opposition parties by publicly reiterating its commitment to hold elections while it undertook measures to entrench itself and consolidate its position" (Noman 1990, 117); the second from 1979 to 1983, when Zia dropped the pretense of being the leader of an interim government and the army tightened its grip; and the third from 1983 to 1988, when the government tried to break its isolation and assimilate civilians into its administration.

The First Phase: 1977–1979

When Zia assumed power in July 1977, he promised new elections in October and released political prisoners. Bhutto's speeches drew millions, and fearing Bhutto's victory if there were elections, Zia canceled the elections, saying that he had "unexpectedly" found "irregularities" in the previous regime and that he needed to clean the government. A special investigation cell was then established to probe into these "malpractices." A number of "white papers" were generated on fraud in the 1977 elections, abuses by the Federal Security Force, and Bhutto's manipulation of the press. Within a month of the takeover, the Federal Investigation Agency (FIA) claimed that Bhutto and Punjab governor Khar were responsible for the murder of Dr. Nazir Ahmad, an ex-member of the National Assembly. Within two months of the takeover, in September, Bhutto was arrested on charges of complicity in the murder of the father of Ahmed Raza Kasuri, a political opponent. As the army had hoped, several political leaders of the PNA demanded that "accountability" should precede the polls. These included important personalities like Asghar Khan, Wali Khan, and Pir Pagoro, some of whom had their own scores to settle with Bhutto and had little chance of defeating Bhutto's PPP in the elections. As noted earlier, after being in jail for about one and a half years, Bhutto was hanged on April 4, 1979, on Zia's orders. The Supreme Court had upheld the verdict of the Punjab High Court by a vote of four to three, split along ethnic lines, with the four Punjabi judges finding Bhutto guilty as charged and the three non-Punjabi judges acquitting him. It is widely believed that Zia had reason enough to eliminate Bhutto physically because a victorious Bhutto would most likely have tried Zia for treason under the 1973 constitution, which prescribed the death penalty for a coup. It is significant that Zia's last promise of an election date was made a few days before the execution. This bait ensured that both the leadership of the PPP and the parties opposed to Bhutto would not attempt jointly to mobilize a mass movement to demand elections and clemency for Bhutto so as not to antagonize Zia into canceling the elections. Shortly after the hanging, elections were canceled and political parties banned. At the international level, Zia's image was tarnished because he was considered a usurper and an executioner. This image was soon to change.

On the economic front, Zia announced the Fifth Plan (1978–1983) in early 1978, emphasizing a shift in strategy so that the private sector would regain the prominence it had lost under the PPP. Accordingly, he instituted constitutional measures to assure private investors that nationalization would occur only under limited and exceptional circumstances and with fair compensation. The rice-husking and flour-milling units were denationalized. Almost all activities were open to private investors, though public-sector enterprises accounted for 40 percent of industrial output. But this time period was also characterized by a worldwide stagflation following the OPEC oil crisis. As such, the country faced the political and economic problems associated with inflation and recession.

Structural changes were also made in religious matters. A genuinely religious man, Ziaul Haq championed a role for Islam that was more state directed and less a matter of personal choice. Just six weeks after the coup, he formed the Islamic Ideology Council to prepare an outline of an Islamic theocratic state. He then announced that Pakistani law would be based on Nizam-i-Mustafa, that is, rule of the Prophet, meaning rule by *Sharia* law. This was one of the demands of the PNA in the 1977 elections. He proclaimed that all laws had to conform to Islamic tenets and values, and he established the Federal Shariat Court to examine laws in the light of Islamic injunctions and to review military and civil verdicts for compliance with Islamic law. In February of that year, new laws were issued that assigned punishments for various violations, *hudood,* including theft, prostitution, fornication, adultery, and bearing false witness. Thus, adultery was punishable by stoning, first-time theft by the cutting off of the right hand, and drinking alcohol by eighty lashes. However, no one was ever stoned to death because such sentences were always reduced upon appeal, and no one had his or her hand cut off because no doctor would agree to amputate the hand surgically, which is required by the antitheft law. The only Islamic punishments actually carried out were whippings, and these were held in public and televised, although the tips of the whip were soft-

ened with padding. Nonetheless, there are many horror stories of women who were raped and got pregnant, but when
they accused the men of rape, they were themselves convicted of adultery and sent to jail if they failed to prove their
charge under Islamic law. Zia also revived an early Muslim
rule of law of evidence by which two women's testimony is
worth one man's in financial matters, and he applied it indis-
criminately to all cases. Zia also began the Islamization of
the financial system regarding the prohibition on interest,
riba, and of the taxation system through promulgating the
Zakat and Ushr Ordinances in June 1980. (*Zakat,* as noted
earlier, is a traditional annual levy, about 2.5 percent on
wealth to be spent on the needy, and *Ushr* is a 5 percent tax
on the produce of land.)

The Second Phase: 1979–1983

Everything changed on December 24, 1979, when the Soviet
Union invaded Afghanistan with 85,000 soldiers. Outside
the city area where the Soviet Army had control, farmers
and nomads in the countryside started fighting back against
the foreign invaders. They called themselves the Mujahideen
(fighters of the holy war, *jihad*). The guerrilla fighting also
extended to Afghans who had taken refuge in Pakistan. Millions of refugees had streamed into Pakistan: men and
women, young and old, many wounded, about 400,000 without an arm or a leg. Within a period of eighteen months,
more than 2 million refugees had poured into Pakistan, and
1.5 million followed later. The Pakistan government put up
camps, mostly in the North-West Frontier Province, near
Peshawar, and provided food, clothing, and medicine to the
refugees. The Pathans or Pakhtuns, known for their hospitality, opened their hearts and homes for their Afghan
(many of them Pakhtun) Muslim brethren. In unparalleled
acts of generosity, many divided their homes in two to
accommodate Afghan families.

Pakistan's proximity to Afghanistan, its help to refugees, and its support the Mujahideen in fighting against Soviet expansion in Afghanistan greatly altered the geopolitical significance of Pakistan for the United States. This could not have come at a better time for Zia. In 1979, the United States had viewed President Ziaul Haq as an executioner and as a dictator who had deposed an elected civilian government, and President Jimmy Carter had cut off all U.S. military and economic aid to Pakistan when Ziaul Haq refused to stop its nuclear weapons program. By 1980, however, the U.S. government needed Ziaul Haq and accordingly changed its priorities. The invasion abruptly ended Pakistan's estrangement from Washington. Within days, Pakistan again became an indispensable frontline state for the U.S. against Soviet expansionism, and an important and valued U.S. ally. President Carter offered aid, which Zia turned down as peanuts. The Reagan administration was more generous. Massive military and economic assistance flowed into Pakistan under Reagan despite Pakistan's continued pursuit of nuclear weapons technology. The United States turned a blind eye to it just as it had been doing toward Israel. About $7 million in aid was sent to Pakistan, including forty-nine F-16 fighter-bombers and one hundred M-48 tanks, and a $3.2 billion package of American military and economic loans. Moreover, American influence in the multilateral agencies enabled Pakistan to reschedule its debt. The flow of foreign assistance also provided a stimulus to the economy, and the average growth in GNP during the period increased to 6.2 percent.

Pakistan's role in the fight against the nine-year Soviet occupation of Afghanistan dramatically changed the Zia government's domestic and international image and influenced the survival of the Zia regime. It gave a measure of credibility and political legitimacy to a regime badly damaged in the aftermath of Bhutto's execution and bolstered the army whose image had been tarnished by the the 1971 war. It also allowed Zia to repeatedly postpone the promised elections while he consolidated his position. The foreign aid–triggered macroeconomic revival became an important means by which Zia could neutralize his opponents. Moreover, the depiction of war by the Mujahideen and the Zia government as *jihad* (holy war) of Muslims against non-Muslims helped Zia to transform Pakistan into an Islamic state, not just in name but in more substantial ways, which, in turn, gained Zia the support of the Middle Eastern Muslim countries, giving him even more international legitimacy.

The Afghan War also led to improved relations between the center and the provinces of Pakistan. The Soviet invasion of a Pathan country made the Pathans question the desirability of a once-sought-after alliance with Russia, which was now seen to be worse than the centralization of the Pakistani political structure. This eroded support for "Pushtunistan," a separate Pathan state merging Pakistan's frontier province with Afghanistan. Moreover, the influx of more than 3 million refugees and the response of the refugees to the Pathans' gracious and unusual hospitality had a corrosive effect on parochial forces in the NWFP. There is plenty of anecdotal evidence of how the Afghan refugees occupied the homes of the Pathans who divided their homes in two to accommodate them, and evicted the original owners. The changed attitudes of Pakistani Pathans toward Afghanistan and the refugees, combined with the migration of Pathan workers to Karachi and the Gulf, have helped facilitate Pathan integration within Pakistan.

At the same time, the war in Afghanistan had other profound and disturbing effects on Pakistani society. First, the influx of more than 3.2 million refugees into its North-West Frontier Province and Balochistan overwhelmed the local economies, stretched the facilities, and strained the infrastructure. It also disadvantaged the local Pakistani Pakhtuns who now had to compete for resources with the refugees. The refugees also brought with them an arsenal of weapons and drugs, creating a *Kalashnikov* culture that led to a dramatic increase in domestic, ethnic, and religious violence, particularly in Karachi, where many of the refugees had migrated.

While Zia's reputation had been somewhat salvaged at the international level, resentment against Zia at home started building up. In February 1981, the officially defunct PPP and other parties joined to form the Movement for the Restoration of Democracy (MRD). It demanded an end to martial law and urged the holding of elections under the suspended 1973 constitution. But the economic boom partly brought about by increasing remittances helped sustain the Zia regime and undermined the opposition's ability to mobilize a popular movement against the military. The opposition could not mobilize key urban centers like Karachi and Lahore or working classes and lower-middle-income groups, who were the beneficiaries of the Middle East migration boom.

The Third Phase: 1983–1988

By 1983, Zia had survived both internal and external threats, and had contained all rival sources of authority. Political parties were banned, and the press and judiciary were marginalized. During this time, Pakistanis were subject to the jurisdiction of military courts. A defendant had no right to a lawyer, no right to a public trial, and no right to an appeal. The press was censored more strictly until 1982. Discontent with Zia's regime increased, and people chafed under his strict, puritanical rule. Anti-Zia riots broke out in Sindh in 1983, killing 600 people and resulting in 7,000 arrests. Zia promised elections for the National Assembly in eighteen months, in February 1985. Local (municipal) elections were held in 1984 on a non-party basis. This veneer of democracy created decentralized institutions at the local level but masked the centralization of political power. Martial law was lifted in December 1985, after eight long years. Three months later, Benazir Bhutto returned to Pakistan to a greeting by 3 million people at Lahore airport. Elections were held for both the national and provincial assemblies in 1985, but political parties were not allowed to participate. The PPP boycotted the elections. The composition of the National Assembly showed a dominance of landlords and tribal leaders, particularly of Punjab and NWFP, who won 67 percent of all the seats. Zia remained president, though martial law was ended. An amended version of the 1973 constitution was reinstated, and the National Assembly was pressured into passing the Eighth Amendment to the constitution, which exempted Zia from any future prosecution for acts in violation of the 1973 constitution. It also gave the president the right to dismiss the prime minister and the provincial governors and to dissolve the national and provincial assemblies anytime, for any reason. After the elections, Zia picked Mohammad Khan Junejo as his prime minister but dismissed him three years later. He also dissolved the National Assembly and the four provincial assemblies in May 1988 on the pretext of a breakdown in law and order across the country, and just four days after the announcement that Bhutto was pregnant. Benazir Bhutto had worked for two and a half years to strengthen the PPP. Elections that were supposed to be held within 90 days of the dissolution were postponed beyond that period to November 16, 1988, presumably to prevent an eight months' pregnant Bhutto from campaigning.

Provincialism and ethnic tensions and violence increased during Zia's rule, and the law-and-order situation kept deteriorating. The Afghan refugees brought thousands of *Kalashnikovs* (original Soviet-made AK-47s) and tons of heroin and opium with them. The spread of this *Kalashnikov* culture led to a sharp increase in armed robberies and kidnappings. At the same time, ethnic tensions increased. Although Zia handled the problem of unrest in Balochistan better than Bhutto, the tensions between Sindhis and non-Sindhis, particularly Muhajirs, increased. Sindhis resented the Muhajirs' economic successes, and Muhajirs resented the job quotas that favored Sindhis. This tension turned into violence in Sindh, which escalated to great heights in the late 1980s. The Muhajirs formed the Muhajir Qaumi Mahaz (MQM—Refugee National Front) to voice their grievances. Ethnic violence in cities and armed robberies in rural Sindh became commonplace.

Zia's death in a still-unexplained aircraft crash on August 17, 1988, along with ten top generals and the U.S. ambassador to Pakistan, ended an era. A joint U.S.-Pakistani committee investigating the accident later established that "the crash was caused by a criminal act of sabotage perpetuated in the aircraft" (Blood 1995, 69). Ghulam Ishaq Khan, chairman of the Pakistan Senate, became the new president of Pakistan under the new constitution, and Mirza Aslam Beg, the only surviving four-star general in Pakistan, became the new army chief of staff. Beg exercised "admirable restraint," and he and Ishaq Khan together announced their intention to hold elections in November 1988. Pakistan prepared for a transition of power. "The prospect for genuine democracy in Pakistan appeared to have dramatically improved, and Pakistan appeared to have reached a watershed in its political development" (Blood 1995, xxxvii).

RETURN TO DEMOCRACY, INSTABILITY, CORRUPTION, AND MISMANAGEMENT: BENAZIR BHUTTO AND NAWAZ SHARIF: 1988–1999

The period from 1988 to 1999 witnessed Pakistan's return to democracy. The restoration of civilian rule ushered in a row of governments between 1988 and 1999, but mostly at the expense of public confidence in democracy. During this period, there were four elections, with Benazir Bhutto and Nawaz Sharif both being returned to power twice. There were also as many as four caretaker governments in between because neither of the elected governments could complete its full term as each was dismissed by the president. The amendment to the 1973 constitution during the

Zia regime had given the president the right to dismiss the prime minister at any time, for any reason, and this right was frequently used during this period. But it has also been pointed out that this may also have been the reason Pakistan's army allowed democracy to resume after Zia's death. Politicians squabbled, as in the earlier civilian governments in the 1951–1958 and 1971–1977 periods, but, to its credit, the army did not seize power and allowed the democratic process to run its course.

The democratic course, however, was very unstable, and governments changed frequently. First, following Ziaul Haq's death in 1988, Benazir Bhutto was elected prime minister and remained so for twenty months, from 1988 to 1990. She was dismissed on corruption charges and was replaced, after a brief caretaker period, by the government of Prime Minister Mian Nawaz Sharif (1990–1993). His government was also eventually dismissed by former president Ghulam Ishaq Khan in a power struggle between the two. Sharif was accused of corruption, particularly in connection with the privatization program. The caretaker government of Moeen Qureshi in 1993 was followed by the return of Bhutto in the 1993 elections. She was again removed from power in 1996 owing to allegations of corruption and mismanagement. Two years later, she and her husband were convicted of corruption. This was followed by the caretaker government of Meraj Khalid and then by the elected government of Sharif from 1996 until 1999. In the mid-1990s, ethnic and religious violence and political turmoil reached new heights. Sharif faced increasing political and military opposition and a deteriorating economy. When Nawaz Sharif removed the army chief of staff, General Pervez Musharraf, from his position while he was flying home from Sri Lanka and prevented his plane from landing at the Karachi airport even though it was short of fuel, supporters of General Musharraf in the army led a coup and removed Sharif from office.

First Benazir Bhutto Government (1988–1990)

On December 1, 1988, Benazir Bhutto became the first female prime minister of Pakistan, the first woman in modern times to lead a Muslim country, and the youngest head of government at the age of thirty-five. Public expectations and hopes were high, particularly among people who were concerned with civil liberty and the status of women following the global revival of fundamentalism. But Bhutto was also Pakistan's weakest leader since the 1950s. She had a weak mandate, getting only 93 of the 205 seats contested in the National Assembly, which was enough to form a majority but only with the support of small parties like the MQM (Muhajir Quomi Mahaz-Refugee National Front) and independent members. Bhutto's thin electoral margin was in part due to the low voter turnout of 42 percent and the inability of millions of her poor supporters to vote in the November 1988 elections since the interim government never gave them identity cards required for registration. She also had less time to campaign as she had prematurely given birth to a son just two weeks after the Supreme Court ruled in October 1988 that political parties could participate in the November elections. Bhutto was allowed to assume power by the army apparently on the condition that Ishaq Khan would continue to be the president, and a powerful one at that, and that the defense budget would not be cut. Eventually, the combination of a weak electoral mandate limiting her ability to enact legislation, her troubled inheritance of complex ethnic problems from Zia's time, her inability to transcend the political legacy and death of her father, and the role played by her husband ultimately affected her management of affairs of the state and dashed the high hopes of many of her supporters. Her rhetoric had promised much but that did not translate into action.

The 1988 elections were different from the earlier elections of 1970 and from the elections that would follow in many ways. Although no single party had been able to win sufficient seats to command a clear majority in the National Assembly, the PPP was way ahead of other parties with its ninety-three seats compared to fifty-five for the alliance led by the Muslim League, the IJI (Islami Jamhoori Ittehad-Islamic Democratic Alliance), followed by fourteen for MQM. But despite being the only party to win seats in all the four provinces, the PPP's vote had split along sharp ethnic and rural-urban lines in the two larger provinces of Sindh and Punjab. In Sindh, the PPP received a clear mandate from rural areas, populated by Sindhis, the ethnic group to which the Bhuttos belong. In the urban areas, populated largely by Muhajirs, particularly Karachi and Hyderabad, the MQM swept through the polls, winning fourteen seats. No other political party won any seat in Sindh. In Punjab, the PPP performed well in the urban areas, particularly among the poor, but the IJI had greater support in the rural areas, particularly among the more afflu-ent. Thus, PPP's real support came from rural Sindh and urban Punjab. Moreover, the precarious nature of the man-date was heightened in the elections to provincial assemblies. PPP's prime rival, IJI, was able to form a government in the key province of Punjab, and PPP formed fragile coalition gov-ernments in Sindh, NWFP, and Balochistan. Following the elections, there was, in fact, a serious debate within the PPP regarding the desirability of forming a government, given these circumstances.

Benazir Bhutto's government faced severe electoral, con-stitutional, and structural constraints from the outset. Elec-toral constraints were an outcome of the 1988 elections lead-ing to vulnerable central government, an opposition government in Punjab, and frail alliances in the other three provinces, as stated earlier. The constitutional constraint was that PPP had to accept a president who had vast powers under the Eighth Amendment provisions of the constitu-tion—a direct legacy of the Ziaul Haq regime and an existing Senate consisting of IJI supporters that had not been dis-

Benazir Bhutto, prime minister of Pakistan (1988-1990, 1993-1996).
(Reuters/Corbis)

solved in 1988. It did not, therefore, have any effective power to enact important legislation. Accordingly, the rich continued to pay almost no taxes, and Zia's Islamization laws remained in force. The size of the defense budget limited the amount that could be spent on the social sectors, including health and education. The structural constraints emanated from problems inherited from past regimes, including ethnic tensions, the aftermath of the continuing U.S.-Pak Afghan policy in terms of a *Kalashnikov* culture in Pakistan, and a liquidity crisis after the end of the Gulf boom.

Benazir Bhutto was often criticized for being autocratic during her first term. Unable to transcend her father's political legacy, she dismissed competent public servants who had earlier been in disagreement with her father. She was criticized for nepotism when she set up the controversial Placement Bureau, which made political appointments to the civil bureaucracy, not on the basis of ability but on personal loyalty to the Bhutto family, particularly during their time of trial in the Zia years. She also appointed her mother, Nusrat Bhutto, as a senior minister without portfolio and her father-in-law as chairman of the parliamentary Public Accounts Committee.

The two problems that plagued Bhutto's government most, however, were the excessive levels of alleged corruption within the PPP, particularly by Bhutto's husband, Asif Zardari, and her government's inability to stop banditry in rural Sindh and ethnic violence between Sindhis and Muhajirs in urban Sindh. Asif Zardari was commonly known as "Mr. 10 Percent," referring to his share in all major deals made by the government. Violence in Karachi and Hyderabad killed more than 500 people in riots and terror bombings, and reached such heights that the army asked for emergency powers in Sindh to control the violence. But Benazir refused to institute martial law in her home province. There was a general sense of disillusionment as her government failed to deliver the promised employment and economic development programs. Inflation and unemployment were high, and drug abuse problems continued to grow.

Despite the weaknesses of the Bhutto government, her contribution to the restoration of democracy in Pakistan was significant. Her government ended censorship, released political prisoners, and lifted the ban on labor unions, student organizations, and political activity in general. She emphasized a private-sector-led economy. In sharp contrast to the PPP's party manifesto in the 1970s under Zulfiqar Ali Bhutto,

Benazir Bhutto's election manifesto did not promise land reforms or nationalization. This was a reflection both of the shortcomings of past policies, particularly the massive nationalization program of the seventies, and a changing world climate in favor of market reforms, privatization, and the free enterprise system. In the same vein, the PPP agreed to sign agreements with the International Monetary Fund (IMF) for the much-needed Structural Adjustment Loans (SALs) that laid down conditionalities (conditions that had to be met) in terms of both micro-pricing and macro-policy issues.

A prolonged struggle between Bhutto and the chief minister of Punjab, Nawaz Sharif of IJI, culminated in President Ishaq Khan siding with Sharif against Bhutto. As a political power broker, Benazir was no match for her main rival. Instead of reaching a political accommodation with Sharif, she pursued a course of confrontation, including unsuccessful efforts to overthrow him in the provincial assembly. In addition, she alienated her coalition partner, the MQM, by not really sharing power and spoils, resulting in their withdrawal from the government in October 1999. Benazir herself narrowly survived a no-confidence motion in the National Assembly. Finally, using his dismissal powers under the Eighth Amendment to the constitution, the president dismissed Bhutto's government on August 6, 1990, dissolved the National Assembly as well as the Sindh and NWFP provincial assemblies, and scheduled new elections for October 24, 1990 (rather than the due date of 1993). The Bhutto government was charged with inability to restore law and order in Sindh, and Bhutto, her husband, and some of her cabinet members were charged with corruption in the awarding of government loans and the sale of public land, but not found guilty then.

Caretaker Government of 1990

President Ghulam Ishaq Khan appointed Bhutto's leading opponent, Ghulam Mustafa Jatoi, the leader of the Combined

Opposition Parties in the National Assembly, as the caretaker prime minister for the interim period till the next elections. Jatoi's government instituted accountability proceedings against those charged with corruption and imprisoned Bhutto's husband, Asif Zardari, setting up seven courts to investigate the corruption charges. Zardari was also charged with kidnapping and blackmail. Bhutto called her dismissal "illegal, unconstitutional, and arbitrary," and her supporters have claimed that charging Bhutto was discriminatory since her government was no more corrupt than other governments in Pakistan's history, and no other government was ever so charged. The PPP's demand that Sharif's Punjab government during the same time be similarly scrutinized was rejected.

First Nawaz Sharif Government (1990–1993)

At the October 24, 1990, elections, the IJI, a coalition of nine political parties united against Bhutto, won by a huge margin, getting 105 out of 207 contested seats, compared to PPP's 45. Two weeks later, on November 6, 1990, the new National Assembly chose Nawaz Sharif, the leader of the largest party in the IJI coalition, the Muslim League, to be prime minister of Pakistan. Sharif was the owner of a large industrial conglomerate, the Ittefaq Industries, one of the largest companies, owning four textile mills and a steel mill. He had also served as a provincial finance minister under Zia in the early eighties and as Punjab's chief minister after 1985, under both the Zia and Bhutto regimes. Bhutto charged the government with massive election rigging, but most foreign observers did not support her claim.

The 1990 elections brought the conservative establishment—generals, businessmen, and religious leaders—to power for the first time in Pakistan's history of popular elections. It was a surprise that so many Pakistanis voted against Bhutto. It is true that the government-controlled television channel had hardly given her campaign any news coverage, but the real reason Bhutto lost support was the public's general belief that the alleged corruption charges against her husband were valid. Although Pakistanis expect corruption from government officials, they still believe that their top leaders should not be above the law. This was also the first time in the history of Pakistan that a head of government was so charged. Moreover, Sharif had a track record, as chief minister of Punjab, of delivering the things that common people want most: roads, electricity, telephones, schools, clean water, and sewage facilities. In contrast, Benazir Bhutto had not been so successful in delivering what she had promised during her tenure, partly because of her weak electoral position.

Nawaz Sharif's rise to power "marked a transition in the political culture of Pakistan—a power shift from the traditional feudal aristocracy to a growing class of modern entrepreneurs" (Blood 1995, 230). Not surprisingly, Sharif was a vigorous proponent of the reprivatization of industries that had been nationalized by Zulfiqar Ali Bhutto in the seventies. The steel mill owned by his family, Ittefaq Industries, had also been nationalized in 1972, but Ziaul Haq privatized and sold it back to the owners in 1977. Sharif's economic reform package focused on privatization and deregulation. By 1992, about twenty public industrial enterprises had been denationalized, two banks were sold to private investors, and plans were under way to privatize several utilities. By 1994, proposals to abolish state monopolies in insurance, telecommunications, shipping, port operations, airlines, power generation, and road construction were well under way. The Sharif government also carried out reforms that removed the impediments to private investment, such as government sanction requirements. Critics pointed to the fast pace of the reforms and the adverse impact on the more vulnerable groups in society. Benazir Bhutto particularly criticized Sharif's privatization program as "loot and plunder" and organized widespread protest marches against the government. She conducted a relentless campaign to oust Sharif.

Nawaz Sharif waves to supporters in Murree, Pakistan, on September 30, 1990. (Reuters/Corbis)

The Sharif government's record was mixed. Its success in passing the *Shariat* Bill, which declared the *Quran* and the *Sunnah* to be the law of the land, did not satisfy either the rightists who thought that the bill did not go far enough or the secular people who thought that a theocracy was being established. Moreover, rampant crime and terrorism continued to plague the country, particularly in Sindh, where kidnappings, bombings, and murders continued rampant. Furthermore, the government budget deficit increased, eventually bringing the country to the brink of insolvency. A combination of economic problems, persistent violence, corruption, and the power struggles of the leaders finally proved too much for the government.

Differences over policy matters, particularly over the power to appoint the top army commander, surfaced between the president and the prime minister. In early 1993, the president brought charges of "corruption and mismanagement" against Nawaz Sharif, as he had before brought against Bhutto. Again empowered by the Eighth Amendment provisions of the constitution, Ishaq Khan dismissed Sharif, dissolved the National Assembly, appointed Balakh Sher Mazari as caretaker prime minister, and announced a new timetable for elections. But this time the Supreme Court declared the president's action unconstitutional, restoring both the prime minister and the National Assembly. Manipulating provincial politics, Ishaq Khan then dissolved the provincial assemblies in Punjab and the NWFP. The army intervened in mid-1993, acting as an arbiter to break the stalemate. To its credit, the army did not take over and did not take advantage of the political situation.

Caretaker Government of Moeen Qureshi (1993)

In July 1993, the acting president, Wasim Sajjad, installed a caretaker government led by Moeen Qureshi, a former World Bank senior vice president, with the mandate to preside over new elections for the national and provincial assemblies. Being outside the military-bureaucratic-landlord-industrialist establishment, and using the brief tenure and temporary nature of his government to his advantage, Qureshi initiated an impressive number of much-needed reforms in Pakistan, for which he came to be known as "Mr. Clean" during his three-month tenure. Asserting that the nation was near insolvency, he initiated a number of measures to impose fiscal discipline. To reduce the trade deficit, he devalued the currency so that it came closer to the free-market exchange rate of the rupee. He cut farm subsidies and public service expenditures to reduce the government budget deficit. Accordingly, there were sharp increases in prices of wheat, electricity, and gasoline. As part of the austerity measures, ten embassies were closed down and fifteen ministries were abolished. New taxes and stiffer enforcement of existing taxes were imposed. Perhaps the most striking feature of Qureshi's reforms was the temporary levy on agricultural output, a step that no other government before him had dared to take in the face of strong resistance by the landed aristocracy, which has always dominated the parliament. He also published lists of 5,000 loan defaulters and prevented politicians (who comprised 15 percent of the defaulters) from running for office if they had not repaid their overdue loans. These politicians had outstanding loans to the tune of $2 billion that had been procured on easy terms in exchange for past political favors. These politicians included Benazir Bhutto, her husband, and Nawaz Sharif's brother. Drug barons, some of whom were members of national and provincial assemblies, were permanently barred from contesting elections. On the whole, his government had set a standard against which past and future governments would be judged.

Qureshi fulfilled his primary mandate of holding new elections for the national and provincial assemblies in October 1993, which international observers hailed as the fairest in Pakistan's history. Although Sharif's Pakistan Muslim League received more of the popular vote than Bhutto's PPP, Bhutto won a narrow plurality of seats in the National Assembly, getting eighty-six seats compared to Sharif's seventy-two seats in a 217-seat national assembly. But Bhutto was able to form a coalition government with 121 seats. Her position was further strengthened when a PPP member, Farooq Leghari, won in

the presidential elections held in November 1993, defeating
Acting President Wasim Sajjad, who was backed by Sharif.
Leghari promised to support a constitutional amendment to
curb the power of his office granted by the controversial
Eighth Amendment of Ziaul Haq and to challenge restrictive
laws of Islamic courts relating to women.

Second Benazir Bhutto Government (1993–1996)

Benazir Bhutto's second coming to the pinnacle of Pakistani
politics in October 1993 was heralded by her supporters as
redemptive. She promised to strengthen democratic institutions and to pursue her reform program, which she had been
unable to do during her first tenure as prime minister. Her
program included addressing the ethnic problems, strengthening the national treasury, reconstructing the financial system, enhancing social services, and enforcing women's rights.
In 1994, the Bhutto government announced its intention to
continue the policies of both deregulation and liberalization
carried out by the Sharif government, as well as the tighter fiscal policies of the caretaker government. Accordingly, her
government budget of June 1994 lowered import duties,
broadened the tax base, and held down defense spending. The
government also indicated its intention to increase the proportion of expenditure going to health and education, particularly for women. Pakistan also received a preferential SAL
(Structural Adjustment Loan) of $1.4 billion from the IMF on
the condition that a three-year program be implemented to
make structural changes in the economy, such as reducing
government expenditure and the budget deficit. These
measures were expected to increase GDP (gross domestic
product) by 6.5 percent per year and to lower inflation to no
more than 5 percent. But performance fell short of expectations due to a serious drought, a major flood, and the onset of
the leaf curl plant virus that devastated cotton production.

Benazir Bhutto with the author at the home of Middle Tennessee State University's president, following her keynote speech in 2002. (Yasmeen Mohiuddin)

Moreover, problems involving an inefficient bureaucracy, weak infrastructure, widespread tax evasion and corruption, neglect of social development, high defense spending (more than 25 percent of government expenditure), and rapid population growth continued to plague the economy at a time when both inflation and unemployment were high.

Not the least of the problems was the continuing law-and-order situation and unprecedented level of violence in Sindh. In mid-1995, there were widespread reports of human rights violations, including torture of prisoners, extrajudicial killings, and arbitrary arrest and detention. An added dimension of the violence situation was the operation of pervasive narcotics syndicates in Karachi and Peshawar. Pakistan had become one of the leading sources of heroin supply to the United States and Europe, meeting 20 to 40 percent of the U.S. and 70 percent of the European demand. Moreover, in mid-1995, Karachi was torn by ethnic riots as religious, political, and criminal gangs fought for control. Since Karachi, a city of 12 million, is the economic hub and the nerve center of Pakistan, any unrest there is contagious. Many foreign observers believe that Karachi presents the greatest risk as well as the greatest potential for the nation's future. Most of the agitations that have eventually toppled governments in Pakistan have originated in Karachi, including those of the Democratic Action Committee (DAC) against Ayub Khan, the PNA (Pakistan National Alliance) against Bhutto, and the MRD (Movement for the Restoration of Democracy) against Zia.

The lawlessness in Karachi, the rampant ethnic and religious violence, the absence of rule of law, and nepotism, combined with charges of continuing corruption on the part of the Bhutto family and close associates, cost Benazir Bhutto her government. President Leghari dismissed her government on charges of corruption and misgovernance in November 1996 and appointed Meraj Khalid as the caretaker prime minister for the interim period until the 1997 elections.

Second Nawaz Sharif Government (1997–1999)

Nawaz Sharif won the 1997 general election by a landslide, becoming Pakistan's most powerful elected leader since martial law ended in 1985. The election results clearly demonstrated the electorate's ability to throw out the old guard via the ballot. In each general election of the past decade, the vote had been against the previous government. Using his two-thirds majority in the parliament, Sharif wasted no time in repealing the controversial Eighth Amendment to the constitution, which had allowed the president, usually with military backing, to dismiss elected governments. This fate had befallen the government of Benazir Bhutto in 1990 and Sharif in 1993 at the hands of President Ghulam Ishaq Khan, and

Bhutto again in 1996 at the hands of President Leghari, always on charges of corruption and misuse of power. Sharif then proceeded to oust the president, replacing him with his own choice of Rafiq Tarrar. Moreover, in late 1997, the chief of army staff, General Jehangir Karamat, was forced to resign after he proposed military representation in a National Security Council of Pakistan, which Sharif took as a threat. He appointed General Pervez Musharraf as the army chief of staff. Musharraf was considered a tolerable replacement, and possibly a seat-warmer for Lieutenant General Khwaja Ziauddin, a Sharif family friend and head of the Inter-Services Intelligence agency (ISI), Pakistan's equivalent of the CIA. He was perhaps also chosen because he did not have a strong power base since he was a Muhajir and was perceived as less likely to ever overthrow Sharif.

Instead of using his two-thirds majority in the parliament to work for stability and development, Sharif followed Ziaul Haq's example by trying to expand his power. He forced the ouster not only of the president but also that of the Supreme Court chief justice in 1997. His government harassed and jailed a number of journalists, and cracked down on the parliamentary opposition. His main political rival, Bhutto, was convicted of corruption. Even his own party, the Pakistan Muslim League, was not spared, and he was known to be intolerant of dissent within his own party. There were widespread fears that Sharif would amass even more power by enacting legislation to amend the constitution to make Muslim *Sharia* the law of the land and to use it as a tool of repression.

The prime minister's management of the economy made it extremely vulnerable. Despite Pakistan's foreign debt of $32 billion, Sharif pushed for expensive public works projects. The International Monetary Fund at one point decided to withhold a $280 million installment of its $1.56 billion loan to Pakistan, owing to a dispute over power prices. There was widespread evidence of fiscal gloom as economic growth rates decelerated, inflation peaked, debt burden escalated, poverty increased, and Pakistan's credibility with international finance institutions reached an all-time low. A report by the Mahbub ul Haq Human Development Center linked a tripling in the suicide rate since 1997, particularly among unemployed married men with children, to the condition of the economy (Bloch 1999).

In October 1999, when General Pervez Musharraf was returning from an official visit to Sri Lanka, Sharif fired Musharraf, announced his replacement on national television, and gave orders to thwart the scheduled landing of Musharraf's airplane at Karachi. Instead the pilot was instructed to land at Nawabshah, 220 kilometers north of Karachi, where police were waiting to arrest the general. But the military, seeing this coming, is said to have drafted coup plans in the event Sharif dismissed the army chief. Accordingly, Musharraf's colleagues staged a coup while the general was still in the air and seized control. The plane ultimately landed with only five minutes' worth of fuel left. Sharif's attempt failed primarily because of the army's inherent unity and its culture where loyalty to the army is still stronger than ethnic loyalties. It also failed because Musharraf had recently consolidated his control by replacing two of the country's nine corps commanders, the backbone of military control, with men he could trust.

The coup was not only bloodless but also popular. The *Time* correspondent wrote: "No shots were fired; there were no tanks or troops in the streets. None of that was necessary because the public was evidently happy to see Sharif go. Outside PTV (Pakistan television station), a crowd gathered and someone hoisted a sign reading 'long live the army.' In Lahore, Sharif's hometown, residents set off firecrackers. And it wasn't just Sharif the people were glad to be rid of. For Pakistanis across the sociological spectrum—from the landowning feudal gentry to the vast urban poor—Musharraf and his men are not the ones responsible for ruining the country's decade of democracy. That dishonor goes to Bhutto and Sharif" (Spaeth 1999). The former Pakistan ambassador to the United States and a newspaper editor, Maleeha Lodhi, is quoted by the *Times* correspondent to have said, "Those who lament the death of democracy don't understand that it's the people who came in through the ballot box from whom democracy first has to be saved." Similarly, Imran Khan, the Pakistani cricketer-turned-politician, is quoted to have described the system as a "status quo of thieves safeguarding the interest of thieves from the other divide" (Spaeth 1999). He recommended a two-year military regime to cleanse the country.

Democracy's record in Pakistan is indeed poor. Worse still, the failure of elected governments eroded public confidence in democracy. But democracy is not just about elections. It is also about respecting and promoting democratic institutions, establishing the rule of law, showing tolerance for opposing views, and protecting religious and ethnic minorities.

ACCOUNTABILITY, WAR ON TERRORISM, DEVELOPMENT, AND STABILITY UNDER PERVEZ MUSHARRAF: 1999–PRESENT

General Pervez Musharraf became the country's chief executive following a coup d'état on October 12, 1999. He then dissolved the parliament and the state assemblies. Exercising the powers of the head of the government, he appointed an eight-member National Security Council to act as the supreme governing body. Rafiq Tarar, who had been the president of the country during Nawaz Sharif's tenure, remained the ceremonial chief of state. Local government elections were held in 2000. The Supreme Court unanimously validated the coup on May 12, 2000, and granted Musharraf executive and legislative authority for three years from the coup date. It also set a deadline for a general election by October 2002. Musharraf formally became president of Pakistan on June 20, 2001.

Even though Musharraf's coup was not constitutional at the time, most Pakistanis welcomed the change and accepted military rule. Independent polls have usually shown high public approval levels for Musharraf. According to a CNN report, the

President Pervez Musharraf, who has one of the most difficult jobs in the world. (Pakistan Mission to the UN)

memory of the corrupt legacies of Prime Ministers Benazir Bhutto and Nawaz Sharif still lingers, as do massive state debts and corruption charges. This is in sharp contrast to the public perceptions of the current regime's personal credibility. The strengths of Musharraf's regime are many. First, it is believed that there is not even "a whiff of corruption at the heart of the government headed by General Pervez Musharraf," although such beliefs may be exaggerated (CNN 2001). Second, the Musharraf government ushered in an era of relative calm and stability, enabling ordinary people to go about their usual business without the constant fear of violence. Third, there is now a general recognition that elections in Pakistan bring the same "constellation of landlords, industrialists, and . . . bureaucrats" (Hussain 1999, xiii) to power that have dominated the scene under every single government. This is because democracy in Pakistan is based primarily on landownership, unlike Western democracy, so that most people, particularly in rural areas, vote for that person whom the rural elite supports. The freedom to vote scarcely exists, and even so, with a third of Pakistanis falling below the poverty line, the poor believe that the opportunity for economic development is more important than the right to vote. So the general populace values any government, civilian or military, that maintains law and order and establishes the rule of law, holds out the promise of improving living standards for all, and is relatively free of corruption, nepotism, and ethnic and religious discrimination. Musharraf's government, unlike that of his two elected predecessors (Bhutto and Sharif) as well as those of most of his military predecessors, possesses all these characteristics.

Following the September 11, 2001, attacks on the United States, Musharraf's support for the United States in its war on terrorism was indispensable in defeating the Taliban in Afghanistan. In a swift and strategic 180-degree turn of policy, Musharraf ended Pakistan's long-running support of the Taliban, cutting their oil and supply lines, providing intelligence, and becoming a logistics support area for "Operation Enduring Freedom." For all these reasons, and despite his blunt refusal to send any Pakistani troops to Iraq without a UN resolution, he is the target for some among the right-wing religious parties in Pakistan. There have been several assassination attempts on General Musharraf, but he has survived them all.

On the order of the Supreme Court, nationwide parliamentary elections for the national and provincial legislatures were held in October 2002. A pro-Musharraf party, the Pakistan Muslim League (Qayyum Group), won a plurality of the seats in the National Assembly, which was paralyzed for about a year by the opposition. After over a year of political wrangling in the bicameral legislature, Musharraf struck a compromise with some of his parliamentary opponents, the Muttahida Majlis-e-Amal Party, on the promise that he would leave the army on December 31, 2004. This ended the deadlock, giving his supporters the two-thirds majority vote required to amend the constitution (Seventeenth Amendment) in December 2003, retroactively legalizing his 1999 coup, and permitting him to remain president if he met the agreed conditions. The National Assembly also elected Mir Zafarullah Khan Jamali of the Pakistan Muslim League as prime minister of Pakistan. Musharraf now shared power with an elected National Assembly, a Senate, and four provincial legislatures.

On January 1, 2004, in a vote of confidence, Musharraf won by a 56 percent majority (658 out of 1,170 votes) in the electoral college of Pakistan, consisting of both houses of parliament and the four provincial assemblies. According to Article 41(8) of the constitution, he was then "deemed to be elected" to the office of president until October 2007. Although opposition members of the parliament protested and many criticized it, the results of the referendum were also widely accepted both inside and outside Pakistan. Prime Minister Jamali resigned on June 26, 2004, and Muslim League leader Chaudhry Shujaat Hussain became interim prime minister. He was succeeded by finance minister and former vice president of Citibank, Shaukat Aziz, who was elected by the National Assembly as prime minister on August 28, 2004. Musharraf remained president and head of state in the new government. He continues to be the active executive of Pakistan, especially in foreign affairs. On September 15, 2004, Musharraf backed down from his commitment to resign as army chief, which would mean relinquishing his power base to another general, citing circumstances of national necessity. On May 11, 2005, Musharraf barred Benazir Bhutto and Nawaz Sharif from participating in the 2007 general elections. It has been announced that Pervez Musharraf will seek another five-year term as head of state after his current tenure ends in 2007.

Musharraf is considered a moderate leader by most observers, desirous of bridging the gap between the Muslim and Western worlds. He has previously spoken strongly against the idea of the inevitability of a clash of civilizations between them, and he has repeatedly expressed admiration for the secularist reformer of Turkey, Kemal Atatürk, outraging religious leaders in Pakistan. He is the only leader in Pakistan who has dared to be openly critical of religious leaders, complaining that the religious extremists have created a state within a state. He envisions Pakistan as a progressive and prosperous country where there is religious tolerance and respect for rule of law, a high level of human development, and equal opportunities for all. The conventional wisdom has been that it is impossible for any Pakistani leader to survive a showdown with the Islamic radicals. Accordingly, "neither Nawaz Sharif nor Benazir Bhutto even tried to dismantle Zia's legacy" (Jones 2002, 282). Musharraf, on the other hand, has gone some way toward dispelling that myth. In 2002, he announced a whole series of measures designed to control the activities of the radicals, and he banned Lashkar-e-Tayyaba and Jaish-e-Mohammed, the two most radical organizations in Pakistan.

Recently, Musharraf has come under fire in the West for Pakistan's acquisition and testing of nuclear capability and its alleged proliferation, particularly after the disclosure by Dr. Abdul Qadeer Khan, the scientist responsible for the acquisition and testing. Musharraf denied knowledge of Dr. Khan's actions or participation by the Pakistan government or army in the alleged proliferation. His lack of support for Khan has drawn deep domestic criticism among a cross section of people because Dr. Qadeer Khan is respected as a national hero and is known as the father of Pakistan's nuclear program. In contrast to opinion in the West, where India's and Pakistan's tactical capability to launch nuclear strikes on each other and the nuclear arms race between them are seen as posing a threat to global peace, most Pakistanis believe that Pakistan's nuclear capability serves as a deterrent to India's expansionism and to a war between the two countries. The majority of Indians and Pakistanis state that their nuclear capability makes them feel more secure: for them it serves as a deterrent not only to nuclear attack but to conventional war as well (Jones 2002, 213). Musharraf resisted U.S. pressure to hand over Dr. Khan to U.S. authorities and insisted that the Pakistan government would fulfill that responsibility, befitting his reputation as the "man in the middle." Dr. Khan was subsequently pardoned in exchange for cooperation in the investigation of his nuclear-proliferation network.

In 2004, Musharraf began talks with India to solve the Kashmir dispute, although he was chief of the army when conflict erupted in the Indian-held disputed territory of Kashmir at Kargil in 1999. It is reported that Musharraf pulled back from Kargil under tremendous pressure from the United States government exerted through Prime Minister Sharif. "Not even an army chief," writes Jones (2002, 107), "could compromise on Kashmir and expect to survive." But the talks are proceeding well. India has declared a "no first nuclear strike" policy, and Musharraf has offered a "no war pact" to India, although he has said that Pakistan reserves the right to "exercise its nuclear option" in a large-scale war with India. Declaring in May 2005 that he would want the Kashmir issue to be settled in a year's time, Musharraf has indicated a preference for "international guarantees" for implementing such a pact with India. No other leader, especially someone with support in the army, has ever dared to back off from the Kashmir involvement.

The country's economy was on the verge of collapse when Musharraf assumed power in 1999. Recent reports by international financial agencies, including the World Bank and the International Monetary Fund, testify to Pakistan's considerable economic recovery under Musharraf, who has been very open to economic reforms and to modernization. In May 2005, the World Bank extended a three-year, $4.5 billion loan to Pakistan (an average annual loan of $1.5 billion, half of which will be interest-free) to help expedite the country's recovery and to support economic reconstruction and social-sector development efforts. This loan increases the annual lending to Pakistan from about $900 million to $2.4 billion.

A recent CNN report (CNN 2005) has given Pervez Musharraf's government high marks for performance, policy, and good-faith effort on several counts: a fiscal deficit below 6 percent of GDP in 2004–2005, for the first time in eighteen years; an increase in exports; the removal of several state controls; institution of market prices of gasoline; progress of privatization; efforts to curb smuggling and document a largely uncontrolled economy; and plans to build a sustainable tax base. The report points out that the civilian economic team appointed by Musharraf is the best in decades. It concludes that poor governance was the major source of the country's political and economic problems over the past decade and that President Musharraf's government has turned the economy around, after years of mismanagement, corruption, and instability during earlier regimes. The report also asserts that given that 30 percent of Pakistan's population are below the poverty line, it is understandable why to the average Pakistani the opportunity for economic development is more important than the right to vote.

Under Musharraf and after a decade of inward-looking policies, Pakistan embarked on far-reaching structural

President Pervez Musharraf with the author (far left) at his official army residence in Islamabad. The first lady, Sehba Musharraf and the author's daughter, Nazia Siddiqi (far right), are also in the picture. (Yasmeen Mohiuddin)

reforms in November 1999, improving the macroeconomic situation considerably. Thus, GDP grew by an estimated 6.4 percent in 2003–2004 and as much as 8.5 percent in 2004–2005, while inflation remained relatively low at 4.6 percent in the same period. The government privatized several public-sector enterprises, strengthened public and corporate governance, liberalized external trade, and reformed the banking sector. Plans are also under way to reform water, transport, and energy sectors, and to promote education, health, and targeted poverty alleviation programs. Pakistan's reform program, supported by the World Bank Country Assistance, aimed at strengthening macroeconomic stability; improving government effectiveness at the federal, provincial, and local levels by improving transparency and accountability at different state and federal agencies; reducing internal and external debt; improving the competitiveness of the economy and the business environment for growth; and improving equity through support for pro-poor and pro-gender policies and programs.

It is widely believed that no leader in Asia, perhaps in the world, has survived as many serious political challenges as Musharraf, sometimes from conflicting forces: pressure from the United States to change the initial policy toward the Taliban and then to be the frontline ally in its war on terrorism, and to end the one-man rule in Pakistan through national elections; Indian "saber rattling" and a 500,000-troop buildup on its border that could lead to war, with its threat of nuclear engagement; rising levels of extremism and backlash against the United States and himself as an American ally; and the wheeling-dealing and intrigue of Pakistani politics. He has coped well until now, taking a moderate stance on many issues, positioning himself as the "man in the middle." He made a U-turn in his policy in relation to the Taliban after September 11, supporting the United States in the hunt for Osama bin Laden and other 9/11 terrorists. But he has refused to send Pakistani troops to Iraq without a UN resolution. He has also promised to end one-man rule through national elections in 2007. Similarly, he has acceded to India's demand to stop the infiltration of militants into Kashmir and to begin peace talks, but he has also said that Pakistan retains the right to use nuclear power in the event of a major war with India. Again, he has taken a hard line on the country's *madrasas* (religious schools that allegedly preach sectarian violence and hatred of the West), and in so doing he has alienated many of his supporters and generated a backlash. But he has also been very inclusive of religious political parties. It is no surprise that "the world is counting on Musharraf to help steer South and Central Asia from local chaos to regional security, from the brink of Armageddon to Pax Pakistana, and from fundamentalist fervor to secular moderation" (Spaeth 2002).

The pressures on Musharraf increased after the March 2006 visit of President Bush to India and Pakistan. Bush offered significantly different "deals" to the two countries, ostensibly signaling a shift in U.S. interest, support, and alliance away from Pakistan and toward India as well as in the balance of power in the region and the world. This is largely perceived in Pakistan as a reduction in American support for Musharraf, who has conceded so much to the Americans. The general response among Pakistanis is that, once again, the United States has begun to neglect Pakistan now that Pakistan has outlived its immediate usefulness for the Americans— much as happened after the Soviets were defeated in Afghanistan with Pakistan's help. Many Pakistanis consider the United States to be a disloyal and inconsistent friend, support for which has never produced long-lasting dividends. The opposition by the religious parties, who accuse Musharraf of fighting a war against his own people in the tribal areas for the sake of the United States, may be on the increase. The army has lost 400 soldiers in the last two years fighting against religious extremists in the NWFP. Tensions have mounted further in the NWFP and Balochistan over the sharing of natural gas. But recent polls in 2006 show Musharraf's continuing popularity, primarily because of his contributions to the improvement of the economy and the law-and-order situation, as well as to check on corruption and good governance.

CONCLUSION: CHALLENGES AND FUTURE PROSPECTS

Since Pakistan's independence in 1947, periods of civilian rule have alternated with military regimes. The three groups that have wielded tremendous power in Pakistan, more in some regimes than in others, include the landed aristocracy or feudals, the military, and the bureaucracy. The *ulema* and clerics also wielded much power during the regime of Ziaul Haq. While the bureaucracy has been a continuing source of stability in the face of political upheaval in Pakistan, and the military is credited for being the most cohesive national institution, the abuse of power by the bureaucracy, the military, the feudals, and the *ulema* has hindered the development of democratic institutions. Even more, the corruption of politicians and elected leaders has eroded public confidence in democracy and has had a devastating effect on the nurture of its institutions, particularly of the rule of law.

Jinnah envisioned Pakistan to be a constitutional, parliamentary democracy informed by Islamic values of social justice. Jinnah's death in 1948 and Liaquat's assassination in 1951 before his government could draft a constitution plunged Pakistan into seven years of political chaos, with six prime ministers sworn to office in seven years. Constitution making was delayed until 1956 because of the reluctance of West Pakistani bureaucrats and politicians to share power with those in the eastern wing, and particularly because of the opposition by feudals from Punjab. The 1956 constitution represented the dominance of civil servants rather than the legislature and the precedence of administrative over legislative and judicial power.

The abuse of power by the bureaucrats, the failure of civilian political rule, and the squabbling of politicians paved the way for a military coup by General Ayub Khan in 1958, who then became the president of Pakistan. He canceled the parliamentary elections scheduled for 1959, which would have shifted power to a Bengali-dominated legislative government. But martial law was lifted in 1962 and a constitution was framed, establishing a presidential form of government. Adult franchise was limited to the election of Basic Democrats (selected by the civil servants), a system introduced by Ayub Khan that allowed for controlled and indirect participation of the electorate and provided a safe electoral college for the president. The eleven years of Ayub Khan's rule are often known as the golden era of agricultural and industrial development in Pakistan. But his policies also led to a sharp income disparity between East and West Pakistan, and concentration of wealth and power. Dissatisfaction with Ayub's government in East Pakistan and mass demonstrations by students and labor unions in West Pakistan led to his resignation as president in 1969. He handed over power to General Yahya Khan.

Yahya Khan promised to hold nationwide elections in 1970 and to apportion the seats in the National Assembly on a one-person, one-vote basis. East Pakistanis voted overwhelmingly for the Awami League, which demanded autonomy, ensuring a majority for it in the 313-seat National Assembly. But Yahya Khan indefinitely postponed the convening of the National Assembly. A massive military crackdown and the arrest of the Awami League leader for treason led to a civil war, followed by invasion of East Pakistan by Indian troops, surrender of the Pakistani Army, and the creation of Bangladesh in 1971. The majority party in the west wing, PPP, came to power led by Zulfiqar Ali Bhutto.

Bhutto's greatest contribution was his role in drafting a democratic constitution with a modified parliamentary and federal system, which took effect in 1973. Bhutto's policies rewarded the landed aristocracy in Sindh, low-income urban workers, and factions within the army, while targeting the industrialists and civil servants. His large-scale nationalization reduced private investment, caused capital flight, and led to a decline in the industrial growth rate. Bhutto had pledged a more equitable development strategy and participatory government, but his regime became increasingly authoritarian, nepotistic, corrupt, and inefficient. Allegations by the opposition, which was an alliance of nine political parties, about rigging of the 1977 parliamentary elections led to a popular movement against Bhutto, causing the downfall of the PPP government

The 1977 military coup by General Mohammad Ziaul Haq began his eleven-year rule until his death in 1988. Although he promised free elections for national and provincial assemblies within ninety days, he brought criminal charges against Bhutto for alleged conspiracy to murder a political opponent and canceled elections shortly after Bhutto's hanging in 1979. Zia's rule was marked by the Afghan War, resulting in the influx of millions of refugees into Pakistan; the opening up of employment prospects in the Middle East, resulting in large remittances from Pakistani workers abroad; and Zia's advocacy of a more orthodox version of the Islamic economy and society. Pakistan received substantial aid from the United States during the Afghan War, but the refugees brought with them an arsenal of weapons and drugs, a *Kalashnikov* culture that increased ethnic violence and lawlessness in Pakistan. Martial law was lifted in 1985 due to widespread resentment and anti-Zia riots in Sindh. Benazir Bhutto succeeded Zia in 1988 after Zia died in an aircraft crash.

The period from 1988 to 1999 witnessed the return of democracy to Pakistan, but its course was very unstable as governments changed frequently. There were four elections during this period, with Benazir Bhutto and Nawaz Sharif both being returned to power twice, and four caretaker governments serving in between. Bhutto's government was dismissed twice by the president, and Sharif's once, on corruption and mismanagement charges. Bhutto's biggest accomplishment was the restoration of democracy. The two major charges against her were the excessive levels of alleged corruption within the PPP, particularly by her husband, and the inability of her government to control ethnic violence in Sindh. The minor charges included nepotism, autocratic behavior, and inability to enact important legislation. Nawaz Sharif's electoral victory in 1990 marked a power shift away from the traditional feudal aristocracy for the first time in Pakistan's history of popular elections, and toward entrepreneurs, generals, and religious leaders. But rampant crime and terrorism in Sindh and increasing budget deficits plagued the government. After Sharif's landslide victory in the 1997 general election against Bhutto, economic management deteriorated: inflation, debt burden, and poverty increased, while economic growth rates decreased. Sharif also cracked down on the parliamentary opposition, and he was intolerant of dissent even within his own party.

The 1999 coup by General Pervez Musharraf's supporters in the army was not only bloodless but also very popular. A pro-Musharraf party, the Pakistan Muslim League (Qayyum Group), won a plurality of seats in the National Assembly elections of 2002, giving it the two-thirds majority required to amend the constitution permitting Musharraf to remain president until October 2007. He is considered a moderate, modernizing, and noncorrupt leader by most observers, capable of promoting rule of law and religious tolerance. Pakistan's economic recovery under Musharraf has been very impressive: a GDP growth rate of 8.5 percent in 2005, low inflation, and a fiscal deficit below 6 percent of GDP in 2004 (the first in eighteen years). The government privatized several public-sector enterprises, liberalized trade, strengthened public and corporate governance, and improved transparency and accountability at different state and federal agencies.

The challenges and prospects for Pakistan's political and democratic development are linked to its future political leadership. The choice is more likely among previously elected leaders charged with corruption (and some even convicted), a noncorrupt and moderate general, and conservative religious parties. Many in Pakistan, particularly the common person without any vested interest or entrenched loyalties, would like Musharraf to continue, even though he has not been elected in a general election. But democracy is not just about free and fair elections. It is as much or more about establishing the rule of law; protecting the rights of religious and ethnic minorities; championing pluralism, diversity, and basic civil rights and political freedoms; fostering a system of accountability and checks and balances; showing tolerance for political opposition and public discussion of failures and transgressions; being open to intellectual influences from elsewhere; and providing the opportunity for citizens to participate in political discussion so as to influence public choice. In the words of Nobel laureate Amartya Sen, "democracy has demands that transcend the ballot box" (Sen 2003, 29). And Pakistanis can draw on their own intellectual heritage of public reasoning from their history in the Indian subcontinent, Iran, and the Middle East, which has been neglected in Western literature on the history of democracy (Sen 2003).

References and Further Reading

Bloch, Hannah. 1999. "A Strongman Shaken." *TIME Asia* 154(15), October 18, 1999. http://www.time.com/time/asia/magazine/99/1018/pakistan.nawaz.html.

Blood, Peter R. (ed.). 1994. *Pakistan: A Country Study* (Area Handbook Series). Washington, DC: Library of Congress.

CNN Report. 2001, June 20. http://archives.cnn.com/2001/WORLD/asiapcf/south/06/20/pakistan.economy/index.html.

———. 2005, July 23. http://www.infopak.gov.pk/Factsheets/Economic_Prf/cnn_economy.htm.

Human Development Report 2003. 2003. New York: Oxford University Press.

Huntington, S. 1968. *Political Order in Changing Societies.* New Haven, CT: Yale University.

Hussain, Ishrat. 1999. *Pakistan: The Economy of an Elitist State.* Karachi, Pakistan: Oxford University Press.

———. 2003. *Economic Management in Pakistan 1999–2002.* Oxford: Oxford University Press.

Islam, Nurul. 1981. *Foreign Trade and Economic Controls in Development: The Case of United Pakistan.* New Haven, CT: Yale University Press.

Jones, Owen Bennett. 2002. *Pakistan: Eye of the Storm.* New Haven, CT: Yale University Press.

Kardar, Abdul Hafiz. *Failed Expectations.* Lahore, Pakistan: Book Traders.

Kibria, Ghulam. 1999. *A Shattered Dream: Understanding Pakistan's Underdevelopment.* Karachi, Pakistan: Oxford University Press.

New York Times International. 2006. March 4.

Noman, Omar. 1990. *Pakistan: A Political and Economic History since 1947.* London: Kegan Paul International.

Sen, Amartya. 2003. "Democracy and Its Global Roots." *The New Republic.* October 6, 2003: 23–35.

Spaeth, Anthony. 1999. "Under the Gun." *Time* (Asia Edition) 154(16), October 25, 1999. (http://www.time.com/time/asia/magazine/99/1025/cover1.html).

———. 2002. "Dangerous Ground." *Time* (Asia Edition). (http://www.time.com/time/asia/covers/1101020722/story.html).

Tonchev, Plamen. 2003. *Pakistan at Fifty-five: From Jinnah to Musharraf.* European Institute for Asian Studies, BP 02/03, 8 EUR Series.

Weaver, Mary Ann. 2002. *Pakistan: In the Shadow of Jihad and Afghanistan.* New York: Farrar, Straus and Giroux.

World Development Report 2005. 2004. Washington, DC: The World Bank.
Ziring, Lawrence. 1999. *Pakistan in the Twentieth Century: A Political History*. Karachi, Pakistan: Oxford University Press.

CHAPTER FOUR

Pakistani Institutions and Contemporary Culture

RELIGION AND SOCIETY

As noted earlier, an overwhelming majority of 97 percent of Pakistanis are Muslims (77 percent being *Sunnis* and about 20 percent *Shi'ites*), and Hindus, Christians, and other religious minorities each account for about 1 percent of the population. More than 300 million Muslims today live in the two Muslim countries of South Asia (Pakistan and Bangladesh), more than all the people in the Middle East and North Africa combined, and one out of every six people in the world is Muslim.

Religion plays a central role in Pakistani society, culture, and personal life. It is not so much a matter of individual belief but of revealed truth and obvious duty. "Islam" is the Arabic word for "submission" (to the will of God), and the one who submits—a Muslim—is a believer who achieves peace, or *salaam*. It is a monotheistic religion. The central belief in Islam is that there is only one God, Allah, and that the Prophet Muhammad was his final messenger. Though not often highlighted in the media, Islam is also in the Judeo-Christian tradition that regards Abraham (Ibrahim), Moses (Moosa), and Jesus (Isa) as prophets, with belief in angels, Holy Books, Heaven and Hell, and the Day of Judgment. Unlike Jews but like Christians, Muslims believe in the virgin birth and the miracles of Jesus. In fact, Jesus is mentioned ninety-three times in the Quran, the holy scripture of Islam, and the Virgin Mary is mentioned more often in the Quran than in the Bible. Unlike Christians but like Jews, Muslims do not believe that Jesus (or anyone else) is the son of God, who alone is the creator, all-powerful, all knowing, omnipresent, and invisible.

The Quran, the holy scripture of Islam, is considered by believers to be truly the word of God, as it was received by the Prophet in a series of revelations from God transmitted through the angel Gabriel. It consists of 114 *suras,* or chapters. Muslims believe the Quran is the blueprint for humanity, and hence plays a pivotal role in Muslim social organization and values. It is of great unifying importance because almost all Muslims learn to read it in Arabic, regardless of their native language and despite the fact that the Quran is very likely to have been translated into their own language. Although there is no room in Islam for new revelations or further additions to "the word" because Muhammad was the last of the prophets, and the Quran is believed to be eternal, absolute, and irrevocable, there was a provision for *ijtehad* (new interpretations), but in practice, it has been rarely used.

The Prophet's life is considered exemplary, and his statements and actions, referred to as the *hadith,* established precedents for Muslims to follow. The Quran and the *hadith* together form the *sunna,* a comprehensive guide to spiritual, ethical, and social living. There are five pillars of Islam, to which every Muslim is supposed to adhere. The first is recitation of the testimony or *shahada* (*kalma* in Urdu), the affirmation of the faith: "There is no god but God (Allah), and Muhammad is his Prophet." The second pillar is *salat (namaz* in Urdu),* the obligation for a Muslim to pray at five set times during the day, facing Mecca: just before dawn, midday, midafternoon, sunset, and nightfall. The third pillar of Islam is *zakat,* the obligation to provide alms for the poor and disadvantaged. The fourth is *sawm (roza* in Urdu),* the obligation for all Muslims (except the sick, the weak, pregnant or lactating women, soldiers on duty, and minors) to fast from sunrise to sunset during Ramadan, the ninth month of the Muslim calendar, in commemoration of the beginning of the Prophet's revelations from Allah. During the fast, eating, drinking, smoking, and sexual intercourse are forbidden. The final pillar is *hajj,* the pilgrimage to Mecca during *Zilhij,* the twelfth month of the Muslim lunar calendar, at least once in one's lifetime, required only of adults who are physically and financially able to do so. The *hajj* is a unifier of the greater Muslim *umma* (community of believers) as all Muslims, regardless of status, race, color, or national origin, draped in a white seamless garment, stand side by side to pray and perform other rituals. The pilgrimage at any other time of the year is referred to as *umra* (visitation). At various times of political crisis in Pakistan, almost every major leader has left for Saudi Arabia to perform *umra.*

Although *jihad* is not one of the five pillars, it is an important element of Islam. Often misunderstood in the West as a fanatical holy war, the most important *jihad,* or "struggle," is the one within each individual to control desire or lower the self; the outer one is to preserve the faith. People who fight the outer *jihad* are Mujahideen, such as the Afghanis against the Soviet invasion. The Quran also specifies the code of conduct in daily life, which is very similar to the Jewish practice, such as the prohibition on the consumption of pork (also alcohol for Muslims), the requirement that animals be slaughtered in a ritual manner (*halal,* similar to *kosher*), and the obligation to circumcise sons. The Muslim calendar, like the Jewish, is based on the lunar system and consists of 354 days, 11 days shorter than the solar year. Accordingly, each solar year, Ramadan arrives about 11 days earlier than it did the year before, occurring during various seasons in different years.

The two most important Muslim holidays are *Eid-ul-Azha* and *Eid-ul-Fitr. Eid-ul-Azha* is celebrated to commemorate the occasion of Abraham's readiness to sacrifice his son, Ismail, on God's command when Allah rewarded his obedience by replacing his son with a sheep. Families sacrifice ani-

mals (goats, sheep, and cows), giving one-third of the meat to
the poor. *Eid-ul-Fitr* marks the end of the month of fasting.
Like Christmas or Hanukah, both of these holidays are times
of feasting, family reunions, and gifts of money from the older
to the younger relatives. The whole month of Ramadan is
very special. Those who fast eat a meal, called *sehri,* before
dawn and one after sunset, called *iftar.* It is said that fasting
is practiced more than prayers.

There are two major sects in Islam, the Sunnis and the
Shi'a, whose beliefs differ on the rule of the Rashideen
Caliphate after the death of the Prophet. The Sunnis accept
the temporal authority of the four caliphs (Abu Bakr, Omar,
Usman, and Ali), and the Shi'a accept only that of Ali, the
Prophet's cousin and husband of his daughter, Fatima, and
believe that their descendants should have been the hereditary leaders of Islam. The Sunnis conform to one of the four
major schools of jurisprudence, the *Hanafi, Shafai, Hum-
bali, and Maliki.* The Hanafi school is predominant in Pakistan. The Shi'as trace their lineage directly to the Prophet
through his daughter, Fatima. Most of the Shi'as believe in
Twelve Imams only, Ali and his eleven direct descendants. A
minority Shi'a group, the *Ismailis,* follows a similar lineage
until the sixth imam, a different seventh imam (a younger
brother, Ismail), from whom the line continues down to the
present day. The current leader is known as His Highness,
Prince Karim Agha Khan. Unlike Christians, and also unlike
the Shi'a sect, there is no organized body of clerics or religious hierarchy in the Sunni tradition, or any requirement of
training or scholarly accomplishment for the imam (prayer
leader). Accordingly, in the rural areas, the *imam* is typically
not educated but delivers sermons on Fridays, presides at
weddings and funerals, and teaches the Quran to children.
But the *ulema,* Muslim scholars trained in Islamic theology,
have provided the orthodox leadership to the Muslim community and unofficially interpreted and administered religious laws.

Muslims offer prayers during Eid-ul-Fitr holiday in Lahore. (Moshin Raza/Reuters/Corbis)

In addition to Sunni and Shi'a traditions, Sufism is Pakistan's mystical tradition, emphasizing the love of God rather than the fear of God. Instead of the ritualistic observance of faith, Sufism is based on a direct, unstructured, personal devotion to God. In the fourteenth and fifteenth centuries, Sufi saints, called *pirs,* converted low-caste Hindus to Islam by the millions in India. Two Sufis whose shrines receive thousands of pilgrims each year are Data Ganj Baksh in Lahore (ca. eleventh century) and Shahbaz Qalander in Sehwan, Sindh (ca. twelfth century). Because Islam was also spread in South Asia by Sufis through the conversion of Hindus, in addition to being spread through the descendants of the Arab general, Muhammad-bin-Qasim, it accommodated some pre-Islamic influences, resulting in a religion traditionally more flexible than that in the Arab world.

The first to propose the idea of a Muslim state in the Indian subcontinent was Muslim poet-philosopher Sir Muhammad Iqbal, whose 1930 proposal called for the Punjab, Sindh,

Balochistan, and the North-West Frontier Province to form a Muslim state. In 1947, Pakistan emerged as a religion-state rather than a classical nation-state, the only modern nation besides Israel that was intentionally formed as a religious homeland for a community. But although Jinnah's demand for Pakistan as a separate homeland for Muslims, where they would be free to practice their religion, was based on the importance of Islam in the lives of Muslims, he represented a secular vision. In the very first meeting of Pakistan's Constituent Assembly on August 11, 1947, Jinnah had said that "you are free, you are free to go to your temples, you are free to go to your mosques, or any other place of worship. . . . Hindus would cease to be Hindus and Muslims would cease to be Muslims, not in the religious sense, because that is the personal faith of each individual, but in the political sense as citizens of the State" (Kibria 1999, 113).

As for other leaders and politicians of Pakistan's early years, most of them, being largely landed magnates and tribal chiefs, had jumped on the Muslim League bandwagon, enabling it to score a landslide victory in the 1946 elections, which paved the way for the creation of Pakistan, not so much because they supported an Islamic state but more because they were concerned about the Congress's plan for land reforms, which would have adversely affected them (Alavi 2002). However, the vision of Pakistan as a Muslim-majority state in which religious minorities would share equally in its development was questioned as early as the 1950s, and the debate continued into the 1990s and beyond. Because no politician could afford to be denounced as anti-Islamic, successive governments found it increasingly difficult to suppress demands for an Islamic state. General Zia's regime pursued an Islamization program that was considered by many as not protecting minorities and women. The Shariat Bill, passed in May 1991, requiring that all laws in the country conform to Islam, threatened to jeopardize the 1961 Muslim Family Laws Ordinance of Ayub Khan, and the blasphemy law was resented by non-Muslims. Zia's policies were in contrast to the popular culture, in which most people are "personally" very religious but not "publicly" religious and do not want to live in a theocracy. An unexpected outcome was that by legislating what is Islamic and what is not, and who is Muslim and who is not, factionalism increased. Blood (1995) notes that "Islam itself could no longer provide unity because it was then being defined to exclude previously included groups. Disputes between Sunnis and Shi'as, ethnic disturbances in Karachi among Pakhtuns, Sindhis, and *muhajirs,* increased animosity toward Ahmadiyyas, and the revival of Punjab-Sindh tensions can all be traced to the loss of Islam as a common vocabulary of public morality" (129).

The debate continues between the modernists and the Islamic radicals, who are influenced by two different schools of Sunni Islamic thought on the Indian subcontinent, the *Deobandis* and the *Barelvis.* The *Deobandis* believe in a literal and austere interpretation of Islam, and the *Barelvis* in a more moderate and tolerant one. The Islamic radicals are described by many in the West as fundamentalists, which is an unsatisfactory label used for any Muslim who challenges any aspect of the Western way of life: Pan-Arab nationalists, Palestinian activists, Islamic extremists, and even religious moderates. The Islamic radicals believe in a return to the *Sharia,* as practiced in the early days of Islam. Pakistani politicians of the 1950s came down firmly on the side of the modernists in constitution making but were reluctant to offend the Islamic radicals and say clearly that they did not want an Islamic state. In the 1960s, Ayub Khan tried to confront the radicals through his Muslim Family Laws Ordinance, though unsuccessfully. Bhutto in the 1970s did not even try and gave in to radical demands for declaring *Ahmedis* to be non-Muslims, even though he was known to be the most modernist leader. In the late 1970s and the 1980s, General Zia, the first leader in thirty years to side with the Islamic radicals, tried to Islamicize the economy, as well as the legal and education systems. Benazir Bhutto and Nawaz Sharif did little to dismantle Zia's legacy: Bhutto, though privately modernist, did not confront the radicals, and Sharif supported them. General Musharraf, on the other hand, distanced himself from the radicals early on when, in 1999, he said, "Islam teaches tolerance not hatred; universal brotherhood and not enmity; peace and not violence; progress and not bigotry . . .I urge [the *ulema*] to curb elements which are exploiting religion for vested interests and bring bad name to our faith" (Jones 2002, 19). Again, in June 2001, he spoke to the clerics as no one had dared to since the 1950s when he said, "We never tire of talking about the status that Islam accords to women. We only pay lip-service to its teachings. We do not act upon it" (Jones 2002, 20). This was the clearest statement of Islamic modernism ever made by a Pakistani leader after Jinnah. Although he was not successful in his attempts to change the blasphemy law and had to back down, he persisted in controlling sectarian and ethnic violence.

LANGUAGE AND ETHNIC GROUPS

The people of Pakistan represent a wide variety of cultures, languages, art, and literature. There are five major ethnic groups in present-day Pakistan: the Punjabis, the Sindhis, the Pathans, the Balochis, and the Muhajirs. Before 1971, the Bengalis constituted another ethnic group, the largest one in Pakistan of that time. The ethnic composition roughly corresponds to the linguistic distribution of the population. The most common languages in Pakistan are Punjabi, Sindhi, Pakhtu or Pashto, Balochi, and Urdu, although there are more than twenty spoken languages. The Punjabis constitute about 60 percent of the population, Sindhis 12 percent, Pathans 8 percent, Muhajirs 8 percent, Baluchis 4 percent, and others 8 percent. All of these languages belong to the Indo-Aryan branch of the Indo-European language family. There are also several subgroups that consider themselves distinct, such as the Saraiki speakers of southern Punjab, the Hindko speakers of the NWFP, the Brohis of Sindh and Balochistan, and the Persian-speaking Hazaras of Balochistan. The Brahui language, and other Northern Areas languages such as Shina, are related to the Dravidian language family. Each group is concentrated in its home province, except for Muhajirs, who migrated from India, mostly at the time of partition in 1947, and settled mostly in urban Sindh. The Punjabis and Sindhis live in the river plains of the Indus in the provinces of Punjab and Sindh, respectively; the Pathans live in the mountainous region of the North-West Frontier Province; and the smaller but distinct nationalities (people of Chitral, Gilgit, and Hunza, and the Kalash) live in the extreme north in the Northern Areas. The Baloch and some Pathans live on the Balochistan Plateau in the Balochistan Province.

Urdu is Pakistan's official language and the mother tongue of the Muhajirs. More than 75 percent of all Pakistanis and 95 percent of city dwellers understand Urdu. It evolved around the twelfth century before the reign of the Sultanate of Delhi from a *lingua franca* through the interaction of different languages spoken by the Sultanate's soldiers. By the seventeenth century, Urdu had incorporated many Persian, Arabic, Sanskrit, Hindi, and Turkish words, and had transformed into a developed, literary language. Spoken Urdu is very similar to spoken Hindi, the language of northern India. But the script is entirely different. The Urdu script is very similar to Arabic and is written from right to left. Each of the major languages—Punjabi, Sindhi, Pushto, and Balochi—shares the same Arabic-Persian script and is classified as an Indo-European language. Sindhi is the most developed of all the regional languages. Since 1947, Urdu has been the medium of instruction at public schools and the main language of television and radio broadcasts. Urdu was chosen as the national language by the founders of Pakistan because it symbolized the shared identity of South Asian Muslims and was considered to be geographically neutral, which would prevent the dominance of one region over another. But this move was unpopular in East Pakistan, where Bengali was spoken, leading to language riots in Dhaka in the early 1950s. It became more politicized over the years. Since the Muhajirs settled largely in Sindh, the movement for the promotion of the Sindhi language was expressed in opposition to Urdu, leading to clashes between Sindhis and Muhajirs. The language riots broke out in 1972 when the government announced its decision to grant special status to the Sindhi language in Sindh. (See Part 2 for more details.)

English is also used for official business, in university classrooms, army manuals, technical training, courts above the village level, government documents, legal contracts, and American movies. It is the language of the elite and the educated, who speak it fluently, switching back and forth from English to their national or regional language in midsentence. Their children start studying English at the age of four or five. It is also the medium of instruction in private schools. In the public schools, it is taught as one subject out of many. Still, many Pakistanis know at least some English.

Punjabis

Punjabis constitute about 60 percent of Pakistan's population and 80 percent of its army. They form a distinct and recognizable group, are typically taller than other Pakistanis, and have a lighter skin. They have a great reputation as warriors. The dominance of Punjabis in the military hierarchy has meant their dominance in government as well, particularly during the frequent military rule in Pakistan. Punjab's landed elite has always been dominant in the upper echelons of civil and military bureaucracy, which is resented by the underrepresented groups such as Pakhtuns, Baloch, and particularly Sindhis. The struggle for democratic rule in Pakistan has been synonymous with movement against ethnic domination of the Punjabis. Having diverse origins, the Punjabis are a coherent ethnic community that has historically placed great emphasis on both farming and fighting. Punjab is the agricultural heartland of Pakistan and pioneer of the green revolution. Most of the farms are owner-operated, but big landlords and tenant farms dominate the south. Punjabis are typically divided into "functional *quams*" or "agricultural tribes" based on descent and traditional occupations, which gives the group its name and its position in the social hierarchy. Distinctions based on *quam* are particularly important social markers in the rural areas. Kinship obligations are central to a Punjabi's identity. The Punjabi language, based on Sanskrit, has a rich oral tradition of poems, songs, folktales, and romances, the most famous being the love story of Heer Ranjha written by the eighteenth-century Punjabi poet Waris Shah.

Sindhis

Sindhis make up 12 percent of Pakistan's population and half of the population in the Sindh Province. The name "Sindh" comes from "Sindhhu," a Sanskrit word for the Indus River, which is also the source for words such as "Hindu," "India," and "Indus." The feudal structure is strong in Sindh, with 50 percent of the farms being tenant-operated. The large landowners (*waderas*) exercise great influence in their areas and can still exact tributary labor. It is believed that many of them give protection to *dacoits* (bandits) to terrorize the area, and as such dacoities are very common in rural Sindh. It is a place where tribal and village lords hold the most power, and it is known that villagers cannot vote against the landlord's wishes in Sindh even in democratic elections.

When millions of Hindus and Sikhs left for India after partition, about 7 million Muhajirs took their place and, with hard work and entrepreneurship, which are characteristic of all migrants, became very successful. This caused resentment in Sindh, often leading to violence. During Zulfiqar Ali Bhutto's term, some rectifying measures were taken to increase Sindhi participation in government and to promote the Sindhi language. Nonetheless, Sindh became an ethnic battlefield within Pakistan and one of the most violent places in Pakistan. The 1980s were marked by repeated kidnappings in the province, both political and criminal. The interior of Sindh became unsafe for road and rail travel because of the persistent fear of dacoits. Sectarian violence also took place against Hindus in 1992 following the destruction of the Babri Mosque in Ayodhya, India, by Hindu extremists who wanted to rebuild a Hindu temple on that site.

Muhajirs

Muhajirs constitute only 8 percent of Pakistan's population and 50 percent of the population of Karachi and Hyderabad, Pakistan's largest and fifth largest cities, respectively. Unlike other ethnic groups in Pakistan, the Muhajirs have no common racial features or character traits. At the time of partition in 1947, about 5 to 7 million refugees from cities all over India crossed the border from India to Pakistan. The only thing they had in common was their search for refuge from the ethnic violence in India, their burning desire to live in the new Muslim nation, and their missionary zeal to fight against heavy odds to make their dream come true. Most of them settled in Sindh, particularly in Karachi. The Muhajirs are the only people in Pakistan who speak Urdu as a native language, although several dialects depend on the part of India from which they migrated.

Since most Muhajirs had lived in cities for several generations, they are often more educated and are considered to be more sophisticated than other Pakistanis. Many had upper-class education and professional skills. Moreover, exposure to and involvement in the freedom movement in India had made them politically aware. Like immigrants all over the world, they were risk takers and had entrepreneurial ability. Their lack of a support system and roots in the areas that became

Pakistan created a work ethic that depended only on effort rather than connections. Not surprisingly, they held a disproportionate share of jobs in business, finance, government, and the Civil Service after partition. Accordingly, they displaced native Sindhis from positions of prominence. This led to resentment against the Muhajirs, particularly by Sindhis who resented their success, and later by other ethnic groups. In the 1970s, under the Bhutto government, the Sindhis succeeded in getting the federal government to reduce the Muhajirs' share of new jobs in the Civil Service. There have been occasional outbreaks of violence against the Muhajirs in Sindh. To protest against this quota, several Muhajirs joined the MQM (Muhajir Quami [National] Movement), a genuinely grass-roots party, and voted overwhelmingly for it in several elections. The late 1980s and early 1990s marked MQM's high point, when it secured thirteen of Karachi's fifteen seats in the 1988 National Assembly elections, sweeping the religious parties and feudal leaders in Sindh out of office.

Pakhtuns

The Pathans, or Pakhtuns or Pushtuns, make up 8 percent of Pakistan's population and 45 percent of Afghanistan's. Warlike and hardworking, they are easily identifiable physically as they are typically tall, slender, often light-skinned, and darkhaired. Some have blue eyes and are believed to be the descendants of the European soldiers in the army of Alexander the Great. The Pathans are the world's largest autonomous tribal group, and the most researched of all ethnic groups in Pakistan. They are concentrated in the North-West Frontier Province, and also in Balochistan and in southern Afghanistan.

The West's fascination with Pathans originated because they are one of the few peoples who were able to defeat the advances of British imperialism. In 1937, the Pakhtuns wiped out an entire British brigade. The two most ferocious tribes are Wazirs and Afridis. The Wazirs in the FATA region (Federally Administered Tribal Areas) are considered to be the most violent of all the Pakhtuns. Throughout the 1930s, more troops were stationed in Waziristan in the southern part of the North-West Frontier Province than in the rest of the subcontinent. The Pathans are very proud that none of the numerous conquerors who came through their lands could assimilate them. Similarly, the fight put up by the Afridis of the Khyber Pass forced the British to send more than 40 military expeditions between 1858 and 1902, and in 1897, 40,000 troops were required to quell the Afridis. The Afridi tribesmen who have lived in the pass for millennia have made war or extracted toll from the users. They are all armed, usually with rifles, ranging from old British Lee Enfields to modern Russian *Kalashnikovs,* but sometimes automatic pistols and submachine guns. Other tribes include the Khattaks, Turis, Daurs, Mahsuds, and Yusufzais.

The Pathans have a deep, powerful, and male-centered code of conduct, the *Pakhtunwali* (Way of the Pakhtuns), which governs all their actions. Adherence to this code is central to identity as a Pakhtun. The *Pakhtunwali* has four parts: *nang* (honor), *melmastia* (hospitality), *badal* (revenge), and *nanwatai* (formal abasement). The first dictate of this code is the notion of honor, *nang*. Without honor, life for a Pakhtun is not worth living. Honor refers to the duty of a Pashtun man to defend the honor of the women of his family or clan. It demands the maintenance of sexual propriety, chastity, and good repute of his mother, daughters, sisters, and wife (or wives) to ensure his honor. Offenses to one's honor must be avenged, or there is no honor. Partners in illicit sexual liaisons are killed if discovered. If a Pakhtun man suspects his wife, sister, or daughter of sexual impropriety, he will kill both the offending male and his own female relative; these killings are the only ones that do not demand revenge, and neither is the killer punished by the local *jirga* (council of male tribal leaders). A direct outcome of this code of ethics is that women are mostly restricted to private, family compounds in much of the North-West Frontier Province. They are rarely to be seen on busy streets in the Frontier. When they do venture out of the house, most wear a *burqa,* a tent-like cloth that covers them from head to toe except for a small, net-like mesh at the center of the face on the eyes. Many women who wear a *burqa* believe that it protects them from the unwanted gaze of unfamiliar men. The tradition and practice of *purdah* (veiling or covering) is more common among the Pathan than other Pakistani women.

The second dictate of *Pakhtunwali,* or *melmastia,* is to provide hospitality to all strangers and guests. Even the poorest Pakhtun village has a guesthouse to accommodate visitors. Hosts, regardless of position, serve meals to guests and sit with them as equals because the host gains honor by serving his guest. The duty of hospitality takes precedence over the demand for revenge. Even if an enemy seeks refuge or safe passage, it must be given for as long as the person is within the precincts of one's home. Refuge must extend to the point of being willing to sacrifice one's own life to defend one's guest, but it is a great humiliation for a Pakhtun to ask for refuge from an enemy. In fact, it was the obedience to the customary dictates of hospitality by Pakistani Pakhtuns that made them initially welcome and supported 3 million Pakhtun refugees from Afghanistan with minimal tension. By the early 1990s, however, all Pakistanis, including the Pakhtuns, were frustrated with the violence overflowing from Afghanistan into Pakistan.

The third aspect of the Pashtun code is *badal,* or revenge, by which Pashtun men are duty-bound to seek revenge for offenses, hostilities, or insults to their honor. If an enemy kills your brother, then honor demands that you kill several members of the enemy's family in return. This has led to endless feuds and counterfeuds that can go on for years, and the quest for revenge can pass from father to son. Almost all Pakhtun men own rifles, many own machine guns, and some even own light artillery. Another trait of the Pakhtuns is their intensely egalitarian ethos within a clan: the tribal leader is considered the first among equals. Pakhtuns do not have chiefs: a *khan* or *malik* is only a first among equals. This sense of equality is evident in the structure of the tribal *jirga,* at which issues of common interest are debated, ranging from disputes between local lineage sections to relations with other tribes or with the national government. Although the council can make and enforce binding decisions, within the body itself all are considered equals. Similarly, a Pakhtun domestic is free to help himself to food at his employer's table and to participate in conversation. In modern government, Pakhtun bureaucrats are far more accessible to ordinary people than are Punjabi or Sindhi officials. *Nanwatai,* the fourth aspect of the code, is meant to preserve the lives of the losers. The losers in a fight are expected to show total submission to the victors, who are expected to be merciful and generous.

At every level of Pakhtun social organization, groups are split into a complex and shifting pattern of alliance and enmity. Hence, a man's greatest rival for women, money, and land (*zan, zar,* and *zamin,* respectively) is his first cousin— his father's brother's son—even though the same man may be his staunchest ally in the event of attack from the outside. Most Pakhtuns are pious, highly devout Sunni Muslims, praying five times a day, fasting during the month of Ramadan, and giving alms to the poor. The typical Pathan family grows wheat on its own land, has some sheep and goats, and may have a small orchard. About 68 percent of farms are owner-operated. Since the 1980s, many Pakhtuns have entered the police force, Civil Service, or military, and have virtually taken over the country's transportation network.

Many Pakhtuns live beyond the boundaries of the North-West Frontier Province. About 500,000 Pakhtuns live in the Northern Areas, where they are a majority. Many live in the mountainous tribal areas within the NWFP, but Pakistani laws and taxes do not apply in these tribal areas. Governance issues are handled by the *jirgas.* About 2 million Pakhtuns live in northeast Balochistan, as do 700,000 refugees from Afghanistan, half of whom are ethnic Pakhtuns. The Baluchis fear domination by the Pakhtuns because of sheer numbers. Tribal society and periodic struggle between Pakhtun and Baluch tribes for control ends in violence. Lastly, more than a million Pakhtuns live in Karachi, where they have monopolized the private transport sector. The Pakhtuns are also believed to have brought the gun culture to Karachi, where there is a proliferation of guns—including clones of Uzis and *Kalashnikovs,* which have exacerbated much of the violence.

Balochi

Balochis, the second largest tribal group in Pakistan, live in the arid areas of Balochistan, in southwest and central-west Pakistan, inhabiting one of the most barren landscapes on earth. Like the Pakhtuns, their original territory extends beyond the national borders so that only 70 percent of the Baloch live in Pakistan, the remaining 30 percent being in Iran and Afghanistan. Only the hardiest people can survive in Balochistan, and the Balochis are legendary for their endurance, good humor, and hospitality. The Balochis are a hardy people who have adapted to survive in the harsh and inhospitable landscape of Pakistan's huge salty deserts. The Baloch tribe claims an ancient Semitic lineage and traces its origin back 4,000 years to Aleppo in Syria, from where they migrated, between the sixth and the fourteenth centuries, slowly eastward. Most Baloch speak Balochi, part of the Iranian group of Indo-European languages. One-fifth of the Baloch speak Brahui, a Dravidian language that may derive from the language of the ancient city of Mohenjodaro, 4,500 years ago.

Like the Pakhtuns, the Baloch abide by a code of honor that calls for revenge, hospitality, and punishment of death for illicit sex. But unlike the Pakhtuns, the Baloch are not egalitarian. Rather, Baloch society is stratified and has been referred to as "feudal militarism." The head of the tribe, the *sardar,* is very powerful, and his word is law. Most *sardars* discourage education, resist change, and block economic development to retain control. It is no surprise that the Baloch are the poorest and the least educated people in Pakistan. The economic activities in this harsh environment are confined to pastoral nomadism, dryland and irrigated agriculture, and fishing. Irrigated farming is done near oases either through open channels bringing water from riverbeds or through subsurface drains that channel groundwater to the fields, known as *karez.*

Others

The mountain valleys and the hillsides are the homelands not only of the Pathans, but also of other ethnic groups. Other mountain peoples "across the roof of Pakistan" are the Kohistanis, the pagan Kalash of the Chitral highlands, and the Hunzakut. Most of the people of Gilgit and Hunza belong to the Ismaili sect of Shi'ite Muslims, being followers of the Agha Khan. Boorishki and Shina are the main languages. Their women wear colorful baggy trousers, knee-length shirts, and embroidered flat-topped caps. Smaller tribes include the Bajaur, Mohmand, Khyber, Orakzai, Kurram, and North and South Waziristanis.

Ethnic identities and tribal loyalties that shape people's hearts and minds are especially strong in Pakistan. The prominent tribal chief of Balochistan, Nawab Akbar Bugti Khan, said, "I have been a Baloch for several centuries. I have been a Muslim for 1,400 years. I have been a Pakistani for just over fifty" (Jones 2000, 109). Language is an important marker of ethnic identity, but there are other differences too. Ethnic hierarchies exist even within classes. Ethnic allegiance has been the basic unit of political organization in Pakistan. Accordingly, political parties are based on regional lines. No political party could claim support across the nation. The politics of ethnicity is so pervasive that it affects even tasks such as conducting the decennial censuses. The decennial censuses were conducted in 1981, 1994, and 2001. The 1991 census was not carried out until 1994. It has been argued (Blood, 1995, 91) that the government felt that ethnic and religious tensions among Punjabis, Sindhis, Muhajirs, and Pakhtuns, and between the Sunni Muslim majority and religious minorities, "were such that taking the census might provoke violent reactions from groups who felt that they had been undercounted." In fact, ethnic struggles have been a primary source of political conflict in Pakistan. It was ethnic tension and the mishandling of it that ultimately led to the dismemberment of Pakistan and the creation of Bangladesh as an independent country in 1971. More recently too, there has been significant loss of life and property, and such lawlessness that three elected governments were dismissed from 1988 to 1999 for their inability to maintain law and order, among other charges.

FAMILY AND KINSHIP

Social life in Pakistan revolves around family and kin, even among members of the most Westernized elite. The family or household is the primary kinship unit and the basis of social organization, providing its members with both identity and protection. A 1980 study (Weston 1992, 161) of more than 100,000 IBM employees around the world found that Pakistan is one of the most family-oriented countries in the world. Most Pakistanis live in "joint" or extended families that include a married couple, unmarried children of all ages and both sexes, married sons and their families, widowed daughters, father's parents, and sometimes widowed sisters of the father (paternal aunts). When a son marries, his wife is expected to move in with her in-laws, just as a daughter is expected to leave her natal home and live with her in-laws. It is almost unheard of in Pakistan for adult and unmarried sons and daughters to live in separate apartments in the same city as their parents, even if they are working. It is equally unheard of for old parents to live by themselves. On the whole, the culture places less value on individualism and independence and more on community and interdependence. Whether the joint or extended family system endures or not depends on the preferences and personalities of the individuals involved, particularly the women (mother-in-law, sisters-in-law, and daughters-in-law), and the degree of influence of the mother relative to the wife.

Status and power within the family depend on both age and gender. The father is the head of the family and is always obeyed by all in the family (though he defers to his father and mother), but sisters and younger brothers often defer to older brothers too. The mother has a lot of power, and even married children seek the mother's approval in most matters. The importance of the extended family system and family relationships, and the reverence for age in the Pakistani culture, are even reflected in vocabulary and language. Urdu and all regional languages contain deferential names and titles for each of the following relatives: older brother; older sister; father's mother, father, older brother and his wife, younger brother and his wife, and sister and her husband; mother's mother, father, brother and his wife, and sister and her husband. These words have no equivalent in the English language, where there is no distinction between maternal and paternal grandparents, uncles, and aunts, or between younger and older sisters and brothers. Age is so revered in Pakistan that even older family friends, neighbors, friends of friends, and customers are not addressed by their name, but are just called by the gender- and age-appropriate title, or simply the English equivalent, that is, "aunt" or "uncle." It is no surprise that almost all Pakistanis and South Asians are shocked when they hear some Westerners addressing their parents by their first names.

Old people in Pakistan are revered for their wisdom and have an honored place in society. Old parents or grandparents live in the family and are involved in decision making. In fact, old-age homes or nursing homes are nonexistent in Pakistan, and Pakistanis abhor the idea. The widespread use of these facilities in the West has created an impression in Pakistan, exaggerated though it may be, of ungrateful, materialistic children thinking only of themselves. Almost all Pakistani parents think of their children before themselves and make great personal sacrifices to provide a better life for their children. It is very common for men, and much more so for women, to stay in unhappy marriages or not remarry primarily because of the adverse impact of divorce on their children. Once a couple has children, everything in life is geared to the well-being of the children. The children, for their part, always hold the parents in high regard, are very polite and respectful to them, and take care of them in old age.

In the rural areas, *biradari* (male kin through patrilineage) plays a significant role in social relations. A *biradari* may be located in a single village, or many villages, cities, and provinces. Members of a *biradari* celebrate the major life events together. The *biradari* also serves as a mutual aid society, helping members in getting loans, employment, and dowries for their daughters (if poor). Although descent is patrilineal, women maintain relations with their natal families throughout life, particularly their brothers, who serve as a fallback in case of divorce or widowhood early in marriage. Although society is organized based on kinship in Pakistan, it is not rigidly stratified. No formal caste system exists among Muslims in Pakistan, unlike in the Hindu society of India or Nepal. There is a hierarchy of social groups, but that is based on traditional functions or roles in society, such as the *mochis* (shoemakers), *dhobis* (washermen), *julahas* (weavers), *lohars* (blacksmiths), *bhangis* or *jamadars* (janitors), and *kumhars* (potters), all of whom are at the bottom of the hierarchy.

Marriages are typically arranged by parents and are a means to cement social ties and build new relationships. As in many parts of West Asia, people prefer to marry their cousins; the Western taboo of somewhat recent origin against marrying one's cousin does not exist in Pakistan. About 50 percent of all marriages are between cousins, mostly between the children of two brothers, in part because property exchanged at marriage then stays within the patrilineage. Many other arranged marriages are between children of family friends, or friends of friends, or within the *biradari* in the same village or outside—those whose families have known each other for long and are not strangers. The relationship between in-laws extends beyond the couple and well past the marriage event. If a marriage is successful, others will follow between the two families, reinforcing the links through the generations. The marriage of Benazir Bhutto, the Oxford- and Harvard-educated daughter of Zulfiqar Bhutto, the former prime minister of Pakistan, was arranged by her mother just a year before Benazir herself became the prime minister of Pakistan. At one extreme, there are some marriages, about 5 percent, in which the groom and the bride have not seen each other and do not meet till the wedding. There are also some marriages that are forced by a father despite a daughter's protest, but they are shrinking in number. The choice of the partners in the arranged marriages is dictated by pragmatic considerations, and romantic attachments have little role to play. Marriage is a contractual arrangement, typically negotiated between two male heads of household, and the terms are noted, by law, at the local marriage registry.

At the other extreme are "love marriages" in which the man and the woman choose each other. These marriages are becoming more frequent now that there are more opportunities for interaction due to both higher female enrollments at co-ed schools and colleges and larger numbers of women in the workforce. But such marriages are still the exception because romantic love is a dangerous thing in Pakistan: it

A Pakistani bride, Samnita Burney, wears the traditional heavily embroidered red wedding outfit and lots of gold jewelry. (Samnita Burney)

The hands of a bride-to-be are adorned with mehndi *(henna) before her wedding. (Samnita Anwar)*

adversely affects a woman's reputation, particularly if the romance does not end in marriage, and it reduces her chances of marriage to anyone else. Pakistani society does not tolerate "shopping around" or short-lived relationships. The standards of morality for women are quite rigid in all areas of Pakistan, and much more rigid than they are for men. Love and sex typically take place within the confines of the marriage, and premarital and extramarital sex, forbidden by the Quran, is very rare, particularly among the middle class. On the whole, arranged marriages are more successful in Pakistan than love marriages for several reasons: lower expectations, higher comfort level because of preexisting bonds (sometimes of blood relationships) not only with the spouse but more importantly with the in-laws, greater social acceptability, greater compatibility in terms of socioeconomic status and family values, and faith in parents' choice.

A typical woman's life is difficult during the early years of marriage, when she has to adjust to all her in-laws in their home where she is a new arrival, particularly her mother-in-law, who typically has more influence over her son (the woman's husband). Her status improves if she has brought a good dowry from her natal home, consisting of household goods, clothing, jewelry, furniture, electric appliances, and/or cash, and when she bears sons. There is a strong preference for sons in Pakistan, as in the rest of South Asia, including India, Bangladesh, and Nepal. Because of the patrilineal system, sons are considered a greater asset and a more reliable source of security in old age than daughters, who have to be protected and for whom a dowry has to be arranged.

STATUS OF WOMEN

The status of women in Pakistan, as in the rest of South Asia, varies across classes, age groups, regions, and the rural-urban divide. Middle-class women in Pakistan have had a long history of being educated and involved in public roles, going back to the launching of a modest school for girls at Aligarh in 1906 by Dr. Shaikh Mohammad Abdullah, an activist for Muslim women's education. This school later became the first college for Muslim women in pre-partition India. Fatima Jinnah, Quaid-e-Azam's sister, played a major role in the independence movement of Pakistan and ran for president in the 1960s against Ayub Khan but lost because that election was not fair. Pakistan was also the first Muslim country to have an elected female head of government when Benazir Bhutto became prime minister in 1988. Currently, Pakistan's high commissioner to the United Kingdom since 2003 has been a woman, Dr. Maleeha Lodhi. She is and has been Pakistan's longest-serving ambassador to the United States (1994–2003). In 1994, *Time* magazine cited her as one of 100 people in the world who will help define the twenty-first century and, in 2002, *Newsweek* listed her among seventy-seven world figures changing the world (*The News* 2003). Recently, Presi-

One of the earliest graduates of the Shaikh Abdullah Girls College at Aligarh (the first for Muslim women in India), Dr. Bismillah Niaz Ahmed (the author's mother), is seen here with a British member of Parliament in 1963. (Yasmeen Mohiuddin)

dent Pervez Musharraf appointed Shamshad Akhtar as the governor of the State Bank of Pakistan, which is the central bank of the country, similar to the Federal Reserve Board (the Fed) in the United States. She is the first woman to hold this job. There are also many women politicians, cabinet ministers, ambassadors, college presidents, university professors, judges, physicians, engineers, pilots, and bankers. But at the other end of the spectrum, large numbers of women in Pakistan have limited access to education, although Islam emphasizes education for both men and women. Moreover, poor women, particularly in rural areas, have very limited access to resources like credit, technology, training, health care, wage labor, and political power. Many have limited power even in their homes, and some are subjected to violence, mostly because of tribal and feudal attitudes toward women. In terms of differences by age, women of all classes gain status and respect as they grow older, which may be different from the Western culture. Women in Pakistan also gain status if they are married and have children, particularly sons.

The social and cultural context of Pakistani society is predominantly patriarchal. Embedded in local traditions and customs, these patriarchal structures are much stronger in the rural and tribal setting, establishing male authority over women's lives. There is a barrier between "private space" (i.e., the home), which is defined as a woman's world, and "public space" (i.e., the rest of the world), which belongs to men. This inside-outside, private-public dichotomy is maintained through the institution of *purdah*, the concept of honor linked to women's sexuality, restrictions on women's mobility, sex segregation, and the internalization of patriarchy by women themselves (ADB 2000). As a consequence, women have lower status than men, as reflected in gender gaps in education, health, labor force participation rates, political participation and power, treatment by law, and property rights. Data on some of these indicators show that considerable gender gaps exist in Pakistan, more so than in some of its

South Asian neighbors, in primary, secondary, and tertiary enrollments, literacy rates, and seats in parliament (Table 4.1). Moreover, despite the religious and legal right to inherit and own property, women hardly own any property. A micro-level survey of 1,000 rural households in 1995 in the Punjab found that only 3.6 percent owned land in their own name, and less than 1 percent (9 out of 1,000) had control over it (ADB 2000, x). Some laws are even discriminatory against women, and violence toward them ranges from domestic to societal, such as honor killings. On the whole, Pakistan ranks 120th in 144 countries in terms of the gender-sensitive development index (GDI) (Table 4.1). It ranks 58th in terms of the gender empowerment measure (GEM) out of 70 countries (compared to 69th rank for Bangladesh and 67th for Sri Lanka). The GDI and GEM are composite indices estimated by the United Nations, the GDI measuring average achievements in health, education, and standard of living, adjusted for gender gaps; and the GEM measuring gender inequality in economic and political participation and decision making. Pakistan's relatively better ranking on GEM is due to the high percentage of seats in the parliament held by women (22 percent compared to 2 percent in Bangladesh, 9 percent in India, 6 percent in Nepal, and 4 percent in Sri Lanka) (Human Development Report 2003, 316).

Pakistani women work extensively in both the rural and urban areas of the country, but their economic activities are unnoticed, disregarded, or invisible. Official statistics such as the decennial population censuses, the annual labor force surveys, and the UN reports (based on country data) severely underreport the female labor force participation rate, which represents the percentage of adult women in the labor force. But the census of agriculture and district-level sample village studies show that 73 percent of adult women are economically active. There are several reasons why the myth of the nonworking Pakistani woman persists, particularly among the middle class; the urbanites; government officials, including

Table 4.1   GDI, GEM, and Gender Gaps in Literacy, Health, and Income

	Bangladesh	India	Nepal	Pakistan	Sri Lanka
Female Share of Non-agricultural Wage Employment (%), 2001	23	17	—	8	47
GDI Rank (out of 144)	112	103	119	120	80
GEM Rank (out of 70 countries)	69	—	—	58	67
Life Expectancy at Birth (years), 2001					
Female	60.9	64	58.9	60.3	75
Male	60.1	62.8	59.4	60.6	69.6
Adult Literacy Rate (% age 15 and above), 2001					
Female	30.8	46.4	25.2	28.8	89.3
Male	49.9	69	60.5	58.2	94.5

Source: United Nations Development Program. 2003. *Human Development Report 2003.* New York: Oxford University Press. Pp. 204, 315–316.

planners and administrators; and even many academicians, despite evidence to the contrary. This perception keeps women out of the purview of institutions that could provide productive resources or support services to them and thereby could enhance their productivity (Mohiuddin 1997, 168).

The most important reason for this misperception is the physical (and psychological) invisibility of women outside the home due to the ideal of female seclusion and the practice of *purdah* (wearing of the veil). Thus, most of the Pakistani towns and cities are "male towns," where the streets, market-places, shops, factories, offices, restaurants, and cinemas are marked by the virtual absence, or scant presence, of women. There are hardly any women petty sellers or vendors and few female buyers because men typically do the shopping for the family. The physical invisibility of women leads to their statistical invisibility. The emphasis on seclusion and physical segregation, or the censure on intermingling of sexes, is so strong that most women and their families prefer that women who do work have jobs that guarantee segregation. Such jobs include those that can be conducted within the privacy of the home or in a sexually segregated environment. Thus, low-skilled and poor rural women work on the family farm mostly as unpaid family helpers or as domestic servants (working in people's home at a time when the master of the house is away at work) in the town or city, or as home-based workers in the city (working at home at tasks such as stitching clothes, making lace, weaving baskets, embroidering and crocheting, and making food products for sale by male relatives or middle-men). On the other hand, high-skilled and richer women may become teachers and doctors (mostly gynecologists) or other professionals. Most of the work at the lower end is not easily visible to the enumerators and data collectors, who are mostly men. Nor can they obtain information directly from the women about their work because of the seclusion ethic. Accordingly, the enumerators rely on indirect information about women's work from male family members, who are likely to underreport it. Moreover, if a woman's "visible" productive work overlaps with her household chores, as it often does, the woman is counted out of the labor force and categorized as a "housewife," even though she makes a significant contribution to productive activities. In addition, questionnaires may be poorly constructed, having been designed by male experts who may not have enough insight into women's issues to be able to extract information from unwilling male proxy respondents and untrained male enumerators.

Women's Work in Rural and Urban Areas

In reality, women are major contributors to the economy of the country in the rural and the urban (both informal and formal) sectors. In rural areas, women participate extensively in crop production activities, such as sowing, weeding, harvesting, threshing, crop processing, and storage; more in the later

Village women with pitchers on their heads walk through the desert in search of water in Cholistan, eastern Pakistan, during the deadly drought of May 2000. (Reuters/Corbis)

phases in the crop production cycle; as well as in livestock activities, such as maintaining animals, cutting fodder in the fields for animal feed, cleaning animal sheds, collecting manure for use as fuel or fertilizer, milking cows, and selling milk. Rural women are also engaged in crafts like embroidery, tailoring, crocheting, flower making (silk and glass), carpet weaving, mat making, basketry, handloom production, miscellaneous handicrafts (doll making, jewelry, papier-mâché, etc.), leather work, pottery, and ceramics, as well as construction, fisheries, and food processing. In addition, women are almost totally responsible for such time-consuming tasks as fetching water and fuel and collecting fodder, which are not counted as agricultural work. On the whole, rural women in Pakistan work long hours at tasks that are physically demanding and sometimes dirty (e.g., cleaning the cowshed, making cow dung cakes) (Mohiuddin 1988, 14–17).

In the urban areas, women are engaged in either informal or formal work. Formal work includes industrial occupations (factory work) and service occupations (government jobs or the professional category). Women's work in formal jobs is counted in the official labor force statistics, such as labor force surveys, population censuses, and other government documents. Informal work is carried out at a large number of individually or family-owned small-scale production and service activities that use indigenous inputs, labor, and simple technology. These workers are self-employed and do not enjoy job security, decent working conditions, minimum wage laws, and old-age pensions. Worker productivity and income tend to be lower in this work. Examples are home-based workers, hawkers, street vendors, mechanics, carpenters, small artisans, handicraft workers, potters, and barbers. At the same time, the informal work provides flexibility to workers in terms of time and location of work since some of this work can be done at home. While it is not socially acceptable for Pakistani women to do all types of informal work, activities where sex seclusion can be ensured are acceptable, such as home-based work, work in homes of others (such as domestics), or in-home businesses and occupations. Accordingly, there has been an increasing influx of women into these activities of the urban informal labor market.

Domestic service has recently emerged as the single largest source of employment for poor women in Pakistan's urban informal areas, especially in Karachi (Mohiuddin 1992, 64). Female domestics, popularly known as *masees* (meaning aunts), typically work in three or four houses part-time on a regular basis at one or more of the following chores: washing dishes, washing clothes, cleaning and sweeping, and cooking. Their low wages have made it possible for most middle-income households to afford *masees,* at least for the most arduous tasks. The recent surge in demand for female domestic servants has been brought about in part by increasing amounts of home remittances sent by middle-class Pakistanis

Women work at sewing machines in a family garment business in Faisalabad, established with a loan from the local nongovernmental organization (NGO). (Caroline Penn/Corbis)

working in the Gulf States and in Western European countries, and in part by a rise in the labor force participation and in college enrollment for middle-class females in Karachi. At the same time, the number of *masees* has increased significantly as a result of the migration of thousands of poor families from Bangladesh in the 1970s as well as rural-to-urban migration from within the country.

At an intermediate level between formal and informal work, or between factory and home-based work, in terms of income is "workshop production" or "subcontracting." Subcontracting is fairly common in the garment industry in Pakistan. The growth of garment workshops in large cities in Pakistan has been quite phenomenal during the last few years. Drawing in poor and lower-middle-class women workers of all ages, these small workshops segregate jobs by gender, with women concentrated in low-skilled, low-paying jobs. Thus, operators are usually women, whereas supervisors, cutters, and master tailors are mostly men. Women carry out the manual work of embroidery, thread cutting, and button stitching. There are even some workshops that will hire men only. Generally speaking, women's wages are lower than those of men, whether in the same workshop for different functions or for the same function in a different workshop.

Although a majority of women in Pakistan do work, very few are regularly employed in formal jobs. The seclusion ethic dictates that educated middle-class women should be employed as professionals (in private or government service as doctors or teachers, for example) and uneducated poorer women as factory workers. In both work environments, segregation is maintained. For example, for female professionals, there are all-female schools, colleges, bank branches, and wards in hospitals. For factory workers, such an environment is created by confining women to particular departments or activities, which then become all female. Packing, sorting, and spinning are examples of such all-female activities within the relevant industries. Within the formal sector, women are

Pilot Ayesha Rabia Naveed (left) and copilot Sadia Aziz in the cockpit of a passenger plane in January 2006. This Pakistan International Airlines flight was the first where both the pilot and copilot were women. (AP Photo/Pakistan International Airlines)

concentrated in a few industries and occupational groups. Within the industrial sector, the tendency is to relegate women to temporary, casual, or contract work and to the least-skilled, lowest-paid, and most casual jobs. In addition to textiles, women are employed in food processing as well as in dairy, bakery, and poultry production. In all these industries, women are concentrated in packing and sorting, which is an almost entirely female activity.

In urban areas, about a third of all employed women are included in the occupational category of "professional and technical workers," where they work primarily in the government sector (such as in nationalized banks, the media, and health and education services), but also in the private sector. Women are actually overrepresented in the professions. If we measure the representation of women in the professions vis-à-vis their representation in the labor force, the index is about 3, meaning that women's share in the professional labor force is three times their share in the total labor force. This might appear strange at first, but on closer examination we find that the high demand for professional women does not violate the rules of seclusion, but indeed is a necessary result of those rules. More specifically, there is a demand for professional women because the seclusion ethic requires that girls be educated by female teachers in special schools for women and that women be taken care of by female health personnel and female social workers. Thus, there are only female teachers and administrators in all-girl schools and colleges, and about 98 percent of gynecologists are women. In a way, women professionals benefit from the seclusion ethic in terms of job opportunities and upward mobility in all-female institutions (such as schools, colleges, bank branches, and hospital departments), which are fairly widespread in Pakistan. Similarly, there is no wage discrimination in the case of professionals. This may be due, in part, to the high demand for them, the importance of the government as an employer (with published uniform pay scales and grade levels similar to a Civil Service wage matrix), and the low overall female participation rates, even in the formal sector.

Pay Equity and Occupational Segregation

The existence of equal pay for equal work in Pakistan, particularly in the government sector and for professional and technical workers, needs further elaboration. It may, at first, seem strange to find equal pay in a male-dominated society when such pay equity does not exist in most Western industrialized societies. The reason for this wage equality is that the government has published uniform pay scales and grade levels in the form of a Civil Service wage matrix. This wage scheme even influences the private sector, particularly for professional and technical workers, because of the relatively large size of the government sector, which includes almost all educational institutions, health organizations, banks, transport and communications networks, and others. In the government sector, the pay scales establish a benchmark for wages in the private sector. Although in the government sector women are overrepresented in the lower grades and underrepresented in the higher grades, they all receive the same pay as men within the same grade.

Women are secluded by the *purdah* system (visible or invisible), and even nonsecluded women are greatly affected in their decision making, and especially in the choice of occupation, by the general attitude in favor of seclusion. In my research on women's employment, I have argued that the underlying reason for sex segregation in general, and occupational segregation by gender in particular, is religion in the sense that Islam discourages the intermingling of sexes, though not employment per se. Accordingly, occupations that guarantee segregation (such as agricultural work within the home compound, home-based work, and domestic service) are considered respectable for poorer women, and jobs in all-female schools, colleges, dispensaries, bank branches, and departments in private organizations (such as computer departments in banks) are deemed desirable for the more affluent. Conversely, occupations in which contact with male strangers cannot be avoided are usually associated with promiscuity, loss of respect, and diminished marriage prospects for single girls. Thus, in clerical and sales occupations where women cannot avoid male contact, the number of female workers as a percentage of males in 1990 was only 5 to 13 percent in the Muslim countries of Africa and Asia and 3 percent in Pakistan. Contrast this with the figures of 107 to 335 percent in industrialized countries: 201 percent in the United States, 70 to 90 percent in Latin America, 65 percent in East Asia, and 100 to 150 percent in sub-Saharan Africa (United Nations Development Program 1995, 57–59). In fact, the most common feature of women's employment pattern in the Muslim countries of Africa, Asia, and the Middle East is the low percentage of women in sales, trade, and commerce. The association of respectability with seclusion possibilities thus explains the choice of occupations by Pakistani females.

EDUCATION

Education affects all types of human development outcomes. It is more than just a source of knowledge. It promotes better hygiene and increases the use of health services, gradually contributing to a healthier population as death rates decline. As more children survive, families have fewer children. Lower infant and child mortality reduces fertility rates. Educating women is particularly important for any society because of the synergies among investment in women's education, children's welfare, and reductions in fertility and poverty. Educated girls and women have fewer children, seek medical attention sooner for themselves and their children, and provide better care and nutrition for their children. This reduces disease and increases the chance of children surviving past age five. Educated women also bring more income into the family and are more likely to spend it on the family compared to men. The benefits of girls' education accrue from generation to generation. Moreover, tolerance of diverse viewpoints, respect for human rights and dignity, appreciation of cultural diversity, and the fostering of civic responsibilities all come with good education.

Pakistan's system of education is patterned largely on the British system, with formal education beginning at age five with five years of primary education, followed by five years of secondary education. Students take the matriculation exam (popularly called matric) in the tenth grade at age fifteen. Those who pass the exam enter the higher secondary level, known as intermediate at four-year colleges, and take the Higher Secondary Certificate (HSC) exam after two years of study. Another two years of study are needed for the bachelor's degree from the college, which precedes a graduate degree (master's) at the university level. Unlike the United States where universities offer both undergraduate and graduate classes, universities in Pakistan are typically confined to graduate studies at the master's and Ph.D. levels. Professional degrees such as those in medicine and engineering require five and four years of study in medical and engineering colleges, respectively. Vocational institutions offer technical and nontechnical certificates in a variety of fields.

There are several different types of schools, colleges, and universities in Pakistan, depending on the source of funding: government or public, private, church (known as convents or missionary schools), and the army. First, there are government/public elementary schools in most villages and urban neighborhoods that are free of cost, but they are crowded and often have poor facilities. But many villages do not have middle schools. The government runs some secondary schools and colleges, which are not free but heavily subsidized, as are public universities. In most public secondary schools, all courses in the curriculum, such as mathematics, natural sciences, social studies (history, geography, civics), and Islamic studies, are taught in Urdu, although English is taught as a language. The declining proficiency in English and of the overall standard of public education has created a huge demand for, and investment in, private schooling at all levels, from the elementary to the university level. The medium of instruction for all courses in these institutions has always been English. The tuition and fees at these schools are twenty to thirty times higher than those at public schools. Then, there are the schools that were traditionally known for quality—the missionary schools, at both the secondary and collegiate levels. They were often managed and operated by Christian nuns, before they were nationalized in the 1970s (and denationalized to some extent later). They also used English as the medium of instruction. Moreover, the army runs cantonment schools for the children of its officers throughout

Pakistani schoolboy in a rural village in Hunza reads aloud to his classmates. (Jonathan Blair/Corbis)

Pakistan, which are often the best schools in rural areas. They are also subsidized. Finally, there are religious schools, or mosque schools or *madrasas,* where traditionally students are instructed in the Quran (and often encouraged to memorize it), some Arabic language, and Islamic studies. In the 1980s, under Ziaul Haq, a large number of *madrasas* opened as thousands of mosques were encouraged to function as elementary schools.

As Table 4.2 shows, there are about 151,000 primary schools, 16,000 high schools, 1,346 colleges, and 95 universities in Pakistan (53 public and 42 private). The enrollments are about 18 million at the primary level, 1.6 million at the secondary level, and 966,000 at the college level. Among the literate population, about 12 million have a primary-level education, about 7 million have passed high school, about 1.7 million have college degrees, and only 619,000 have university-level education. Women constitute 33 percent of college

Table 4.2   Number of Schools, Enrollments, and Literate Population by Level of Education, 2002–2003

	Total Number	Total Enrollments	% Female	Literate Population	% Female	Teachers	% Female
Schools							
Primary Schools	150,809	18,220,000	41.3	11,781,000	38	434,000	44
Middle Schools	28,021	3,918,000	39.6	8,168,000	31	236,000	62
High Schools	15,623	1,589,000	41.4	6,759,000	31	278,000	47
Secondary & Vocational Institutions	451	69,000	15	—	—	—	—
Teacher Training Institutions	92	16,000	48	—	—	—	—
Colleges	—	—	—	1,712,000	33	—	—
Arts and Science	964	802,000	49	—	—	—	—
Professional (Medicine, Law& Engineering)	96	49,000	27	—	—	—	—
Others (Commerce, Education, etc.)	286	115,000	24	—	—	—	—
Universities	95	—	—	619,000	26	—	—

— *Not available*

Source: Government of Pakistan, Ministry of Economic Affairs and Statistics, Statistics Division. *Statistical Yearbooks 2004 and 2005, and 1998 Population Census.* http://www.statpak.gov.pk/depts/fbs/statistics/social_statistics/datasheet_student_per_teacher.pdf.

and 26 percent of university graduates. They also make up 27 percent of students enrolled in professional colleges (varying from 55 percent in medical to 2 percent in engineering colleges). While public schools are segregated by sex from the fourth grade onward, at the secondary level, some schools are coeducational and others are exclusively for female students. The same is true at the college level. Moreover, there is at least one medical college exclusively for women. But all universities are coeducational.

Pakistan's economic growth has been quite impressive in recent decades, at more than 6 percent per annum from the 1950s (and as high as 8.5 percent in 2005). Reductions in poverty have also been impressive, from 33 to 18 percent. But Pakistan's educational performance during its more than fifty-year history has been dismal, in terms of both quantity and quality. Countries with the same per capita income and even those that were less advanced have surpassed Pakistan because they invested in education in the right way. There are several challenges in the education sector: high levels of illiteracy; low enrollment ratios at the primary, secondary, and tertiary (higher education) levels; high dropout rates; wide gender gaps; rural-urban differences in these enrollment rates and other education outcomes; deteriorating quality; and high level of waste and inefficiency in the system. The gap between Pakistan and other developing countries has been widening on many counts at an accelerating rate. By all criteria, Pakistan's educational system is at the bottom of the international ladder. The fact that Pakistan has managed to obtain such high growth rates in spite of such a fragile educational base is considered one of the central paradoxes of the Pakistani economy.

Pakistan's adult illiteracy has historically been high, both in absolute terms and in comparison to other countries (Table 4.3). Currently, the rate is 56 percent, which means that about six out of ten people—seven out of ten women and four out of ten men—are illiterate. Moreover, the illiteracy rate in rural areas is as high as 66 percent. There are regional variations too, with the highest level of illiteracy in NWFP and Balochistan. Moreover, Pakistan's primary enrollment ratio, showing primary school–age children who are enrolled in school, is among the 20 lowest in the world out of 175 countries. At 66 percent, it is not only below that of Sri Lanka and Bangladesh, but also below the average for developing countries (82 percent) and for South Asia (79 percent). The female primary enrollment ratio (PER) is even lower, being 56 percent at the national level and less than 10 percent in Balochistan and Sindh. Although the gender gap in enrollments has decreased somewhat over time, the rural-urban disparity in

PER widened during the 1990s, partly due to decades of neglect of the education sector by successive governments. The low gross enrollment rates are accompanied by relatively high dropout rates of about 15 percent. Only about half of those who enroll in school stay on until the fourth grade in Pakistan, in comparison with an average of about two-thirds for all low-income countries. Dropout rates, in grades 1 through 3, are higher for girls—only 3 percent of rural girls are in school by the age of 12 (compared to 18 percent of boys) and less than 1 percent are in school by the age of 14. The reasons for low enrollments and high dropout rates are primarily on the supply side—not enough school buildings and shortages of teachers, particularly female teachers. Many poor parents in Pakistan are reluctant to send their daughters to school, not only because of the direct costs in terms of fees, uniforms, and books and the indirect costs in terms of losing their help in household chores, but also because of safety issues and the absence of female teachers. It has been observed that if the right type of school is available (sex-segregated), where some teachers are female, which is within relatively close and safe walking distance from home, and which has sanitation facilities with some privacy, parents are more than willing to send their daughters to school.

Table 4.3   Education Indicators, 2001

	Adult Literacy Rate (%)	Primary Enrollment Ratio (%)	Combined Enrollment Ratio (%)
Bangladesh	40.6	89	54
India	56.5	77	56
Nepal	42.9	72	64
Pakistan	44.0	66	36
Sri Lanka	91.9	97	63

Source: United Nations Development Program. 2003. *Human Development Report 2003.* New York: Oxford University Press. Pp. 238–239 for columns 1 and 3; pp. 271–272 for column 2.

The combined primary, secondary, and tertiary enrollment ratio is 36 for Pakistan, the lowest in South Asia, and 20 percentage points below India and 18 below Bangladesh (Table 4.3). Historically, Pakistan has placed greater emphasis on tertiary education than on basic primary and secondary education, and public educational expenditure has been concentrated at the tertiary level. The gaps between the social and private rates of return are highest at the university and college level because of high subsidies at that level. Thus, a disproportionately higher percentage of the limited educational expenditures has been allocated to tertiary education. On the whole, the education sector has been underfinanced for years. The expenditure on education since independence has been 1 to 2 percent of GNP, lagging behind most developing countries, which spend 3 to 4 percent of their GNP on education. Budgetary shortfalls, large military expenditures, and huge fiscal deficits account for this meager allocation of resources to education. Similarly, educational expenditures as a percentage of all government expenditures are only about 8 percent, the lowest in South Asia. At all levels of education, there is a scarcity of qualified teachers, good textbooks, research facilities, and scientific equipment. As a consequence, the richest and the brightest students leave Pakistan to study in Great Britain and the United States, many among them never returning home, causing "brain drain" from Pakistan. Furthermore, many universities, particularly in Sindh, became very politicized in the 1990s, embracing the culture of violence. In view of the growing criticism of Pakistan's educational policy and its inadequate attempts to boost literacy, the Social Action Plan (SAP) under the World Bank and a whole new policy package under Pakistan's Eighth Five-Year Plan (1993–1998) were designed to improve educational performance, with particular emphasis on female literacy in rural areas and training of teachers. But the SAP did not attain most of its objectives, owing to problems in governance and leakage and waste of funds.

But there is hope as never before. Over the past fifty years, most developing countries achieved advances in education and health that took nearly 200 years in the developed countries (World Development Report 2005). Sri Lanka added twelve years to life expectancy at birth in just seven years from 1945 to 1952. China added thirteen years to life expectancy from 1953 to 1962. Between 1960 and 1980, Botswana more than doubled its gross primary enrollment ratio (GPER), from 41 to 91 percent. And in Zimbabwe the GPER rose from 75 percent in 1960 to 124 percent in 1985. The state of Kerala in India has health indicators similar to those of the United States despite a per capita income that is 99 percent lower and an annual spending of just $28 a person. Cuba's per capita income is only a small fraction of that of the United States, yet it has the same infant mortality rate. More recently, the literacy rates and school enrollments in Pakistan have shown a significant improvement, and there is increasing hope that a reduction in corruption and an improvement in governance that have been occurring recently will go a long way toward solving the country's educational problems, provided they are combined with sound and innovative educational policy. Such a policy should be outcome- and people-oriented, based on decentralization and improved implementation, and should improve access for the underprivileged groups and regions while at the same time rewarding merit and meeting the emerging challenges of globalization.

References and Further Reading

Alavi, Hamza. 2002. "Misreading Partition Road Signs." *Economic and Political Weekly,* November 2–9.

Asian Development Bank. 2000. "Women in Pakistan." Country Briefing Paper.

Blood, Peter R. (ed.). 1995. *Pakistan: A Country Study* (Area Handbook Series). Washington, DC: Library of Congress.

Economic Indicators Pakistan. 2003. Islamabad, Pakistan: Federal Bureau of Statistics (FBS), Government of Pakistan.

Human Development Report 2003. 2003. New York: Oxford University Press.

Hussain, Ishrat. 1999. *Pakistan: The Economy of an Elitist State.* Karachi, Pakistan: Oxford University Press.

Jones, Owen Bennett. 2002. *Pakistan: Eye of the Storm*. New Haven, CT: Yale University Press.

Kibria, Ghulam. 1999. *A Shattered Dream: Understanding Pakistan's Underdevelopment*. Karachi, Pakistan: Oxford University Press.

Mohiuddin, Yasmeen. 1988. "Women and Agricultural Credit." Report, Identification Mission, Pakistan Agriculture Credit VII Project, Agriculture Operations Division of the Europe, Middle East and North Africa Region Country Department 1 (EM1AG), The World Bank.

———. 1992. "Female-headed Households and Urban Poverty in Pakistan," in Nancy Folbre, Barbara Bergmann et al. (eds.), *Issues in Contemporary Economics*, Vol. 4: *Women's Work in the World Economy*. Hong Kong: Macmillan, pp. 61–81.

———. 1995. "Country Rankings of Women's Status: An Alternative Index." *Pakistan Development Review* 34(4), 1025-1039.

———. 1997. "Gender Inequality in the Pakistan Labor Market: Myth and Reality," in J. Rives and M. Yousefi (eds.), *Economic Dimensions of Gender Inequality: A Global Perspective*. Westport, CT: Praeger, pp. 167–184.

Mumtaz, Khawar, and Yameema Mitha. 2003. *Pakistan: Tradition and Change*. An Oxfam Country Profile. London: Oxfam.

The News. 2003. http://lists.isb.sdnpk.org/pipermail/gsd-list/2003-October/001261.html.

Pakistan Census of Agriculture. 1998. Lahore, Pakistan: Agriculture Census Organization, Gove.nment of Pakistan.

Statistical Pocketbook: Pakistan. 2003. Islamabad, Pakistan: Federal Bureau of Statistics (FBS), Government of Pakistan. http://www.statpak.gov.pk/.

Statistical Yearbook Pakistan. 2005. Islamabad, Pakistan: Federal Bureau of Statistics (FBS), Government of Pakistan. http://www.statpak.gov.pk/depts/fbs/statistics/social_statistics/datasheet_student_per_teacher.pdf.

Weaver, Mary Anne. 2002. *Pakistan: In the Shadow of Jihad and Afghanistan*. New York: Farrar, Straus and Giroux.

Weston, Mark. 1992. *The Land and People of Pakistan*. New York: HarperCollins.

World Development Report 2005. 2004. Washington, DC: The World Bank.

PART TWO
REFERENCE SECTION

Key Events in Pakistani History

Early Civilizations and Ancient Empires
The period includes early civilizations and ancient empires and continues up to the Mughal period.

4000–1500 BCE	The Indus Valley civilization flourishes and then declines.
1500–500 BCE	Aryans from Central Asia conquer the Indus region and introduce their Vedic religion.
327 BCE	Alexander the Great reaches the Punjab and defeats King Porus.
321 BCE–319 CE	Mauryan, Kushan, and Gupta empires; the golden age of Sanskrit learning and literature and Hindu culture; spread of Buddhism.
711 CE	Muhammad bin Qasim, an Arab general, conquers Sindh and incorporates it into the Umayyad Caliphate.
1021	Mahmud of Ghazni from Afghanistan conquers the Punjab and makes Lahore its capital.
1206	Qutb-ud-din Aibak becomes the first ruler of the Sultanate of Delhi. A *lingua franca* evolves through the interaction of different languages spoken by the Sultanate's soldiers, which will later develop into the Urdu language in the fourteenth century.

The Mughal Period (1526–1858)
The Mughal period begins with the foundation laid by Babur.

1526	Babur, a descendant of Timur from Central Asia, defeats the Lodhi Sultan in the first battle of Panipat and lays the foundation of the Mughal Empire.
1556–1605	Reign of Akbar the Great, bringing prosperity and reforms, and uniting South Asia.
1605–1627	Reign of Jahangir. East India Company opens first trading post (factory) in 1612.
1628–1658	Reign of Shah Jahan, builder of the Taj Mahal.
1658–1707	Reign of Aurangzeb, last of the great Mughal rulers.
1739	Persia's Nadir Shah invades Delhi, marking the decline of Mughal power.

The British Period (1757–1947)

The period begins when the British establish a foothold with their victory over the forces of the Nawab of Bengal at the battle of Plassey. British colonialism continues until independence of India in 1947.

| 1757 | Battle of Plassey and British victory over Mughal forces in Bengal; conventional date for beginning of British rule in India. |
| 1857–1858 | Uprising, called the First War of Independence by the Indians (often referred to as Indian Mutiny or Sepoy Rebellion by the British). The East India Company is dissolved and rule of India under British crown begins, marking formal end of Mughal Empire. Large-scale massacres, executions, and destruction by the British. Emperor Bahadur Shah II exiled to Burma. |

1906	All-India Muslim League founded.
1909	Morley-Minto Reforms establish separate electorates for Muslims.
1916	Jinnah's Lucknow Pact creates a brief Hindu-Muslim unity.
1920	Gandhi becomes the leading force in the Congress Party.
1928	The Congress Party opposes separate elections for Muslims.
1930	Allama Muhammad Iqbal, the poet-philosopher, advocates a separate Muslim state. In 1933, Chaudhry Rahmat Ali coins the name "Pakistan."
1937–1939	Congress Party governments alienate the Muslims.
1940	The Muslim League passes the historic Pakistan Resolution in Lahore.
1946	The Muslim League sweeps in the elections, winning 90 percent of the legislative seats reserved for Muslims.
1947	Legislation is introduced in the British Parliament in June calling for the independence and partition of India. Communal rioting and mass movements of population begin following the announcement of arbitrary boundaries between India and Pakistan and the disorganized transfer of power by the British. In the next few months this results in 250,000 to 1 million deaths and 11 to 17.5 million refugees. (About 8 million Muslims leave their home in India for Pakistan, and about 6 million Hindus and Sikhs leave their home in Pakistan for India.)

Independent Pakistan (1947–2006)
With the dawn of independence, a new era begins in
Pakistan.

1947   With the partition of British India, Pakistan
                is created on August 14, 1947, out of terri-
                tory on the eastern and western flanks of
                India. East Pakistan incorporates East
                Bengal, and West Pakistan incorporates the
                northwestern provinces. Quaid-e-Azam
                (Great Leader) Muhammad Ali Jinnah
                becomes the governor general of Pakistan;
                Liaquat Ali Khan becomes prime minister.
                First Indo-Pakistan war over sovereignty of
                Kashmir, leading in October 1951 to a divi-
                sion of Kashmir, based on a UN-arranged
                cease-fire in 1949 between India and
                Pakistan.

1948   Jinnah dies in September; Khwaja
                Nazimuddin becomes governor general. In
                January, Mohandas Gandhi is assassinated
                by a Hindu fanatic. Prime Minister Liaquat
                Ali Khan and Indian prime minister
                Jawaharlal Nehru sign pact to protect
                minorities in both countries. Pakistan allies
                itself with the West, while India allies with
                the Soviet bloc. Since then, Pakistan has
                remained a loyal ally of the United States.

1951   Assassination of Prime Minister Liaquat Ali
                Khan at a rally in Rawalpindi begins an era
                of political corruption and chaos.
                Controversy surrounds murder. Suspicion
                remains that it was plotted by factions
                within the government. Nazimuddin
                becomes prime minister, but real power lies
                with bureaucrats. Nazimuddin's undemocrat-
                ic dismissal by Governor General Ghulam

Mohammad in 1953 exposes the facade of parliamentary democracy.

1954   Constituent Assembly declares Urdu and Bengali the official languages of Pakistan following the 1952 language riots in East Pakistan, which were in protest of central government attempts to impose Urdu as the only official language. Pakistan signs mutual defense agreement with the United States.

1955   The four provinces of West Pakistan are merged into One Unit, a scheme to achieve parity vis-à-vis East Pakistan, provoking considerable resentment in East Pakistan as well as among the smaller provinces of West Pakistan.

1956   The Constituent Assembly adopts the first constitution on March 23, 1956, after a delay of nine years; outlines a framework for a parliamentary democracy; and the country is officially named the Islamic Republic of Pakistan.

1958   Governor General Iskander Mirza abrogates the constitution and enforces martial law with General Ayub Khan as chief martial law administrator. Shortly thereafter, Mirza is sent into exile; General Ayub Khan becomes president. The coup d'état is followed by the dissolution of the National Assembly. Parliamentary elections, scheduled for early 1959, are canceled, and political parties are banned.

1959   System of Basic Democracies established to provide a safe electoral college for the president. The Ayub government announces the Family Laws Ordinance in 1961 restricting polygamy.

1965   Brief seventeen-day war with India over the disputed Kashmir territory.

1966   East Pakistan's major political party, Awami League, puts forward a six-point platform, which proposes a confederation of the two regions. Mujibur Rahman, leader of the Awami League, is subsequently charged with treason.

1969   Demonstrations and strikes fueled by growing class conflict and regional tensions force Ayub Khan to resign; General Yahya Khan imposes martial law, dissolves national and provincial assemblies, becomes president, and promises elections on March 26.

1970   Yahya honors his pledge to hold free elections on December 7 to form a parliamentary government, the first general elections since independence. The Awami League, led by Mujibur Rahman, secures an absolute majority in the new National Assembly with 160 seats, all in East Pakistan. The Pakistan Peoples Party (PPP), led by Z. A. Bhutto, emerges as the dominant political force in West Pakistan but does not secure any seat in East Pakistan.

1971   The West Pakistan–dominated central government postpones convening the National Assembly, and the army refuses to transfer power to the Awami League, fearing implementation of the six-point program. In late March, the army launches a massive military offensive against the Bengalis, causing millions to flee to India. Mujibur Rahman is arrested and sent to prison in West Pakistan. East Pakistan attempts to secede, beginning a civil war. On April 17, East Pakistan for-

mally declares its independence as the
nation of Bangladesh, and a government-in-
exile is formed in India at Calcutta. India
invades East Pakistan. On December 16, the
India-Pakistan war ends with the surrender
of 90,000 Pakistani troops and the creation
of Bangladesh. Yahya resigns and hands
power in the truncated Pakistan to Zulfiqar
Ali Bhutto, who becomes chief martial law
administrator of West Pakistan.

1972   Martial law is lifted, an interim constitution
is enforced, and Bhutto becomes prime minister. The PPP government nationalizes large
industries. Land reforms are announced.
Through the good offices of Pakistan, con-
tacts are established between the United
States and China. Pakistan arranges Henry
Kissinger's groundbreaking visit to China
through Pakistan.

1973   Parliament approves new constitution, the
third since independence but the first to
have the support of all political parties.
Ethnic divisions continue to plague
Pakistan. The Balochistan provincial government is dismissed, and the provincial government in the North-West Frontier
Province (NWFP) resigns in protest. Bhutto
negotiates successfully with India for the
release of Pakistani prisoners of war held
since December 1971.

1974   Islamic Summit of Muslim heads of state is
held at Lahore, symbolizing Pakistan's closer
association with the Muslim world.

1977   PPP government rigs parliamentary elections. Taking advantage of widespread rioting and protest, General Ziaul Haq over-

throws Zulfiqar Ali Bhutto in a military coup. Zia arrests Bhutto, declares martial law, and promises fresh elections within ninety days of the coup. Bhutto is charged with murder of a political opponent.

1978   Ziaul Haq becomes nation's sixth president, replacing Fazal Elahi Chaudhry. Zia proceeds with his version of Islamization of the economy and society, and introduces his idea of an Islamic penal code.

1979   Zulfiqar Ali Bhutto is executed on April 4 on disputed conviction for conspiring to commit a political murder. Political parties are banned, and political activity is declared a punishable offense. The Soviet Union invades Afghanistan in November. About 5 million Afghan refugees enter Pakistan, creating great economic problems for Pakistan. U.S. president Jimmy Carter offers US$400 million military assistance to help Pakistan defend itself against Soviet threat, an offer rejected by Zia as "peanuts." In 1981, the United States begins massive military and economic aid to Pakistan. American support for Zia's government breaks the regime's isolation, which grew out of revulsion at Bhutto's hanging. For the next ten years, Pakistan bears the brunt of the confrontation with the USSR as a proxy for the West and endures great suffering in the process.

1985   Zia holds nonparty elections in February to provide civilian buffer for military rule. He names Mohammad Khan Junejo as prime minister and declares himself "elected" as president after referendum on Islamization. In July, Movement for the Restoration of

Democracy (MRD) launches campaign against the government, demanding new general elections. Benazir Bhutto is arrested in Karachi. Martial law is lifted in December.

1986–1987   Pakistan acquires the capability to build nuclear weapons.

1988   Junejo is dismissed and parliament is dissolved. The civilian facade crumbles. In August, Ziaul Haq, the U.S. ambassador to Pakistan, along with top army officials, is killed in a mysterious airplane crash near Bahawalpur in Punjab; sabotage is suspected. In November, Benazir Bhutto and her Pakistan Peoples Party win 39 percent of the vote in the general elections. In December, Benazir Bhutto is sworn in as the first female prime minister of a Muslim nation, and Ishaq Khan, chairman of the Senate, is sworn in as acting president. General Aslam Beg becomes chief of the army staff. PPP and MQM parties sign "Karachi Declaration," an accord to restore peace in Sindh; Pakistan and India sign accords at a summit in Islamabad, including agreement not to attack each other's nuclear facilities.

1989   The Soviet Union completes withdrawal of its troops from Afghanistan due to heavy losses inflicted by Pakistan Army and Afghan Mujahideen. The international community, including the United States, abandons war-devastated Afghanistan. Pakistan is left with the burden of millions of Afghan refugees, political chaos in Afghanistan, and a dangerous gun and drug culture at home.

1990   President Ishaq Khan accuses Bhutto's government of corruption and removes her from office in November; Ghulam Mustafa Jatoi becomes the caretaker prime minister until general elections in October; Nawaz Sharif is elected prime minister.

1991   Prime Minister Sharif liberalizes the economy, lifts controls on foreign currency, and announces pro-investment policies. Sharif faces widespread public opposition to his support for the Gulf War. Shariat Bill is adopted by the National Assembly.

1993   President Ishaq Khan dismisses government of Prime Minister Sharif in June, citing corruption. World Bank senior vice-president, Moeen Qureshi, is named caretaker prime minister pending elections in October. Wassim Sajjad becomes acting president. India rejects Pakistan's proposal to sign regional nuclear test ban treaty. In October, Bhutto's PPP wins slim margin in national elections and builds coalition government; Bhutto is appointed prime minister for the second time. In November, Farooq Leghari, a Bhutto nominee, is elected president.

1994   Peace talks with India break down over Kashmir. Terrorist attack on streets of Karachi in August kills two American employees of United States consulate and draws international attention to mounting law-and-order problems in Pakistan.

1996   In November, President Leghari accuses Bhutto's government of corruption, removes Bhutto from office, dissolves parliament, and calls elections for February 3.

1997   Pakistan Muslim League wins general elections by landslide margin, and Sharif becomes prime minister for second time. In December, President Leghari resigns after a six-month legal battle to have Sharif investigated for misuse of power during his first premiership. Mohammad Rafiq Tarar becomes president.

1998   On May 11 and 13, India explodes five nuclear devices under the desert at Pokhran in Rajasthan. In response, Pakistan detonates two nuclear devices on May 28 under the Chagai Mountains in Balochistan.

1999   Former prime minister Benazir Bhutto and her husband, Asif Zardari, are sentenced on April 15, in absentia, to five-year jail terms on charges of corruption. Border skirmishes erupt between Pakistan and India in June over infiltrators who seized hilltop positions on the Indian side of the line of control. In July, Pakistan orders the infiltrators to withdraw from Kashmir, ending the standoff with India. In October, Sharif dismisses the chief of army staff, General Pervez Musharraf, and gives orders that the airplane on which Musharraf is returning from an official visit to Sri Lanka not be allowed to land at Karachi, even though it is short of fuel and might crash. Senior army officers stage a coup while the general is still in the air and seize control. Sharif is removed from office on October 12, and Musharraf becomes the country's chief executive. Parliament and state assemblies are dissolved. Tarar remains the chief of state.

2000   The Supreme Court unanimously validates the coup on May 12 and grants Musharraf authority until October 2002, which is the

	deadline set for a general election. Local government elections are also held.
2001	Musharraf formally becomes president of Pakistan on June 20. Following the September 11, 2001, attacks on the United States, Musharraf helps the United States in its fight against global terrorism by cutting the oil and supply lines of the Taliban and providing intelligence and logistics support for Operation Enduring Freedom. Musharraf declines to send troops to Iraq without a UN resolution.
2002	In elections ordered by the Supreme Court for the national and provincial legislatures, which take place in October, Pakistan Muslim League (Qayyum Group, a pro-Musharraf party) wins a plurality of the seats in the National Assembly.
2003	Musharraf strikes a compromise with the opposition, the Muttahida Majlis-e-Amal, and promises to leave the army on December 31, 2004. Constitution amended (Seventeenth Amendment) in December, retroactively legalizing Musharraf's 1999 coup and permitting him to remain president if he meets the agreed conditions. Mir Zafarullah Khan Jamali of the Pakistan Muslim League is elected prime minister.
2004	In a vote of confidence on January 1, Musharraf wins a 56 percent majority in the electoral college of Pakistan, consisting of both houses of parliament and the four provincial assemblies. According to Article 41(8) of the constitution, he is "deemed to be elected" to the office of president until October 2007. Results of the referendum are

widely accepted both inside and outside
Pakistan. Prime Minister Jamali resigns on
June 26, and Shaukat Aziz is elected prime
minister in August. In September, Musharraf
retracts his commitment to step down as
army chief, citing circumstances of national
necessity.

2005 Musharraf remains president and head of
state. In May, he bars Benazir Bhutto and
Nawaz Sharif from participating in the 2007
general elections. It is announced that
Musharraf will seek another five-year term
as head of state after his current tenure
ends in 2007. On October 8 Pakistan is
struck by the most calamitous earthquake in
its history, with a magnitude of 7.6 on the
Richter scale. The earthquake affects the
Northern Areas of Pakistan, causing life and
property damage at an unprecedented level.
As of November 8, the government's official
death toll is 87,350. Some estimate that the
death toll could reach over 100,000. Millions
are rendered homeless.

2006 President Bush visits India and Pakistan in
March. The different "deals" struck with the
two countries are widely perceived in
Pakistan as evidence of America's reduced
support for Musharraf and Pakistan, even
though Musharraf has conceded so much to
the Americans. A general concern arises
that U.S. interest in Pakistan may be short-
lived, repeating the history of U.S. withdrawal of support to Pakistan after the
defeat of the Soviets in Afghanistan with
Pakistan's help, giving the religious parties
ammunition against Musharraf.

Significant People, Places, and Events

Afghan Refugee Emergency. The Afghan refugee situation represents one of the world's largest and most prolonged refugee emergencies. Currently, about 2.5 million Afghan refugees are living in Pakistan. There have been at least four major waves of refugees pouring in from Afghanistan into Pakistan. The first large refugee exodus occurred after the Soviet invasion of Afghanistan in 1979. Continuous flows ensued for the following ten years as anti-Soviet Mujahideen (Muslim guerrilla fighters) fought with Soviet forces. By 1990, there were about 3.9 million Afghan refugees settled in Pakistan. After the Mujahideen victory in 1992, a large number returned to Afghanistan, and Amnesty International reported that only 1.4 million remained in Pakistan by 1994. But since then, wave after wave of refugees has fled Afghanistan. The second wave came as a result of factional fighting following the Mujahideen victory and pre-Taliban-era abuses, combined with severe droughts. The third exodus occurred in response to the fighting that took place as the Taliban rose to power and in reaction to the human rights violations by the Taliban. The fourth and most recent wave of Afghan refugees came to Pakistan to escape the air strikes and bombing by U.S. military forces against the al-Qaeda camps, and the related conflict involving Taliban and Northern Alliance forces. It was reported that around 2,000 Afghans were escaping into Pakistan every day at that time. Several thousand continue to flee or attempt to flee Afghanistan. Although the Pakistan government officially closed its border with Afghanistan in November 2000 to stop new flows of refugees, it has granted entry to the most vulnerable. Refugees who have entered unofficially have also been allowed to remain inside Pakistan.

Agha Khan Rural Support Program (AKRSP). Expanding the range of development options in the Northern Areas of Pakistan, AKRSP is one of the two important NGOs (the other being the Orangi Pilot Project) that have had a major impact on development in both the government and nongovernment sectors of Pakistan. The AKRSP pioneered the approach of building Village Organizations (VOs), with community-based, self-help, separate groups for poor men and women, and then launching development activities through these groups. Such activities have focused on health, education, and livelihood opportunities in the Northern Areas, particularly Gilgit. This highly successful program has received very favorable evaluations from the World Bank and independent organizations, and is being replicated in other countries.

Ali, Chaudhri Rahmat (1897–1951). Belonging to a group of Indian Muslim students at Cambridge in Britain that had issued a pamphlet, *Now or Never,* demanding the partition of India into regions, Chaudhri Rahmat Ali came up with the name *Pakistan,* in 1933, for the northwest region of India. In Urdu and Persian, Pakistan means Land of the *Paks* or the Pure, and it is also an acronym: "P" is for Punjab, "A" for Afghania (referring to the North-West Frontier Province), "K" for Kashmir, an "I" that occurs in English but not in Urdu, "S" is for Sindh, and "TAN" is for Balochistan.

Badshahi Mosque. The most impressive building in Pakistan is the Badshahi Mosque in Lahore, built during the rule of the Mughal emperor, Aurangzeb, in the early 1670s. It is the second largest mosque in the world, with a capacity to hold up to 100,000 people. The courtyard, the largest in the world, measuring about 528 feet by 528 feet, is surrounded by huge walls of red sandstone. Three enormous onion-shaped domes of white marble stand at the farthest end of the courtyard. Each of the four minarets is 67 feet in circumference and 175 feet high (Amin et al. 1982, 155).

Bhutto, Benazir (1953–). Bhutto became the first female prime minister of Pakistan, the first woman in modern times to lead a Muslim country, and the youngest head of government at the age of thirty-five in 1988. She is the daughter of Zulfiqar Ali Bhutto, Pakistan's prime minister from 1971 to 1977, who was imprisoned in 1977 and subsequently executed. Bhutto assumed the leadership of the party formed by her father, the Pakistan Peoples Party (PPP). After many years of detention and exile, Benazir Bhutto returned to Pakistan in 1986, and following Ziaul Haq's death in a plane crash in 1988, was elected prime minister and remained so for twenty months, from 1988 to 1990. Although she was ousted from office in 1990 on corruption charges, she came back to power in the 1993 elections. Bhutto was again removed from power in 1996 amid allegations of mismanagement and corruption, particularly by her husband, Asif Zardari. She is currently living in exile in Dubai.

Bhutto, Zulfiqar Ali (1928–1979). Leader of the Pakistan Peoples Party (PPP), Bhutto assumed power as president and chief martial law administrator of Pakistan in 1971, after the separation of East Pakistan following a brutal civil war and the surrender of the Pakistan Army in the war with India. Within one year, the 1973 constitution came into effect, guaranteeing freedom of speech and a judicial system with due process. The constitution addressed the standing controversies about the role of Islam; the sharing of power between the federal government and the provinces; and the division of responsibility between the president and prime minister, with a greatly strengthened position of the prime minister. Widespread nationalization was carried out. Bhutto's regime became increasingly authoritarian and corrupt. The alleged rigging of the 1977 parliamentary elections by the PPP was the final blow, galvanizing nine opposition parties from across the ideological spectrum into forming a united front, the Pakistan National Alliance (PNA), to lead a popular movement against Bhutto, causing an abrupt downfall of the PPP government. On July 5, General Mohammad Ziaul Haq, army chief of staff, abruptly took over as chief martial law administrator to supervise fair elections, but instead arrested Bhutto on September 3, 1977. On April 4, 1979, by Zia's order, Bhutto was hanged.

Chughtai, Abdur Rahman (1897–1975). Acclaimed as the foremost national painter of Pakistan, Chughtai revived and developed the traditional Mughal style of miniature painting. His paintings are regarded as classics. He was a master of figural painting and portraiture. He is also well-known for his watercolors.

East Pakistan. At the time of partition in 1947, East and West Pakistan formed the two wings of Pakistan, separated by 1,000 miles of Indian territory. Regional disparities between the two wings and underrepresentation of Bengalis increased under the regime of Ayub Khan. The Awami League, which had won almost all the seats in East Pakistan in the 1970 elections, demanded autonomy for East Pakistan. The West Pakistani politicians and the army regarded the demand for complete autonomy by the Awami League and its leader, Sheikh Mujibur Rahman, as equivalent to secession, and as such, unacceptable. The Awami League was outlawed, and Mujibur Rahman was arrested for treason. The massive military crackdown was followed by a brutal civil war and military intervention by India that ultimately led to the surrender of the Pakistan Army and the loss of East Pakistan, which became the independent nation of Bangladesh on December 16, 1971.

Edhi, Abdul Sattar (1928–). Edhi is to Karachi what Mother Teresa was to the poor of Calcutta. He is one of the world's foremost benefactors of the poor. He started his social work with the purchase of an old van that he used to go around the city of Karachi, providing medical help to the poor and bathing and burying unclaimed bodies. As news of his work with the poor spread, and donations started pouring in, his operations expanded so that now the Edhi Foundation is the largest welfare organization in Pakistan. It has over 300 centers across the country, in big cities, small towns, and remote rural areas, that provide medical aid, family planning, and emergency assistance through its network of 3,500 workers and thousands of volunteers, air ambulances that provide quick access to far-flung areas, a fleet of regular ambulances, and wireless communication systems. The foundation's activities include a 24-hour emergency service across the country that provides free shrouding and burial of unclaimed dead bodies; shelter for over 6,000 destitute, orphans, and handicapped persons; free dispensary and hospital services to over 1 million persons annually; rehabilitation of drug addicts, family planning and maternity services; animal shelters, and national and international relief efforts for the victims of natural calamities, including refugees in the United States, United Kingdom, Canada, Japan, and Bangladesh. In Karachi alone, the Edhi Foundation runs eight hospitals, eye clinics, diabetic centers, a cancer hospital, mobile dispensaries, two blood banks, and *langars* (free community meals for the poor). The Edhi Foundation refuses to take any aid from the government, thereby maintaining its independence.

It is widely known that Edhi ambulances are the first to arrive at any disaster scene and start rescue operations, whether it is a train accident, a bomb blast, or an ethnic/religious riot. They go to places where even government agencies hesitate to venture. This is because Edhi's mission of service and humanitarianism for the past forty-five years has known no barriers of religion, caste, creed, or national boundaries; consequently, he is respected among followers of all religions, sects, and ethnic groups in Pakistan. In 1985, Edhi received the highest national award from the government of Pakistan (known as the Nishan-e-Imtiaz), and he and his wife Bilquees received the internationally prestigious Magasayay Award from the government of the Philippines in recognition of their services.

Despite their fame, Edhi and Bilquees are down-to-earth persons, who still bathe the unclaimed dead bodies themselves and do not seek publicity. They have had little formal education, but organize mass campaigns against illiteracy and narcotics and campaigns in favor of population control and basic hygiene. To date, their grass-roots-level, lifetime work for the poor and needy remains unparalleled in Pakistan and perhaps in the world.

Eid-ul-Azha. Celebrated on the tenth day of the last Islamic month of *Zilhij,* Eid-ul-Azha occurs about two months after Eid-ul-Fitr. Eid-ul-Azha is celebrated to commemorate the occasion when the prophet Abraham was ready to sacrifice his son, Ismail, on God's command, and Allah rewarded his obedience by replacing Ismail with a sheep. Families sacrifice goats, sheep, and cows, giving one-third of the meat to the poor. Like Eid-ul-Fitr, it is a time of special prayers, feasting, family reunions, and celebration for three days.

Zilhij is the month of pilgrimage to the holy city of Mecca in Saudi Arabia for Muslims from all over the world. Eid-ul-Azha is celebrated in Mecca by pilgrims as one of the rites of *Hajj,* the fourth pillar of Islam. The *Hajjis* (pilgrims) are accorded great respect and are welcomed with garlands and special parties in their honor upon their return.

Eid-ul-Fitr. One of the two most important holidays in Pakistan, as in other Muslim countries, *Eid-ul-Fitr* marks the end of the month of fasting, Ramadan. Like Christmas or Hanukah, this is a time of feasting, family reunions, and gifts of money from the older to the younger relatives. New outfits are bought for children and other family members. Glass bangles (many bracelets) are particularly popular for girls. Women dress in elaborately embroidered outfits and gold jewelry. They often apply *mehndi* (henna) to their palms for adornment. The *Eid* day begins with a special breakfast of sweet vermicelli (a type of very fine spaghetti) cooked in milk, with saffron, dried fruits, and nuts. The men and boys gather in a mosque, or a nearby park or other open space, for the special *Eid* prayers. From there, they typically go to the cemetery to say special prayers for dead relatives. All day, families and friends visit one another and are served a large array of delicious foods. Muslims greet each other with *"Eid Mubarak"* (Eid greetings). The celebrations continue for a total of three days.

Faiz, Faiz Ahmad (1911–1984). Considered one of the greatest modern Urdu poets, Faiz writes poetry that expresses his socialist leanings. His politically motivated work was banned from Pakistani television and radio by most military governments. However, his romantic poetry is enjoyed by millions and is sung on radio, television, and in film.

Ghalib, Mirza Asadullah Khan (1797–1869). An iconic figure and the most widely admired and quoted poet of the Urdu language, who lived well before the creation of Pakistan, Ghalib has influenced generations of poets, songwriters, painters, and other artists who have translated his poetry into their art forms. The painter Sadequain is one such example. Ghalib is most famous for his *ghazals* (a poetry form that has five or more two-line couplets in which the last words of the second lines rhyme with each other). Many of his *ghazals* are memorized, as Pakistanis generally adore poetry and frequently recite it, a tradition not known in the West.

Harappa. Located in the Punjab, Harappa is one of the two main sites of the Indus Valley civilization, which was a major center of civilization that flourished between 4000 and 2500 BCE. The Harappans developed an advanced urban culture with a diversified social and economic system, remarkable town planning, a written language, centralized administration, extensive commerce, and trade with ancient Egypt and Sumer in southern Mesopotamia.

Independence Day. Pakistan came into existence as an independent Muslim state on August 14, 1947, with two parts, East and West Pakistan, separated by 1,000 miles of Indian territory. With 70 million people, Pakistan became the fifth most populous country in the world at that time (now the sixth). It also became the world's most populous Muslim country at that time. Independence Day in Pakistan is celebrated with great fervor. The flag of Pakistan is based largely on the flag of the All-India Muslim League, which led the independence movement. It is dark green in color with a vertical white stripe on the left. It has a white star and crescent, the traditional symbols of Islam. The dark green stands for the nation's Muslim majority, and the white stands for the religious minorities, symbolizing respect for all religions.

Indus Valley Civilization. One of the first great civilizations of the world, it extended along the Indus River between 4,000 and 6,000 years ago, around 2500 BCE, and flourished for about a thousand years. It is now agreed that the Indus Valley civilization was the first organized urban settlement in the world. It produced sophisticated irrigation systems, houses of burnt bricks, crafts, well-planned drainage systems, and town planning models. The first forms of writing, not yet deciphered, were also discovered in the ruins at Mohenjodaro in Sindh and Harappa in the Punjab.

Iqbal, Sir Muhammad (1877–1938). A great Islamic poet and philosopher of the early twentieth century, educated and knighted in England, he became president of the All-India Muslim League in 1930. He was the first to articulate the notion of a separate Muslim homeland in the Indian subcontinent. He considered Muslims to be a nation based on unity of language, race, history, religion, and identity of economic interests. He proposed the establishment of a confederated India to include a Muslim state, consisting of the Punjab, the North-West Frontier Province, Sindh, and Balochistan. Three years later, a group of Indian Muslim students at Cambridge in England issued a pamphlet, *Now or Never,* opposing the idea of a federation and demanding partition into regions, the northwest becoming the nation of Pakistan.

Muhammad Iqbal is Pakistan's most famous poet. Using the poetic vocabulary of classical Persian and Urdu, Iqbal imbued Urdu poetry with faith and action, always seeking to rekindle the spirit of Muslim brotherhood in the modern world. In his greatest collection of poetry, *Bal-e-Jibril* (Gabriel's Wing), Iqbal asks Muslim youth to renounce both Western materialism and Eastern mysticism, because only men of faith and action could change the world. Iqbal has sometimes been compared to John Milton, the author of *Paradise Lost,* because of the quality of his work, the religious themes of his poetry, and his role in politics of the time.

Islamabad. Newly built in the foothills of the Himalayas, Islamabad is the capital of Pakistan and center of the government. Rawalpindi, its twin older city, is the headquarters of the army and the site of textile mills, iron foundries, and locomotive works. The population of Rawalpindi is about 1.4 million, and that of Islamabad is 0.5 million. The largest mosque in the world, the Faisal mosque, is in Islamabad. It was constructed in the early 1980s as a gift from Saudi Arabia.

Jalandhari, Hafeez (1900–1982). The creator of the national anthem of Pakistan, Jalandhari is one of the most famous Urdu poets of Pakistan. His fame rests on his long poem *Shahnama-i-Islam,* in four volumes, which is a record of the glorious history of Islam in verse. It is in the manner of *Shahnameh* (Book of Kings) of Firdausi, the Iranian poet who wrote the greatest national epic in world literature (60,000 couplets). Jalandhari is also known as Firdausi of Pakistan.

Jinnah, Mohammad Ali (1876–1948). Regarded as the father of the nation, Mohammad Ali Jinnah—or Quaid-e-Azam (Great Leader) as he is called—was the founder and the first governor general of Pakistan. Without his leadership in the 1930s and 1940s, Pakistan would never have been created as an independent state. He won independence for Pakistan within seven and a half years of formally demanding it at the annual session of the Muslim League session in 1940 (known as the Pakistan or Lahore Resolution), because of his vision, his formidable negotiation skills and political acumen, and above all his tireless effort and complete devotion.

Born in Karachi, Jinnah was a brilliant lawyer who studied in England and began his career as an enthusiastic liberal in Congress when he returned to India. He began working for Hindu-Muslim unity, believing it to be the key to India's independence from Britain. Jinnah was a unifier and not a separatist, as his record shows. Almost to the moment of transfer of power, Jinnah was still searching for a way to bridge differences between himself and his Hindu counterparts. In 1913, he joined the Muslim League but continued his membership in Congress as well. Almost single-handedly he built the League into the broad-based political party that in the 1940s unified India's 100 million Muslims behind the demand for Pakistan. Jinnah became the sole spokesman for, and the undisputed leader of, the Indian Muslims.

On September 11, 1948, just thirteen months after independence, Quaid-e-Azam Mohammad Ali Jinnah died of lung cancer at the age of seventy-one. Jinnah wanted Pakistan to be a democratic, multiethnic, and multireligious polity, informed by Muslim values. Most Pakistanis believe that had he lived for even one more year, he would have been able to transform his vision into reality. Even today he has no rival. He was and is the Quaid-e-Azam. Many people throughout the

Muslim world consider Jinnah one of the great Muslim leaders of all time.

Junoon. The most popular band in Pakistan, Junoon produces music that mixes the mystical Urdu poetry of Sufi saints with Punjabi and Sindhi folk music and the rock 'n' roll of the West. Its members are Salman Ahmad, Ali Azmat, and Brian O'Connell. Their music and videos were banned by the governments of Benazir Bhutto and Nawaz Sharif because some of their song lyrics were critical of these governments. The band has also won an award from UNESCO for their achievements toward peace in South Asia, particularly between Pakistan and India.

K2 Mountain. K2 Mountain is Pakistan's highest mountain and the world's second highest after Mount Everest. Lying in the Karakoram Range, it rises 28,252 feet above sea level and is only 800 feet lower than Mount Everest. It is almost twice as high as Mount Whitney, the highest mountain in the contiguous United States. It lies on the border of China and the Northern Areas of Pakistan. It was measured by T. G. Montgomerie of the Survey of India in 1856 and named K2 because it was the second peak measured in the Karakoram Range. In 1861, it was unofficially named Mount Godwin Austen by the British after the surveyor who climbed and surveyed many glaciers in the region. The real name is "Chogori," which in the *Balti* language means the king of mountains, or "Dapsang." There are glaciers thirty and forty miles long on its flanks. Describing it as a cone of ice and limestone, many mountaineers consider it to be the most challenging and ultimate climb, owing to both its natural formation with slopes of 45 degrees or more and its unpredictable weather pattern of sudden and blinding blizzards. Climbers need about 8,202 feet of rope to climb the south-side route and about 16,405 feet for the north ridge route. During the early 1900s, there were five unsuccessful attempts to reach the peak by Anglo-

Swiss, Italian, and American expeditions. The peak was first reached in 1954 by an Italian team led by Ardito Desio. The first official Pakistani climber reached the summit in 1977. The local people scale the mountain with no aids and lead outsiders to the peak as guides. Nanga Parbat, the ninth highest mountain in the world at 26,660 feet, second highest in Pakistan, and nicknamed the "killer mountain," has a terrain much worse than Everest due to unstable glaciers causing vast avalanches, and a longer approach route. It remained unconquered until 1953.

Kalash. A primitive pagan tribe, also known as Kafir-Kalash or "Wearers of the Black Robes". The tribe inhabits the Kalash Valley of the Hindu Kush Mountains, located in the Chitral district of the North-West Frontier Province. Their religion is a unique form of polytheistic paganism involving animal sacrifice, nature and ancestor worship, and belief in saints, fairies, and demons. They are the only community in Pakistan that has not adopted Islam. Their unique religion and culture have attracted a lot of attention from anthropologists and travelers all over the world. There has been some mystery and controversy over their ancestry. Some anthropologists believe that the Kalash descended from the armies of Alexander the Great, which passed this way in the fourth century BCE, and may be a mixture of Indo-Aryans and Greeks. Although there is no written language or recorded history, their spoken language, Kalashwar, is said to include Greek, Persian, and Sanskrit words. The Kalash are light-skinned, and many have blond hair and green or blue eyes, which lends support to the theory about their ancestry. So does the similarity between Kalash women's folk costumes and those in northern Greece.

There are now only about 3,000 Kalash in about twenty villages in three isolated valleys in Chitral—Birr, Bumburet, and Rambur—though this pagan culture once claimed a million followers. Kalash society has adhered to an ancient way of life for centuries despite countless invasions, as reflected in their practice of religion, in houses that they build, and in their clothes. They typically make wood-and-stone, windowless houses, with wooden crossbeams in the masonry that act as cushions to absorb the shock of earthquakes. Architects consider this design to be earthquake-proof to some extent. Women spin and dye their own cloth. They wear gowns, mostly black in winter, and simple bead jewelry. The cowrie-shell headgear of the women is very distinctive and picturesque. However, now the society is changing as increasing tourism and financial need put pressure on Kalash women and girls to perform their religious dances for money, in much the same way as other tribal cultures have responded to such pressures.

Karachi. Pakistan's largest city and commercial-industrial-financial center, Karachi, is a sprawling metropolis of traditional and modern buildings, bazaars, and high-tech shops. Many of the buildings were built in British colonial style, contrasting significantly with the Mughal style of Lahore. Located on the Arabian Sea, Karachi is the main port. With the highest number of migrants from other cities and provinces, it is the ethnic melting pot of Pakistan and a vibrant, spirited city. It is now the capital of Sindh but was the country's capital from 1947 to 1959. Although the capital later moved to Rawalpindi and then Islamabad, Karachi remains the economic center of Pakistan.

The population of Karachi is about 9.3 million, according to the 1998 census, which makes it the seventh most populated city of the world. Its ranking may be higher in reality because cities with a higher ranking report more recent data than 1998, and Karachi's current population is estimated to be about 15 million, much higher than the official 1998 count of 9.3 million. Karachi is the financial capital of Pakistan. It accounts for the lion's share of Pakistan's GDP and a large proportion of the nation's white-collar workers. The city contributes about 70 percent of national revenues. It is also home to the largest stock exchange of Pakistan: the Karachi Stock

Exchange. Most Pakistani banks and multinational companies based in Pakistan have their headquarters in Karachi. Markets offering an endless variety of goods can be found throughout the vast city.

Karakoram Highway. The highest tar road in the world and one of the greatest engineering feats of the twentieth century, it connects Pakistan's capital, Islamabad, to Kashgar in the Sinkiang Province of China. This 800-mile, dual-carriage road runs through some of the world's toughest terrain. It took fifteen years to be completed, and it is said that one life was lost for every kilometer of its length due to avalanches, falling boulders, and other accidents. The highway has provided a vital link to China and has improved trade and communications between isolated villages of the Northern Areas and the rest of Pakistan.

Khan, Abdul Qadeer (1935–). Respected as a national hero and known as the father of Pakistan's nuclear program, the scientist Dr. Qadeer Khan has recently come under fire in the West for his role in Pakistan's acquisition and testing of nuclear capability and its alleged proliferation. The government has denied knowledge of Dr. Khan's actions or its own involvement in this regard. Dr. Khan was subsequently pardoned in exchange for cooperation in the investigation of the nuclear-proliferation network.

Khan, Agha Mohammad Yahya (1917–1980). In 1969, Yahya Khan became the president and chief martial law administrator of Pakistan. Under Yahya Khan the first general elections were held on December 7, 1970, heralded as fair and free by all observers. East Pakistanis voted overwhelmingly for the Awami League, which demanded autonomy for East Pakistan. Yahya tried to persuade Bhutto and Mujib to come to some sort of accommodation, but Mujib insisted on his right as leader of the majority to form the government and Bhutto claimed that there were "two majorities" in Pakistan. When negotiations among Bhutto, Mujib, and Yahya failed, Yahya sent 75,000 West Pakistani troops to East Pakistan in March 1971 for a military crackdown.

War broke out between Pakistan and India when Indian troops invaded East Pakistan in December 1971, when snow in the Himalayas made it impossible for the Chinese, Pakistan's strong ally and India's enemy, to intervene. The East Pakistanis greeted the Indian Army with joy, and within two weeks the Indian Army had captured all of East Pakistan. The Pakistani Army surrendered, and East Pakistan became the independent nation of Bangladesh on December 16, 1971. Yahya Khan resigned in disgrace on December 20, 1971. He had presided over the two most traumatic events in Pakistan's history: the humiliating surrender of Pakistan's army to India and the secession of East Pakistan.

Khan, Akhtar Hameed (1914–1999). Founder of the internationally renowned development projects-turned-models, the Orangi Pilot Project in Karachi and Comilla Cooperatives under the Comilla Rural Academy in East Pakistan (now Bangladesh), Dr. Akhtar Hameed was a scholar, a social worker, a community development expert, and a legend in his own time. As his two-pronged program of rural works and credit and training at Comilla expanded to all of East Pakistan, his name became synonymous with the concept of endogenous rural development. His "research and extension" method of community development is followed today by numerous development agencies and NGOs around the world. His Comilla project is considered by many to be the precursor of world-renowned micro-finance institutions such as the Grameen Bank and Bangladesh Rural Advancement Committee (BRAC) in Bangladesh. He was a recipient of the highest civil awards from the government of Pakistan, including the Nishan-i-Imtiaz, Hilal-e-Pakistan, Sitara-i-Pakistan, and the Magsaysay Award from the Philippines.

Khan, Ghulam Ishaq (1915–). As president of Pakistan from 1988 to 1993, and using the Eighth Amendment to the 1973 constitution of Pakistan introduced by former president Ziaul Haq, which gave the president the right to dismiss the prime minister anytime, for any reason, he dismissed the government of Benazir Bhutto in 1990 on charges of corruption, and of Prime Minister Nawaz Sharif in 1993 on similar charges.

Khan, Liaquat Ali (1895–1951). Pakistan's first prime minister, Liaquat Ali Khan was a member of the nobility who entered politics in 1923 and began working closely with Mohammad Ali Jinnah after joining the Muslim League. He gained the respect of the Muslim community of British India for his role in the struggle for an independent homeland for Muslims, and he was given the title of Quaid-e-Millat (Leader of the Nation). As prime minister, he laid down the foundations of the country's domestic and foreign policies. He was assassinated in 1951 before his government could draft a constitution, which plunged Pakistan into seven years of political chaos and led to a collapse of the parliamentary system.

Khan, Mohammad Ayub (1907–1974). In 1958, General Ayub Khan invoked martial law and made himself president of Pakistan. His coup ended eleven years of unstable democracy in Pakistan and began a new era of military rule that would continue intermittently for thirty-one of the next forty-eight years. The Ayub period is often known as the golden era of economic development in Pakistan. Among Ayub's contributions are his program of agricultural and industrial development, his advocacy for women's rights, and his successful foreign policy, particularly with the United States and China. But his policies also led to sharp interregional and interpersonal inequities in income distribution and in concentration of wealth and power, paving the way for the 1971 dismemberment of Pakistan. The resentment of East Pakistan toward the Ayub government was crystallized in the Six Point program put forward in February 1966 by Sheikh Mujibur Rahman, the leader of the Awami (People's) League, the largest political party in East Pakistan. Mass demonstrations by students and labor unions finally led to Ayub's downfall. Ayub Khan resigned as president in March 1969 and, forever contemptuous of lawyer-politicians, handed over power to his fellow army officer, General Yahya Khan.

Khan, Nusrat Fateh Ali (1948–1997). Regarded as one of the world's greatest singers of Sufi devotional poetry, known as *qawwali,* and the best-known Pakistani folk singer of the last twenty years, Nusrat Fateh Ali Khan enjoyed a huge following that spanned generations. Coming from a family with a 600-year tradition of *qawwali* singing, he became famous for his hypnotic live performances and was known as the King of *Qawwali.* His fame spread throughout Pakistan during the 1970s and then throughout the world in the 1980s. He collaborated with rock singer Peter Gabriel on the soundtrack to the movie *The Last Temptation of Christ* in 1988. He also performed on the soundtrack for the 1995 movie *Dead Man Walking,* and to sold-out audiences at New York's Radio City Music Hall and other cities across the world.

Khyber Pass. One of the most famous mountain passes in the world, the Khyber Pass connects Pakistan with Afghanistan. It is 40 miles long, of which 29 are in Pakistan. The mountains on either side are about 590 to 985 feet high. Since ancient times, the Khyber Pass has been the point of entry to the subcontinent for invading armies, traders, and travelers, partly because it is the widest and lowest of mountain routes from Afghanistan into India, varying in width from about 10 to 450 feet. It was the route used by the armies of the Aryans, Persians, Greeks, Scythians, White Huns, Seljuks, Tartars, Mongols, Sassanians, Turks, and Mughals to enter the Indus Plains. Some of the most well-known invaders who have come to the subcontinent through the Khyber Pass include Alexander the

Great in the fourth century BCE; Sabuktagin, founder of the Ghaznivid dynasty, and his son, Mahmud, in the tenth century CE, who crossed it seventeen times; Genghis Khan and Timurlane in the thirteenth and fourteenth centuries; Babur, the first Mughal, in the sixteenth century; and Nadir Shah from Iran in the eighteenth century. At the same time, it is believed that many invaders did not use the Khyber Pass or used it only once and not again because of the fierce and brave Afridis, a tribe of Pathans described as a "law unto themselves." It has also been a major trade route for centuries.

The Khyber Pass was also at the center of the "Great Game," which was played from 1840 to 1895 between the British and the Russians who wanted to secure it for their respective countries. The Khyber Pass was like a swinging door that both the Russians and the British wanted to use: the Russians to expand from Central Asia to the Indian subcontinent and the British from the subcontinent to Afghanistan. The British used the Khyber Pass during the First Afghan War (1839–1842), the Second (1878–1879), and the Third (1919).

Lahore. With a population of 5.1 million, as reported in the 1988 census, Lahore is the second largest city of Pakistan and the capital of Punjab. It had long been a center of culture and learning, and is the city of Mughal monuments. These include the Badshahi Mosque, built by Emperor Aurangzeb in the early 1670s; the Lahore Fort, a sprawling complex of fortified walls and open-air pavilions built during the reigns of four Mughal emperors between the 1580s and the 1670s; and the Shalimar Gardens, with more than 400 fountains built for Emperor Shah Jahan in 1642.

The streets of Lahore, very similar to the streets of Karachi and other major cities, are jammed with every existing form of transportation for people and goods: cars, vans, pickup trucks, motorcycles, motorized three-wheeled rickshaws, colorful public buses, bicycles, three-wheeled manually pulled rickshaws, horse-drawn taxis called *tongas,* brightly and intricately painted trucks (a unique feature of Pakistan), and animal-drawn wooden carts (pulled by a camel, horse, donkey, or oxen). The bazaars are crowded, tightly packed with open-air stalls beneath centuries-old wooden houses, selling an assortment of goods and services, such as brassware, spices, flowers, jewelry, and clothing, as well as with food vendors, small restaurants, tailors, beauticians, dyers, and others.

Lahore Resolution of 1940. At its annual session in Lahore on March 23, 1940, just seven and a half years before the partition of 1947, the Muslim League passed the Lahore Resolution, often referred to as the Pakistan Resolution, formally demanding independent Muslim states.

Minto, Saadat Hasan (1912–1955). As a short story writer, Minto has published a body of work that has been widely acclaimed. His stories focus on the dark side of life, and his story *"Toba Tek Singh,"* is considered to be one of the best pieces of literature written about the human tragedy experienced during the partition of 1947.

Mohenjodaro. Located in Sindh, Mohenjodaro is one of the two major sites of the Indus Valley civilization, which was a major center of civilization that flourished between 4000 and 2500 BCE. Ruins show that it was well planned, with 30-foot-wide streets laid out at right angles, extensive water supply and drainage systems, and many two-storied shops and houses, all of which indicate an advanced urban culture. Similarly, there is evidence of a written language, use of weights and measures for commerce, and extensive trade. Also see Harappa.

Musharraf, Pervez (1943–). As chief of army staff and chairman of the Joint Chiefs of Staff Committee, Pervez Musharraf became the country's chief executive following a bloodless military coup d'état that removed Prime Minister Nawaz Sharif from office on October 12, 1999. Musharraf formally became president of Pakistan on June 20, 2001. A pro-Musharraf party, the PML-Q (Pakistan Muslim League–Qayyum Group), won a plurality of the seats in the National Assembly elections of October 2002. On January 1, 2004, in a vote of confidence, Musharraf won by a 56 percent majority in the electoral college of Pakistan, consisting of both houses of parliament and the four provincial assemblies. According to the constitution, he was then "deemed to be elected" to the office of president until October 2007.

Musharraf is considered a moderate leader by most observers, desirous of bridging the gap between the Muslim and the Western worlds. He envisions Pakistan as a modern, liberal country in which there is religious tolerance and rule of law. During his rule, lawlessness and corruption have decreased significantly. Recent reports by international financial agencies, including the World Bank and the International Monetary Fund, testify to Pakistan's considerable economic recovery under President Pervez Musharraf, and point out that the civilian economic team appointed by Musharraf is the best in decades.

Musharraf has been astute in his foreign policy. Following the September 11, 2001, attacks, Musharraf's support for the United States in its war on terrorism was indispensable in defeating the Taliban in Afghanistan. In a swift and strategic 180-degree turn of policy, Musharraf ended Pakistan's long-running support of the Taliban, cutting their oil and supply lines, providing intelligence, and becoming a logistics support area for Operation Enduring Freedom. In 2004, Musharraf began talks with India to solve the Kashmir dispute and has indicated a preference for some kind of "international guarantees" for implementation of a "no war pact" with India.

Nazimuddin, Khwaja (1894–1964). Nazimuddin became the second governor general of Pakistan after the death of Mohammad Ali Jinnah. After Liaquat Ali Khan's death in 1951, Nazimuddin naively agreed to resign as governor general and step down to take over as the country's second prime minister. But he inherited an impossible legacy of reconciling opposite views on constitution making. In April 1953, Ghulam Mohammed dismissed Khwaja Nazimuddin, which was totally undemocratic since he still had the support of a majority in the assembly.

Niazi, Imran Ahmad Khan (1952–). Popularly known as Imran Khan, Niazi is regarded as one of the best all-around cricketers in the world. He became a national hero when he led the Pakistan cricket team to victory over the British in the World Cup finals held in Melbourne, Australia, in 1992. At the height of his career, he was the fastest bowler in the world. After his retirement from cricket in 1992, he entered politics and formed his own political party, Tehrik-e-Insaf, in 1996 and announced his candidacy for prime minister. He campaigned on a promise to clean up the corruption that was prevalent in Benazir Bhutto's administration. Although he had many supporters, he lost the election.

Orangi Pilot Project (OPP). One of the two important NGOs, other than the Agha Khan Rural Support Program, that have had a major impact on development thinking in Pakistan, the Orangi Pilot Project was established in Karachi in 1980 by Dr. Akhtar Hameed Khan, the renowned Pakistani community development expert of legendary fame. The Orangi Pilot Project has become one of the best known NGO projects in the provision of sanitation, assisting about one million people in the sixteen years since its inception in Orangi, Karachi's largest *katchi abadi* (slum), with a population of 1.2 million. Using sanitation as an entry point, a range of community development initiatives have been undertaken at Orangi, including health, education, and income-generating activities. The OPP supports local initiatives, uses local resources, and builds on the capability of poor communities to look after themselves. Totally indigenous, the OPP model has not required large funds, foreign or local, or expensive imported expertise. It is now being replicated in numerous settlements in Pakistan, and in urban projects in South Africa, Central Asia, Nepal, Sri Lanka, and India. The OPP received the Habitat Award in 2000.

Pakistan. It is properly pronounced pahk-ih-STAHN. In the United States, where an "ah" usually sounds affected, it is pronounced PACK-ih-stan.

Pakistan Muslim League (PML). One of Pakistan's two largest mainstream political parties, other than the Pakistan Peoples Party, the Pakistan Muslim League originated from the All-India Muslim League, which was founded in Dhaka in 1906 to protect and advance Muslim interests. In 1913, Mohammad Ali Jinnah, the founder of Pakistan, joined the Muslim League, and in 1930, Sir Muhammad Iqbal became its president.

Partition of 1947. The independence of India, after a century of British rule based on their policy of "divide and rule," and its partition into two countries were accompanied by communal violence and large-scale migration of refugees. An estimated one million people were killed in the riots that followed between Hindus and Muslims. It is estimated that between 5.5 and 7.5 million Muslim refugees fled to East or West Pakistan fearing a violent backlash in India, and between 5.5 and 10 million Hindus and Sikhs, not wanting to end up in Muslim Pakistan, left for India across the newly formed border. This exodus created unimaginable hardship, loss of property and life, and terror. People were forced to leave their homes, businesses, employment, schools, possessions, fields, farm animals, and the only life they had ever known.

Political Parties. Pakistan's two largest mainstream parties are the Pakistan Peoples Party (PPP) and the Pakistan Muslim League (PML). In addition, there are a number of other large or politically significant parties as well as smaller organizations. The Awami National Party (ANP), the Muttahida Qaumi Movement (MQM), and the Jamat-i-Islami (JI) are among the parties that have a strong regional, ethnic, or religious base. The Muttahida Qaumi Mahaz (or MQM) (formerly known as the Muhajir Qaumi Movement, the name is still maintained by one or more splinter groups) is often among the three largest groups in the National Assembly. The Muttahida Majlis-e-Amal is a coalition of "religious" parties that controlled the government of two out of four provinces.

Qureshi, Moeen (1930–). A former World Bank senior vice-president, Moeen Qureshi led the caretaker government installed by the acting president of Pakistan, Wasim Sajjad, in July 1993, with the mandate to preside over new elections for the national and provincial assemblies. Being outside the military-bureaucratic-landlord-industrialist establishment, and using the brief tenure and temporary nature of his government to his advantage, Qureshi initiated an impressive number of much-needed reforms in Pakistan and came to be known as "Mr. Clean" during his three-month tenure. Qureshi fulfilled his primary mandate of holding new elections for the national and provincial assemblies in October 1993, which were hailed by international observers as the fairest in Pakistan's history. Moeen Qureshi is currently the chairman and managing partner of the Emerging Markets Corporation, based in Washington, D.C. He serves on the board of the Pakistan National Commission for Human Development and is often consulted on matters pertaining to investment, privatization, and finance by cabinet members of the current government.

Ramadan. The ninth month of the Muslim calendar, the month of Ramadan, which commemorates the beginning of the Prophet's revelations from Allah, is very special in Pakistan. All Muslims (except the sick, the weak, pregnant or lactating women, soldiers on duty, and minors) are obligated to fast from sunrise to sunset during Ramadan. They eat a meal, called *sehri,* before dawn and one after sunset, called *iftar.* It is said that fasting is practiced more than prayers.

Sadequain (1930–1987). An influential artist who embraced modern art, Sadequain initially produced sketches and figure paintings, often based on the poetry of Ghalib, the famous Urdu poet of the mid-nineteenth century in India, and then moved on to calligraphy and murals. Much of his work, including Quranic calligraphy, is displayed in important public buildings throughout the country.

Salam, Abdus (1926–1996). A theoretical physicist, Salam shared the 1979 Nobel Prize in Physics with Sheldon L. Glashow and Steven Weinberg for their independent contributions to the electroweak theory, which is the mathematical and conceptual synthesis of the electromagnetic and weak interactions. It is the latest stage reached until now on the path toward a unification theory describing the fundamental forces of nature. He received several international awards for contributions to peace and promotion of international scientific collaboration. During the early 1970s, Salam played a very significant role in starting Pakistan's space agency, the Atomic Energy Commission, and SUPARCO. He was the first and only Nobel laureate from Pakistan. He was also the first from any Muslim country to receive a Nobel Prize for academic subject-specific work, as the 1978 Nobel Prize to Anwar El-Sadat of Egypt was for world peace.

Sharif, Mian Nawaz (1949–). As the leader of the Muslim League, the largest party in the IJI (Islami Jamhoori Ittehad), a coalition of nine political parties united against Benazir Bhutto, Mian Nawaz Sharif became the prime minister of Pakistan when the IJI won by a huge margin in the October 1990 elections. Nawaz Sharif was the owner of a large industrial conglomerate (including four textile mills and a steel mill) and had served as a provincial finance minister under Zia in the early 1980s, and as Punjab's chief minister after 1985, both under the Zia and Benazir Bhutto regimes. Nawaz Sharif's rise to power marked a power shift from the traditional feudal aristocracy to a growing class of modern entrepreneurs. Not surprisingly, Sharif was a vigorous proponent of the reprivatization of industries that had been nationalized by Zulfiqar Ali Bhutto in the 1970s. However, the Sharif government's record is mixed. Rampant crime and terrorism continued to plague the country, particularly in Sindh. His government was eventually dismissed by President Ghulam Ishaq Khan in a power struggle between the two. Sharif was accused of mismanagement and corruption, particularly in connection with the privatization program.

Sharif returned to power again when he won the 1997 general election by a landslide, becoming Pakistan's most powerful elected leader since martial law ended in 1985. Using his two-thirds majority in the parliament, he repealed the controversial Eighth Amendment to the constitution, which had allowed the president, usually with military backing, to dismiss elected governments. But his mismanagement of the economy was disastrous for Pakistan. Economic growth rates decelerated, inflation peaked, debt burden escalated, poverty increased, and Pakistan's credibility with international finance institutions reached an all-time low. In October 1999, when General Pervez Musharraf was returning from an official visit to Sri Lanka, Sharif fired Musharraf, announced his replacement on national television, and ordered that the airliner on which Musharraf was traveling not be allowed to land at Karachi. The subsequent coup by Musharraf's supporters in the army deposing Nawaz Sharif was not only bloodless but also very popular. Sharif was later brought to trial for his role in diverting the plane and was convicted of hijacking. He is currently living in forced exile in Saudi Arabia.

Ziaul Haq, Mohammad (1924–1988). As chief of the army staff under Zulfiqar Ali Bhutto, General Zia led a military coup on July 5, 1977, and declared martial law, beginning the longest period of rule by a single leader in Pakistan's history. Suspending the constitution, he arrested Bhutto, who was tried and sentenced to death in 1978 on charges of conspiracy to murder a political opponent. Zia's regime was marked by the Afghan War (with its consequences of large aid flows from the United States and the growth of a drug and arms culture in Pakistan), opening up of employment opportunities in the Middle East resulting in large remittances from Pakistani workers abroad, and the imposition of his version of Islam on the economy and society.

As discontent with Zia's authoritarian regime built up, the officially defunct PPP and other parties joined to form the Movement for the Restoration of Democracy (MRD) in February 1981. It demanded an end of martial law and the holding of elections under the suspended 1973 constitution. Widespread anti-Zia riots broke out in Sindh in 1983, and martial law was lifted in December 1985, after eight long years. Elections were held for both the national and provincial assemblies in 1985, but political parties were not allowed to participate. The National Assembly passed the Eighth Amendment to the constitution of 1973, which exempted Zia from any future prosecution for acts in violation of the 1973 constitution, and gave the president the right to dismiss the prime minister and the provincial governors and to dissolve the national and provincial assemblies anytime, for any reason. Ziaul Haq died in an aircraft crash, believed to be an act of sabotage, on August 17, 1988, along with ten top generals and the U.S. ambassador to Pakistan.

Pakistani Language, Food, and Etiquette

LANGUAGE

Pakistan is a linguistic and cultural kaleidoscope, with each of its four provinces being multilingual and multicultural. There are five major languages in present-day Pakistan: Urdu, Punjabi, Sindhi, Pakhtu or Pashto, and Balochi. Although Urdu is the mother tongue of only 8 percent of the population, the Muhajirs, it is the national and official language of Pakistan. More than 75 percent of all Pakistanis and 95 percent of city dwellers understand Urdu. Punjabi is the mother tongue of the Punjabis who live in the river plains of the Indus in the province of Punjab, constituting about 60 percent of Pakistan's population. Sindhi, the oldest of the regional languages, with a rich literature, is the mother tongue of Sindhis who live in the province of Sindh and who constitute 12 percent of Pakistan's population. Pashto, the mother tongue of the Pathans, who live in the mountainous region of the North-West Frontier Province, is spoken by about 8 percent of Pakistan's population. Balochi, the mother tongue of 4 percent of Pakistan's population, is spoken by the Baloch who live on the Balochistan Plateau in the Balochistan Province. All of these languages belong to the Indo-Aryan branch of the Indo-European language family. Before 1971, Bengali was another language, the mother tongue of Bengalis living in East Pakistan and the language of the majority of the population in Pakistan of that time.

In addition to the one national and four major regional languages, there are more than twenty spoken languages. In fact, the same language is not spoken in any one province. The lan-

317

guages spoken in Balochistan include Balochi, Brahui in the Kalat region, Makrani in the coastal areas, Pushto, Saraiki, and Sindhi. Similarly, Pushto, Hindko, and some Saraiki are spoken in the Frontier Province, and in some parts, such as Hazara, even Persian. Sindhis speak Sindhi, Brahui, and Saraiki, and in Karachi, Urdu and Gujrati are spoken. Punjabis speak Punjabi, Saraiki in southern Punjab, and the Potohar dialect of Punjab Province. The Brahui language, and other Northern Areas languages such as Shina, are related to the Dravidian language family. There are other spoken languages in the extreme north in the Northern Areas of Pakistan, which are inhabited by distinct nationalities and people of Chitral, Gilgit, Hunza, and the Kalash. English is also used for official business, as a medium of instruction in public and private universities and professional colleges, in private schools (from first to tenth grade) and undergraduate colleges, government documents, legal contracts, and American movies. It is the language of the elite and the educated, although many Pakistanis know at least some English.

Urdu originated from a lingua franca that had evolved over the centuries through the interaction of different languages before and during the reign of the Delhi Sultanate, around the twelfth century. By the seventeenth century, this lingua franca had incorporated many Persian, Arabic, Sanskrit, Hindi, and Turkish words, and had developed into a literary language. In the colonial period, it was formally called "Urdu." By the end of the British rule in India, Urdu also incorporated scores of English words, such as railway-station, car, motor, bus, bus stop, post office, airport, stationmaster, postman, box, time, line, picture, telephone, telegram, bicycle, tram, petticoat, and many more, and English incorporated several Urdu words, such as veranda (from *baramda*), dacoit (from *daku*), sepoy (from *sipahee*), loot, and pajamas. Urdu was chosen as the national language and the medium of instruction at public schools after independence in 1947 because it had become strongly associated with Muslim nationalism and was not identified with any regional or ethnic group. But this move was unpopular in the linguistically homogeneous East Pakistan, where Bengali was spoken, thus leading to language riots in Dhaka in the early 1950s. The language riots again broke out in 1972 between Sindhis and Muhajirs when the government announced its decision to grant special status to Sindhi in response to the movement for the promotion of Sindhi language in Sindh, which was expressed in opposition to Urdu. It continues to be the main language of television and radio broadcasts, and of the majority of newspapers, magazines, and books.

There are thirty-six letters in the Urdu alphabet, borrowed from its multiple-root languages but more than in any one of them, including English, Persian, Arabic, and many other Indo-European languages. As a result, there are many more sounds in Urdu than in any of these languages. Some examples include the letter "qaaf," a deep, guttural "q" as in the "Quran," distinct in sound from "k" and pronounced correctly by few excluding the Arabs; the letter "ghain," a deep "gh" sound, distinct from "g," as in "Afghanistan," and pronounced incorrectly by most native English speakers; the letter "khe," a guttural "kh" as in "Khan," distinct from "k" and pronounced correctly by few excluding the Germans; the letters "tay" and "dal," which are soft "t" and "d" as in "Tehran" and "Dalai Lama," pronounced incorrectly by most native English speakers though correctly by some Europeans such as Italians; the letters "gaaf" like "g" and "pay" like "p" which are in Urdu but not in Arabic; and the "qaaf," which is in Urdu but not Sanskrit. Urdu also has more sounds than most regional languages of Pakistan. Although spoken Urdu is very similar to spoken Hindi, the language of northern India, the script is entirely different from Hindi but very similar to Arabic and almost the same as Persian. It is written from right to left. Each of the major languages—Punjabi, Sindhi, Pushto, and Balochi—share the same Arabic-Persian script. Sindhi is the most developed of all the regional languages.

Unlike English, in which the sentence (grammar) order is subject-verb-object, the normal sequence in Urdu is subject-object-verb. For instance, "I like apples" in English would be "I apples like" in Urdu. There is, however, flexibility in the sentence formation in both speaking and writing. It is common for people to converse in single words rather than in complete sentences and yet understand each other. Most native speakers of English find spoken Urdu to be very fast, particularly when two Pakistanis are speaking to each other. Culturally, the language reflects a hierarchical social structure, where there is both a social class and age connotation when one addresses others. For instance, the pronoun "you" has three different words in Urdu to differentiate social status and age: *"aap," "tum," and "too." "Aap"* is used for relatives, family friends, neighbors older than oneself, strangers, employers, and those of high status. *"Tum"* is used for people younger than or the same age as oneself and friends. *"Too"* in Urdu is now used mostly by low-income and uneducated people, although a few decades ago, it was also used to address low-class people. Sometimes it is used as an endearment by all classes. It needs to be kept in mind that *"too,"* used frequently in Punjabi, does not have the same connotation as in Urdu and is used in Punjabi the way *"tum"* is used in Urdu. There are hierarchical variations not only for "you," but also for the pronouns "she", "he", "they" as well as for verbs. The other important feature of Urdu is the gender differentiation of the verb. For instance, "I am going" in English would be *"mein jah rahha hoon"* in Urdu if it is a man saying it, and *"mein jah rahhi hoon"* if it is a woman saying it. Every subject and object is either masculine or feminine, and the relevant masculine or feminine verb needs to be used with it. For instance, door is masculine but window feminine, river is masculine but stream feminine, flood is masculine but windstorm feminine, and the relevant verb needs to be used in each case. The masculine words often end in an "aa" sound and the feminine in an "ee" sound.

Pakistan has a rich literary tradition, notably in Urdu, dating back to the sixteenth century. Sindhi is also rich in both language and literature. Punjabi and Pashto have a rich oral tradition of poems and folk songs. Most Pakistanis adore poetry and often memorize and recite poems, a tradition not known in the West. *Mushairas* (poetry readings) are very popular in Pakistan and very widely attended. Mirza Ghalib (1797–1869) is the most admired and quoted poet of the Urdu language, an iconic figure who is most famous for his *ghazals* (a poetry form with five or more two-line couplets in which all the second lines rhyme with each other), which typically describe love and other emotions. Ghazals are sung by popular singers and in concerts, and by ordinary people as well. One of Ghalib's ghazals has been translated as follows (Weston 1992, 205):

Passion feels confined
even in the heart—
the sea's restless surge
absorbed in a pearl.

Sir Muhammad Iqbal (1877–1938), the poet-philosopher who died before his dream of independent Pakistan could be realized, is the national poet of modern Pakistan. Contemporary Pakistani Urdu writers who have won recognition include Faiz Ahmad Faiz (1911–1918), known for both his romantic and socialist poetry; short-story writer Saadat Hasan Minto (1912–1955); and Ahmad Nadeem Qasmi (1916–), among others. The most popular poet of the Sindhi language is the Sufi mystic Shah Abdul Latif (1689–1752), and the most famous poet of the Pashto language is Khushhal Khan Khattak (1613–1689).

The following are some useful survival Urdu expressions. **Us-salam-o-alaikum.** Greetings, meaning "Peace be unto you." Appropriate any time of the day, always when meeting somebody, but sometimes also when saying goodbye. **Valaikum us-salam.** And on you be peace.

Aap kaise hain? How are you?
Khudah Hahfiz, Allah Hafiz. Goodbye, meaning God take care of you.
Kiyah ho rahah hai? What is going on?
Kiyah sub khairyat hai? Is everything okay?
Ach-chha. Commonly used, meaning okay, yes, or good, depending on context. For example, in response to instructions like "come tomorrow," one can say "ach-chha."
Yay Achchha hai. This is good.
Kharahb. Bad.
Nahi. No.
Mehrbani. Please.
Shukriyah. Thank you.
Aap kah nahm kyah hai? What is your name?
Mera nahm Jane hai. My name is Jane.
Mujhe oordoo (Urdu) naheen ahtee. I do not speak Urdu.
Kyah ahp ko angrezee ahtee hai? Do you know English?
Insha'Allah. God willing.
Ek minute. One minute, meaning just a moment.
Intizar kijiyay. Please wait.
Maaf kijiyay. Please pardon me.
Kyah hoa? What happened?
Yay kyah hai? What is this?
_____ Ka-hahn hai? Where is _____?
Kaisay? How?
Is ki kyah keemat hai? What is the price of this?
Kub? When?
Ahp or Tum (the familiar). You.
Bus. Enough.
Khahna, roti. Food.
Pani. Water.
Pakhana/Bait-ul-Khulah. Restroom/toilet/bathroom.
Ek, do, teen, chahr, pahnch. 1, 2, 3, 4, 5.
cheh, saht, ahth, nau, dus. 6, 7, 8, 9, 10.
bees, tees, chalees. 20, 30, 40.
pa-chahs, ek sau. 50, 100.

FOOD AND BEVERAGES

Eating in Pakistan is a time-honored social activity, and Pakistan's cuisine is one of the best in the world. No other food, except perhaps French and Chinese, is as consistently delicious and varied. It is based on grains, lentils, and legumes, as well as meat and vegetables. But the key to Pakistani cooking is the extensive use of spices and herbs, seasonings, and flavorings, which are blended in many different ways, creating dozens of flavors. The typical spices used in most dishes are garlic, ginger, coriander, turmeric, chilies, cumin seeds, pepper, and *garam masala* (a mixture of black spices like cloves, black pepper, cinnamon, big black cardamom, and bay leaves). The additional spices used only for specific preparations are fennel seeds, mustard, nutmeg, mace, poppy seeds, pomegranate seeds, and saffron.

Pakistani food is similar to North Indian food, although the varieties of meat dishes are greater in Pakistan. The widespread Mughal style of cooking in Pakistan emerged from the royal kitchens of the Mughal Muslim emperors of India from the sixteenth to eighteenth centuries. Mughal cuisine includes a selection of meats and poultry cooked in yogurt and selected spices and herbs deep-fried in *ghee* (made from melted butter); tandoori dishes baked in a clay oven; flat breads; and a variety of rice dishes. The daily diet for most Pakistanis typically consists of one staple (bread or rice), dahl, vegetables, and some type of meat if one can afford it. The higher the income of a household, the greater the variety of side dishes to complement the rice and bread. There is tremendous variety in types of bread, forms of rice dishes, choices of vegetables, and meat dishes. Most of the meat and vegetable dishes are cooked by first browning the onions, then adding the spices and browning them, and finally adding the meat or vegetable and cooking on low heat till tender. Each of the ethnic groups is particularly known for certain foods: Punjabis for their sahg, dahl, and breads; Sindhis for their seafood dishes; Pathans for their *chapli kebabs* (fried patties of ground mutton, lamb, or beef mixed with green onions, crushed pomegranate seeds, and other mild spices); Balochis for *sajji* (whole grilled lamb); and Muhajirs for *qorma* (special meat curry).

Common Pakistani Dishes

Dahl. The most common food in Pakistan is dahl, which is a type of soupy stew made with orange, yellow, or black lentils, or *mung* beans. The lentils are boiled with onions, garlic, ginger, turmeric, pepper, and chilies until the liquid has the consistency of porridge. Dahl is garnished with fried garlic, cumin seeds, and oil. Rice is not considered complete without dahl, although dahl is also eaten with bread. Dahl with rice or bread often serves as an entire meal for the poor, but a side dish at almost every meal for the nonpoor. It is a very important source of protein, particularly in the poorer households that cannot afford meat.

Bread. Breads, together with rice, are the mainstay of the Pakistani diet. Most Pakistanis do not use knives and forks. Instead they break off a piece of bread and use it to scoop up dahl or meat or vegetables, avoiding touching it with their fingers. The most common type of bread is *chapati*, which is round and flat like a tortilla. It is unleavened bread made out of wheat flour, cooked in an iron pan on top of the stove on both sides, and then briefly held over a flame till it puffs up and becomes soft. It is also called *roti*, which is also used generically to mean any type of bread, or meals in general. Other breads are *parathas*, which are softer, thicker, and flakier than chapatis because oil is added during the kneading of the flour as well as in the pan frying; *stuffed parathas*, which are parathas filled with potatoes or ground beef; *naan*, made from white flour, which is kneaded with milk and then baked; and *puri*, made from white flour and deep-fried.

Vegetables. Popular vegetable dishes include *alu gobi*

(potatoes and cauliflower); *alu matar* (potatoes and peas); *bhindi* (okra); different greens, including *palak* (spinach), *surson ka sahg* (mustard greens), and *tori;* and *lauki* (squash). All vegetable dishes are cooked either on low heat with only oil, garlic, chilies, and cumin seeds, or curry style, which involves frying first onions and then spices, and cooking vegetables in the mixture.

Meat. Meat is a very desirable food in Pakistan. The affluent eat it at both lunch and dinner, but even the landless villagers can afford to eat it once every week. People in sheepherding areas like NWFP and Balochistan eat it more often than others. The preferred meat is chicken, goat, lamb, and beef, in that order. Chicken is the most prestigious and beef the least—beef is less preferred perhaps because of the impact of Hinduism, which prohibits beef in particular. Like the Jews, Muslims have religious dietary restrictions on consumption of ham and pork in all forms. All Muslims are very particular about this restriction and take great care to follow it, which is more challenging if they live in non-Muslim countries. Moreover, the animals have to be slaughtered in a particular way, making the meat *"halal,"* similar to the Jewish conditions on "kosher."

The favorite meat dishes in Pakistan include mutton or chicken *qorma,* cubes of meat cooked with fried onions, yogurt, and spices in a thick, spicy gravy; *saag gosht,* cubes of mutton and spinach in a thick spicy sauce; *aloo gosht,* cubes of mutton and potatoes in a soupy spicy sauce; *shami kebab,* small patties of minced beef boiled with onions and spices and deep-fried; *kofta,* spicy meatballs of beef in a soupy sauce; and *seekh kebab,* patties of beef, lamb, or chicken mixed with spices, rolled into tubes, and grilled. Barbecued chicken, mutton, and beef are also very popular, both *tikka* style (charcoal grilled) and *tandoori* (baked in a clay oven).

Rice. Rice is cooked in many forms. Apart from plain boiled white rice, there is *khichri*—rice and any of the lentils cooked together with some oil, garlic, ginger, salt, and yogurt; peas or vegetable *pulao*—rice cooked with peas or mixed vegetables in the same way as *khichri; tahiri*—rice cooked with potatoes and spices fried in oil (turmeric, onions, garlic, ginger, coriander, red chilies, and salt); and *pulao*—rice cooked with meat in meat broth. The fanciest rice dish is *biryani*—boiled white rice and *qorma* (meat curry), arranged in layers and steamed. All these forms of rice are full or stand-alone meals, except boiled plain rice, which is served with dahl, vegetables, or meat.

Curry. Curry is not a particular dish or preparation but a method of blending specific spices and of cooking. It involves browning onions in oil, followed by browning spices (ginger, garlic, coriander, turmeric, hot chili pepper, salt), and then cooking meat or vegetables in this sauce.

In addition, there are a wide variety of pickles, chutneys, and sauces, the most popular being *khira raita,* plain yogurt with grated cucumbers and mint; and *imli chutney,* made with tamarind, sugar, salt, and red pepper. The most popular snacks are *samosas,* dough pockets stuffed with beef, mutton, chicken, potatoes, or peas.

Desserts. A Pakistani meal is not complete without dessert. Most Pakistani desserts, unlike Western ones, are made from fresh milk, which is boiled and cooked until it thickens. Nuts like almonds and pistachios, and raisins are added to most desserts. The most common desserts are *kheer* or *firni,* rice pudding; *sheer,* vermicelli noodles cooked with milk and sugar; *zarda,* sweet rice of yellow color; and *shahi tukra* (literally meaning royal pieces), slices of deep-fried bread cooked in cream and sugar and topped with nuts and saffron. In addition, dozens of varieties of sugary sweets, made from milk or grain and known as sweet meats, are sold in sweet meat shops found in every neighborhood.

Common Pakistani Beverages

Tea. As in the rest of South Asia, tea, with milk and sugar, is the most popular drink in Pakistan, particularly in urban areas. Sometimes tea is made with spices such as nutmeg, cinnamon, cloves, and cardamom. Guests who visit home or office are always served a cup of hot tea, often with snacks.

Lass-see. Made from yogurt, *lass-see* is a favorite drink in the summer, particularly in the Punjab. A salty *lass-see*, typical in the Punjab, is a beverage taken with lunch and dinner, which is widely regarded as very healthy for the dry summers of Punjab. The sweet version, taken at no particular time, is very popular all over Pakistan. A sweet *lass-see* with mango juice is very popular at Pakistani restaurants in the United States.

Soft Drinks. Soft drinks, particularly Coca-Cola, have become very popular in Pakistan and are widely available, both imported ones and those that are produced domestically. They are still considered luxury drinks. Fruit juices and drinks have also become more available.

Alcoholic Drinks. There is a religious prohibition on alcohol consumption for Muslims, but this restriction is less strictly followed by Pakistanis and other Muslims than the one on consumption of pork. Although there is a legal prohibition in Pakistan on drinking as well as social censure against it, some Pakistanis consume alcoholic drinks in their homes and private parties, particularly those belonging to the upper classes.

On the whole, the preparation of a Pakistani meal is quite time-consuming, particularly if it is cooked for a large or an extended family. Cooking is almost always the responsibility of women, and most Pakistani men have very little to do with the preparation of a meal. Wealthy and upper-middle-income households often hire a male servant who cooks, shops for groceries, washes dishes, and sets the table. Even middle- and lower-middle-income households hire a female servant, popularly known as a *masee*, who works at one or more of the following chores and charges per activity: washing dishes, washing clothes, and cleaning the house.

ETIQUETTE

Pakistani society has its own set of etiquette and manners, but foreigners are not expected to know it or to abide by it. Still it is important to know it in order to gain a better understanding of the culture. The reader should also note that Pakistani etiquette and manners are undergoing change due to increasing Western influence and globalization.

Greetings. Throughout Pakistan, the greeting when meeting somebody is *"us-salam-o-alaikum,"* meaning peace be unto you. It is used on both formal and informal occasions, and is appropriate any time of the day. Between two people of different ages, the younger person always takes the initiative in the greeting. This greeting may also be used when saying goodbye, although the more common expression is *"Allah Hafiz"* or *"Khuda Hafiz,"* meaning God protect you.

Hospitality to Guests. One of the most enduring traits of Pakistani culture is hospitality to guests. Welcoming and honoring guests and offering them food and drink are a time-honored practice among Pakistanis of all geographic regions and socioeconomic classes. If a guest, whether a relative, friend, neighbor, or friend of a friend, happens to visit a family during lunch or dinner hours, it is expected that the visitor will be offered a full meal. Moreover, the choicest items will be served to the guest. If guests visit at other times, they are still offered something to eat or drink—tea, snacks, or fruits. It is very embarrassing for a host to be unable to offer anything to a guest. There are numerous stories of poor farmers offering fruits or nuts produced on their farms (and their source of income) to visitors when they had nothing else to offer. The culture of sharing food is so pervasive that it is considered highly impolite to eat something by yourself and not offer it to others if you are in the company of others, whether or not it is your home.

Similarly, accommodating guests in your home, whatever its size, number of bedrooms, and number of guests, is very common in Pakistan. People typically say that what matters is room in your heart, and not the number of rooms in the house. It is customary in Punjab for middle-class households to own several sets of blankets and bedding to accommodate guests from out of town. Even among the Pakistani-Americans living in the United States, children are trained to give up their rooms willingly for family and friends who visit from out of town. It is an insult to both the host and the guest if visitors stay in a hotel when visiting friends or relatives out of town.

Respect for Age and Relationships. One of the most deep-rooted Pakistani traditions across every region and class is the tremendous respect for age, particularly for parents. Elderly persons are given more consideration than anyone else in Pakistan, and they are respected for their wisdom. When meeting a group of people, the elderly are to be acknowledged first. This respect for age is reflected in a multitude of customs, rules of conduct, actions, expressions, behavior, demeanor, tone of voice, and language. Examples of this respect include not eating until people older than you have begun to eat, giving a seat on a bus to an unknown older person, getting a parent's approval in the most important decisions of life, and happily agreeing to arranged marriages (arranged by parents) due to a firm belief in parents' love and wisdom. Children are taught deference for all elders and people older than themselves from an early age, whether they are family members, relatives, neighbors, friends, or even strangers. Parents are not only loved but also respected and obeyed. It is considered very impolite to disagree with them, especially in public. It is very common, for example, to find smokers refraining from smoking in front of their fathers out of pure respect, even when they have children of their own.

Forms of Address. In most cases, it is not considered polite in Pakistan to address people older than you by their first names. The proper way is to address by reference to both age and relationship. In fact, Urdu and all regional languages of

Pakistan have distinct words to describe each close relationship within the extended family that have no equivalent in English, such as *dada* and *dadi* (paternal grandfather and grandmother), *nana* and *nani* (maternal grandfather and grandmother), *taya* and *tayi* (father's elder brother and his wife), *chacha* and *chachi* (father's younger brother and his wife), *mamu* and *momani* (mother's brother and his wife), *phoopi* and *phoopa* (father's sister and her husband), *khala* and *khalu* (mother's sister and her husband), *bhabi* (elder brother's wife), and *doolah bhai* (elder sister's husband). Elder brothers are not addressed by their name alone, but either a prefix of *bhai* (brother) is attached to their name or they are just called *bhaijan* (best translated into dear brother, as *jan* means life or soul). Similarly, elder sisters are not addressed by their name alone, but either a prefix of *apa* or *baji* (elder sister) is attached to their name or they are just called *apajan* or *bajijan* (dear sister), or just *apa* or *baji*. Age and relationships are so revered in Pakistan that even older family friends, neighbors, and friends of friends are not addressed by their first name, but are just called by the gender- and age-appropriate titles listed above. As an expression of respect, it is common to call someone of one's father's age "*chacha*," and someone of one's mother's age "*khala*," or simply the English equivalents, that is, uncle and aunt. Those of older brothers' or sisters' age are called *bhai* (older brother) or *baji* (older sister). Even shopkeepers, vendors, and domestics address their customers/ employers as *bhai* and *baji*.

Similar to the tradition of respect for elders and the proper forms of address, there is also the tradition of social hierarchy and respect for higher officials or social ranks. It is quite common for people to address their bosses or teachers as "sir" or "madam" forever, even when they are not their employees and students. Calling them by their first names would be an insult. Unlike the United States, whenever people in Pakistan see their teachers, whether or not they are current students, they greet their teachers with great deference.

Privacy and Personal Space. The Pakistani concept of personal space, or lack of it, is sometimes a source of frustration and misunderstanding among Westerners. As a result of the extended family structure in Pakistan, where an individual is surrounded by people all the time, and the high population density, few Pakistanis value privacy the way most Westerners do. It is very common for Pakistani hosts never to leave their guests by themselves, unattended, at any time, as a mark of their hospitality and concern. Western guests, however, are bothered by it. Pakistani hosts want to be hospitable, not realizing that their Western guests want some privacy and time alone. This misunderstanding is also common between Pakistani immigrants and their American-born children, when the children close the door to their bedrooms just because they want privacy; the parents, not understanding this need on the part of their children, feel shut out.

Subtlety in Compliments, Please, and Thank You. It is not common to pay direct compliments to one another in Pakistan because it may be interpreted as fake. So when someone says, "your clothes look great," they mean "you look great." When someone is praised for his or her success or accomplishments or health, it is very common to preface or end it with "Masha Allah," meaning "by the grace of God." Moreover, compliments are not reciprocated openly but displayed in subtle forms. This subtlety is also evident in responding to a "thank you," in saying "thank you," and in saying "please." For example, a "thank you" may not elicit a reply of "you're welcome." But this is not a sign of rudeness; rather, it signifies humility in that one's action is a matter of duty and not necessarily something that deserves to be thanked, somewhat in the same vein as the British response "don't mention it." Similarly, while Pakistanis may not say please and thank you in words, they express it in a hundred ways through demeanor, tone of voice, and sentence structure. Unlike English, there is no single word for "please" in Urdu, but the sentiment is expressed through qualifying the "verb" in a sentence; for example, verbs like *aeeyay, jaeeyay,* and *kijiyay* mean please come, please go, and please do, respectively. In fact, the humble demeanor and the facial expression showing the relevant sentiments (request for "please," gratefulness for "thank you," and deep regrets for "sorry") serve as substitutes for "please," "thank you," and "sorry."

Modesty and Humbleness. A sense of modesty and humbleness about one's achievements is expected behavior in Pakistan. Open bragging and self-congratulatory statements about oneself are considered impolite, ungraceful, and uncultured. Pakistanis often do not like to use words in the superlative, such as fantastic, awesome, or wonderful, although this is changing with American influence. It is also not considered modest to look directly in the eyes of a senior person, or elder, or someone of the opposite sex. Modesty also requires that one does not speak too much in front of elders and does not use inappropriate language or discuss topics such as sex, pregnancy, and childbirth. Similarly, such topics are not discussed in the presence of the opposite sex.

Public Display of Affection between Opposite Sexes. As in the rest of South Asia, including Bangladesh, India, and Nepal, displaying affection between a man and a woman in public is seen as an immoral act. This is particularly true for women, who will be perceived as having a loose character that would bring disgrace to the family. Even husbands and wives should not kiss or hug in public in Pakistan. Foreigners should refrain from touching a person of the opposite sex.

Taking Shoes Off. It is not customary in most Pakistani homes, unlike India, Bangladesh, and Nepal, to take one's shoes off at the main entryway before entering the home. This tradition is primarily rooted in the Hindu religion where homes are places where gods are kept and worshipped. It is also common in Arab countries. But it has increasingly become common at the homes of Pakistani immigrant families in North America, partly because of Arab influence. However, shoes are always taken off at mosques.

Eating and Drinking. When invited to a Pakistani home, expect to be served a meal that is special and better than what the host typically eats at home. The host or hostess will repeatedly request guests to eat more and take seconds, as an expression of hospitality. It is also the custom for guests to decline the offer, at least the first time. When the host insists again, then the guest will eat more. Pakistanis typically do not use the fork or spoon, but eat with their hands. It is the custom to wash hands thoroughly before and after eating. The rule for dining out in Pakistan is that the person who suggests going out pays, though people often argue over who pays. It is considered very impolite to go Dutch treat, although it is becoming more common with American influence.

Clothes. Pakistan is a relatively traditional and conservative society with regard to clothes and dressing, particularly for women. The preferred clothing allows only minimal body exposure; even men should not wear shorts. Women are expected to avoid low-cut dresses, short skirts, sleeveless shirts, and exposure of thighs and cleavage. The use of Western clothes is rare for women in public places, although jeans are popular among the upper classes. People in Pakistan typically wear light, white, and pure cotton clothes in summer, and heavier ones in winter. Almost everyone, rich or poor, urban or rural, male or female, wears a *shalwar-qameez,* a pair of thin baggy trousers tapered at the ankles and a long, pajama-like shirt that extends down to the knees. Women also wear a *dupatta,* a scarf-like shawl. While almost all women wear *shalwar-qameez* all the time, many middle- and upper-class men wear Western-style clothes (shirts and pants), at least for work.

Nose Blowing. Contrary to the Unites States, blowing one's nose at the dinner table or at an eating place is extremely unsociable.

Shopping. When shopping in Pakistan, it is perfectly acceptable to bargain in open markets, small shops in shopping plazas, and other markets. However, department stores and some shops have fixed prices.

Business Cards. Exchanging business cards is becoming quite common in business meetings and official visits.

Gift Giving. Gift giving is very important in Pakistani culture, whether it is a regular gift, money, a box of sweet meats, or flower garlands. The important occasions that warrant gifts are weddings; birthdays; birth of a child; engagement; graduation; going to or returning from *Hajj, Eid-ul-Fitr,* or *Eid-ul-Azha;* fasting for the first time; and others. Typically, people older in age give money to younger relatives on Eid-ul-Fitr and Eid-ul-Azha, and sweet meats and flower garlands are more common on occasions of *Hajj.*

Punctuality. Pakistanis are very relaxed about time, particularly in social contexts. It is not uncommon for movies, parties, and public events to begin a little late. More recently, weddings have started to begin much later than scheduled.

Pakistan-Related Organizations

BUSINESS AND ECONOMICS

The following is a list of various Pakistani organizations related to trade, commerce, banking, and economic development. Note that telephone calls to Pakistan require a country code (92) and the appropriate city code. The city codes for Karachi, Lahore, and Islamabad are 21, 42, and 51, respectively.

Agha Khan Rural Support Programme (AKRSP)
Head Office: P.O. Box 506, Gilgit Road
Gilgit, Northern Areas, Pakistan
Phone: (92–572) 2480
Fax: (92–572) 2779
E-mail: akrspog@glt.comsats.net.pk
  A nonprofit organization operating in the rural areas of NWFP (Chitral, Gilgit, and Skardu), the AKRSP focuses on poverty alleviation through agricultural and infrastructure development, microcredit, and training, with special focus on women.

Agricultural Development Bank of Pakistan
Zarai Taraqiati Bank Limited
Head Office: 1 Faisal Avenue
P.O. Box 1400
Islamabad, Pakistan
E-mail: adbp@isb.paknet.com.pk
http://www.adbp.org.pk

Allied Bank
Khyaban-e-Iqbal, Main Clifton Road,
Bath Island
Karachi, Pakistan
Phone: (92–21) 111110110

Board of Investment
Karachi Office: Kandawala Building
M. A. Jinnah Road
Karachi, Pakistan
Phone: (92–21) 9215067
Fax: (92–21) 9215078
E-mail: boikarachi@pakboi.gov.pk
    The Board of Investment is a government organization set
up to promote domestic and foreign investment and to
enhance Pakistan's international competitiveness.

Export Promotion Bureau
5th Floor, Block A
Finance & Trade Centre
P.O. Box 1293
Shahrah-e-Faisal
Karachi 75200, Pakistan
Phone: (92–21) 9206487–90
E-mail: epb@epb.gov.pk
http://www.epb.gov.pk
    The Export Promotion Bureau is a government organiza-
tion set up to promote Pakistani exports. Its website includes
an exhaustive list of trade and manufacturers' associations in
Pakistan.

Federation of Pakistan Chambers of Commerce & Industry
(FPCCI)
Head Office: Federation House Sharea Firdousi
Main Clifton, P.O. Box 13875
Karachi 75600, Pakistan

Phone: (92–21) 5873691–94
Fax: (92–21) 5874332
Cable: FEDCOMERC
Telex: 25370 FPCCI PK
E-Mail: fairs@khi.fpcci.infolink.net.pk

An apex body of trade and industry, FPCCI aims to promote, encourage, and safeguard the interest of the private sector in Pakistan and to serve as a bridge between the business community and the government.

Habib Bank
Habib Bank Plaza
I.I. Chundrigar Road
Karachi 75650, Pakistan
Pakistan Phones: (92–21) 2418000 (50 lines)
Fax: (92–21) 2411647
Telex: 20086–20751 HBANK-PK

Karachi Chamber of Commerce & Industry
Aiwan-e-Tijarat Road
Karachi 74000, Pakistan
Phone: (92–21) 2416091/94, 2415435–9
Fax: (92–21) 2416095, 2410587
E-mail: info@karachichamber.com, ccikar@cyber.net.pk
http://www.karachichamber.com

Karachi Cotton Association
The Cotton Exchange
I. I. Chundrigar Road
Karachi, Pakistan
Phone: (92–21) 2425007, 2412570, 2416497, and 2410336
Fax: (92–21) 021–2413035, 2412580
E-mail: kca33@cyber.net.pk
http://www.kcapak.org

338 PAKISTAN: A Global Studies Handbook

Karachi Stock Exchange
Stock Exchange Building
Stock Exchange Road
Karachi, Pakistan
Phone: (92–21) 2415213–15, 2425502–04, and 2419146
Fax: 021–2416072
E-mail: info@kse.com.pk
http://www.kse.com.pk

The Karachi Stock Exchange (KSE) was established in September 1947, immediately following the birth of Pakistan. It has grown from ninety members, six brokers, and five companies with a paid-up capital of Rs. 37 million in 1947 to 200 members, 133 brokers, and 724 companies with a listed capital of Rs. 438.49 billion (US$7.36 billion) in June 2005. The KSE 100 Index closed at 7450.12 on June 30, 2005. Its major functions include listing of companies and monitoring their activities; trading of listed securities; settlement of trading; and market surveillance, administration, and control.

Khidmat Foundation
Head Office: 11-B, P&V Farms, Scheme 2, St. 4
Park Road, Chak Shahzad
Islamabad, Pakistan
Phone: (92–51) 2241503
E-mail: khidmat@khidmat.org
http://www.khidmat.org

An all-Pakistan NGO targeting landless peasants, wage laborers, subsistence farmers, youth, and women, the foundation focuses on projects for urban renewal, eco-friendly environment, solid-waste management, town planning, slum development, as well as consumer protection against unfair trade practices and hazardous conditions in workplaces.

National Bank of Pakistan Head Office
NBP Building Karachi, Pakistan
E-mail: enquiries@nationalbank.com.pk

Orangi Pilot Project and Orangi Charitable Trust
Head Office: Street 4, Sector 5/A, Qasba Township
Karachi 75800, Pakistan
Phone: (92–21) 6658021, 6652297
Fax: (92–21) 6665696
E-mail: opp@digicom.net.pk
An NGO with a track record of success and accountability, the OPP focuses on poverty alleviation in rural and urban areas of Pakistan through community-based efforts.

Overseas Investors Chamber of Commerce and Industry
P.O. Box 4833, Talpur Road
Karachi, Pakistan
Phone: (92–21) 2410814
Fax: (92–21) 2427315
E-mail: info@oicci.org
http://www.oicci.org
The Overseas Investors Chamber of Commerce and Industry stems from the Karachi Chamber of Commerce, which was founded in 1860 and was the oldest Chamber of Commerce in Pakistan. It is a mix of large and small international enterprises in all sectors of the economy, with the aim of promoting the interests of the business community.

Pakistan Carpet Manufacturers & Exporters Association
401-A, 4th Floor, Panorama Centre 1
Fatima Jinnah Road, Saddar
Karachi, Pakistan
Phone: (92–21) 5212189
Fax: (92–21) 5678649
E-mail: pcmeaho@gerrys.net

Pakistan Chamber of Commerce–USA
9700 Club Creek Drive
Houston, TX 77036–7214
Phone: (713) 771–9628

Pakistan Electronics Manufacturers Association
Showroom "B," Al-Haroon 10
Agha Khan III Road
Karachi, Pakistan
Phone: (92–21) 5658872
Fax: (92–21) 5689819
E-mail: Pema@cyber.net.pk

Pakistan Engineering Components & Machinery
Manufacturing Association
10 Nargis Block, Iqbal Town
Lahore, Pakistan
Phone: (92–42) 7841300, 6364065
Fax: (92–42) 7832456
E-mail: grand@lcci.org.pk, ecmma@lcci.org.pk

Pakistan Handicrafts Manufacturers & Exporters Association
13/14 Firdous Colony
New Golimar No. 2
Karachi, Pakistan
Phone: (92–21) 6689085, 6685762, and 5681853

Pakistan Industrial Credit & Investment Corporation (PICIC)
Schon Center
I. I. Chundrigar Road
Karachi 74200, Pakistan

Pakistan Industrial Development Corporation
2nd Floor, PIDC House
Dr. Ziauddin Ahmad Road
Karachi, Pakistan
Phone: (92–21) 5685041–9
Fax: (92–21) 9204376
E-mail: pidc@hki.comsats.net.pk, chpidc@khi.comsats.net.pk,
        pidcops@khi.comsats.net.pk
http://www.pidc.org.pk

Pakistan Information Home Page
http://www.pakistaninformation.com/, http://www.infopak.
gov.pk/, http://www.pakgov.pk/public/county_profile.html
These are comprehensive websites on Pakistan providing
information on the country's history, geography, economy,
cultural heritage, tourism, and government.

Pakistan Textile Exporters Association
30/7 Civil Lines, Near State Bank
Faisalabad, Pakistan
Phone: (92–41) 644750–51, 644754
Fax: (92–41) 617985
E-mail: apcea@fsd.paknet.com.pk

State Bank of Pakistan
I. I. Chundrigar Road
Karachi, Pakistan
Phone: (92–21) 24450298
Fax: (92–21) 9212440
The State Bank is the central bank of Pakistan. It deter-
mines the country's monetary policy, including regulating the
issue of the currency and the keeping of reserves, managing
the credit and monetary system, preserving the par value of
the Pakistani currency (rupee), and maintaining stability in
the economy by controlling inflation and unemployment.

CULTURE, EDUCATION, AND EXCHANGE

Agha Khan University
Stadium Road, P.O. Box 3500
Karachi 74800, Pakistan
Phone: (92–21) 4930051
Fax: (92–21) 4934294, 4932095
E-mail: aku@aku.edu
http://www.aku.edu
Founded by His Highness the Aga Khan and chartered in

1983 as Pakistan's first private university, AKU seeks to provide instruction, training, research, and service in the health sciences through its Medical College, School of Nursing and Teaching Hospital, and Institutes for Educational Development and for the Study of Muslim Civilizations.

Agricultural University Faisalabad
Faisalabad, Pakistan
Phone: (92–411) 601822
Fax: (92–411) 647846
　　Founded in 1909 as Punjab Agricultural College and Research Institute, the university acquired its present status and title in 1961. It offers B.Sc., M.Sc., and Ph.D. degrees under its faculties of Agriculture, Veterinary Sciences, Animal Husbandry, Crop Production, Agriculture Economics and Rural Sociology, Agriculture Engineering and Technology, and Faculty of Science.

Arts Council of Pakistan
M. R. Kayani Road
Karachi 74200, Pakistan
Phone: (92–21) 2635108
Fax: (92–21) 2634055
http://www.un.org.pk/unic/ACP.htm
　　The Arts Council of Pakistan organizes exhibitions of visual arts; performing arts programs, including mimic shows and stage dramas; and cultural exchange programs with other countries.

Chawkandi Art
105 Marine Point
D.C. 1, Kehkashan, Clifton
Karachi, Pakistan
Phone: (92–21) 573582
Fax: (92–21) 575912
http://www.chawkandi.com/main.html
　　Established in 1985, Chawkandi Art is a leading art gallery in Pakistan.

Country Clubs
http://www.getpakistan.com/karachi/clubs.htm
  This site is a good source for country clubs in Karachi.

Cyber Cafes
http://www.getpakistan.com/karachi/CyberCafes1.htm
  This site provides an exhaustive list of cyber cafes in Karachi.

Higher Education Commission
H-9
Islamabad, Pakistan
Phone: (92–51) 9040000–1, 9257651–60
Fax: (92–51) 9290128
info@hec.gov.pk
  The Higher Education Commission (HEC) has been set up to facilitate the development of the universities of Pakistan to be world-class centers of education, research, and development. The HEC also supervises the planning, development, and accreditation of public- and private-sector institutions of higher education.

International Islamic University Islamabad
P.O. Box 1243
Islamabad, Pakistan
Phone: (92–51) 54068
Fax: (92–51) 853360
  Founded in 1980, the Islamic University consists of the faculties of Sharia and Law, Arabic, and Management Sciences; the Institutes of Languages and of Islamic Economics; and the School of Economics, among others.

Lahore University of Management Sciences (LUMS)
Opposite Sector U, DHA
Lahore 54792, Pakistan
http://www.lums.edu.pk

The Lahore University of Management Sciences (LUMS) is a national university, established by sponsors belonging to the country's leading private- and public-sector corporations. Distinguished by its highly competitive admissions process and the quality of its faculty, LUMS offers degrees in several disciplines, including law and policy, science and engineering, business administration, and arts and sciences.

Rafi Peer Theatre Workshop
No. 25, F/3, Block D
National Homes, New Muslim Town
Lahore, Pakistan
Phone: (92–42) 5885074, 5885075, and 5885079
E-mail: rptw@brain.net.pk, rptw@magic.net.pk

Founded in 1974, the Rafi Peer Theatre Workshop is the oldest independent theatre/puppet company of Pakistan. It organizes major international arts festivals and has organized nineteen international festivals of puppetry, theatre, dance, music, and film in the last thirteen years. These festivals have featured over 2,500 performances by approximately 5,000 artists from more than seventy-six countries.

Tehrik-e-Niswan
3-C, Zamzama Commercial Lane No. 3
DHA, Phase 5
Karachi 75600 (3A), Pakistan
Phone: (92–21) 5822721, 5837119
E-mail: tehrik@hotmail.com

Founded in 1980 and working for peace and human rights through theatre and art, Tehrik-e-Niswan is the only group in Karachi that performs street theatre. Focusing on themes such as son preference, child marriage, and dowry, Tehrik-e-

Niswan seeks to raise awareness about gender discrimination and to change attitudes toward women. It also conducts theatre workshops for workers and leaders of community organizations.

University of Karachi
University Road
Karachi, Pakistan
Phone: (92–21) 9243131–42, 8372563
Fax: (92–21) 9243161
E-mail: registrar@ku.edu.pk
http://www.ku.edu.pk, http://www.kucwn.edu.pk
    The University of Karachi, established in 1950, is spread over 1,279 acres of land. About 20,000 students are enrolled in the fifty-one departments functioning under eight faculties, including Arts, Business Administration, Commerce, Islamic Studies, Pharmacy, and Science, as well as twenty-five research institutes and centers. Foreign students from twenty-three different countries comprise about 4 percent of the student body. More than 150 colleges are affiliated with this university.

University of the Punjab
P.O. Box 54590
Lahore, Pakistan
Phone: (92–42) 9231102
Fax: (92–42) 9231103
E-mail: registrar@pu.edu.pk
http://www.pu.edu.pk
    The University of the Punjab is not only the oldest university in Pakistan but also the largest.

USEF in Pakistan (USEFP)–The Fulbright Commission
P.O. Box 1128
Islamabad, Pakistan
Phone: (92–51) 2278344

Fax: (92–51) 2271563
E-mail: info@usefpakistan.org

The United States Educational Foundation in Pakistan (USEFP), established in 1950 by the governments of Pakistan and the United States, is one of fifty-one Fulbright commissions located throughout the world. The foundation is dedicated to improving mutual understanding between the people of Pakistan and the people of the United States of America through educational exchange opportunities. It administers a variety of programs that send Pakistani scholars to American campuses while bringing American scholars to universities in Pakistan. The programs for Pakistani citizens include the following: Fulbright Student Program, Fulbright Scholar Program, Fulbright/USAID Program, Hubert H. Humphrey Program, Foreign Language Teaching Assistant Program, and American Studies Summer Institutes.

PAKISTAN'S GOVERNMENT REPRESENTATIVES IN THE UNITED STATES

Consulates General of Pakistan
Chicago
333 North Michigan Avenue, Suite 728
Chicago, IL 60601
Phone: (312) 781–1831, (312) 781–1833
Fax: (312) 781–1839
E-mail: parepchicago@yahoo.com
Boston
Honorary Consulate General
20 Chestnut Street
Needham, MA 02492
Phone: (781) 455–8000
Fax: (781) 453–1188
E-mail: pakistan@tiac.net

Houston
11850 Jones Road
Houston, TX 77070
Phone: (281) 890–2223
Fax: (281) 890–1433
E-mail: grbaluch@hotmail.com, parephouston@sbcglobal.net
Los Angeles
10850 Wilshire Boulevard., Suite 1250
Los Angeles, CA 90024
Phone: (310) 441–0161, 310–446–6695
Fax: (310) 441–9256
E-mail: info@pakconsulatela.org
New York
12 East 65th Street
New York, NY 10021
Phone: (212) 879–5800, 212–517–7541
Fax: (212) 517–6987
E-mail:nyconsulate@embassyofpakistan.org,
www.pakistanconsulateny.org

Embassy of Pakistan
3517 International Court, NW
Washington, DC, 20008
Phone: (202) 243–6500
E-mail: info@embassyofpakistan.org
http://www.embassyofpakistan.org

United Nations Permanent Mission
8 East 65th Street
New York, NY 10021
Phone: (212) 879–8600
Fax (212) 744–7348
E-mail: Pakistan@un.int
http://www.un.int/pakistan

INTERNATIONAL DEVELOPMENT AGENCIES AND NGOs IN PAKISTAN

Action Aid Pakistan
http://actionaidpakistan.org/
Action Aid Pakistan is an international NGO dedicated to the eradication of poverty, focusing on children, labor, women, and youth. Food security, water and land management, disaster management, citizenship, and peace are some of the issues dealt with using a participatory approach.

Amnesty International
B-12 Shelozon Centre
Gulsan-e-Iqbal
Block 15, University Road
Karachi 75300, Pakistan
Phone: (92–21) 4960661
Fax: (92–21) 4960661

Asian Development Bank–Pakistan
Pakistan Resident Mission
Overseas Pakistanis Foundation Building (OPF)
GPO Box 1863, Sharah-e-Jamhuriyat, G-5/2
Islamabad, Pakistan
Phone: (92–51) 2825011–16, 2087300
Fax: (92–51) 2823324, 2274718
E-mail: adbprm@adb.org
ADB is a multilateral development finance institution dedicated to reducing poverty in Asia and the Pacific. Pakistan has been a member since its establishment in 1966.

GTZ Pakistan
GTZ Office Islamabad House 63/A
Street No. 5
Second Gate No. F-8/3
Islamabad, Pakistan

Phone: (92–51) 2264161
Fax: (92–51) 2264159
E-mail: GTZ pakistan@pk.gtz.de

UNIFEM
www.unifem.undp.org/ec_povh5.htm
The United Nations Development Fund for Women works for women's empowerment and gender equality.

United Nations Development Program (UNDP)–Pakistan
9th Floor, Saudi Pak Tower
61-A Jinnah Avenue, Blue Area
Islamabad, Pakistan
Phone: (92–51) 2800133
http://www.un.org.pk/undp/
UNDP is part of the United Nations. UNDP–Pakistan addresses the issue of poverty eradication and sustainable human development through the three program areas of governance, gender, and sustainable livelihoods. The UN community in Pakistan is extensive, comprising sixteen UN agency offices dealing directly with Pakistan.

United Nations Headquarters
House 26, Street 88, G-6/3
Diplomatic Enclave, Ramna 5
Islamabad, Pakistan
Phone: (92–51) 2270610, 28210122

USAID Mission to Pakistan Diplomatic Enclave
Ramna 5
Islamabad, Pakistan
Phone: (92–51) 2082795
Fax: (92–51) 2870310

\World Bank–Pakistan
www.worldbank.org.pk
  This website provides up-to-date information on World
Bank-assisted programs, data, publications, and other information pertaining to Pakistan.

TOURISM

Adventure Foundation of Pakistan
Garden Avenue, National Park Area
P.O. Box 1807
Islamabad 44000, Pakistan
Phone: (92–51) 2825805, 2272538
Fax: (92–51) 2272538
E-mail: afopak@yahoo.com
www.adventurefoundation.org.pk

Alpine Trekkers and Tours Private Limited
21 Al-Amin Plaza
The Mall
Rawalpindi, Pakistan
Phone: (92–51) 5593149, 2852496, 5519815, 2292126
Fax: (92–51) 2260111, 5517330

American Embassy Diplomatic Enclave
Ramna 5
Islamabad, Pakistan
Phone: (92–51) 2080000
Fax: (92–51) 2276427
E-mail: webmasterisb@state.gov
http://islamabad.usembassy.gov
  The U.S. Embassy provides valuable information to Amer-
ican tourists and travelers planning to visit Pakistan, along
with travel tips and alerts (on security, health, and other mat-
ters). It also provides information on business climate, invest-

ment opportunities, trade rules and regulations, tax laws, and other relevant matters.

Pakistan Sports Board
Kashmir Highway
Islamabad, Pakistan
Phone: (92–51) 920268
Fax: (92–51) 9203077

Pakistan Tourism Development Corporation (PTDC)
22 Saeed Plaza, Jinnah Avenue, Blue Area
Islamabad 44000, Pakistan
Phone: (92–51) 9212722–26
Fax: (92–51) 9219702–08
E-mail: tourism@isb.comsats.net.pk, mdptdc@comsats.net.pk,
        ptdc3@paknet.com.pk
http:// www.tourism.gov.pk

Travel Agents Association of Pakistan (TAAP)
115 Central Hotel Building
1st Floor, Merewether Road
75530 Karachi, Pakistan
Phone: (92–21) 5682748, 5684469
Fax: (92–21) 5682748

http://www.tourism.gov.pk/
http://www.geographia.com/pakistan/
http://offroadpakistan.com/
http://homepages.uel.ac.uk/u0014048/
    These sites give valuable information for tourists and travelers on all topics related to Pakistan.

Lonely Planet Online
http://www.lonelyplanet.com
    This is a good website to visit for travel information on Pakistan.

NATIONAL NONGOVERNMENTAL ORGANIZATIONS (NGOS)

Service Delivery NGOs

Aahung
E-mail: krhp@cyber.net.pk
Registered in 1995, Aahung focuses on health, and its major projects include the Karachi Reproductive Health Project and AIDS Awareness Program.

Adult Basic Education Society
P.O. Box 18
Gujranwala, Pakistan
Phone: (92–431) 266014
Fax: (92–431) 258314
http://abes.cjb.net
The society is working in the field of literacy, health, and primary education in the Punjab, and particularly focuses on nonformal education for girls.

All Pakistan Women's Association
67 B Garden Road
Karachi 74400, Pakistan
Phone: (92–21) 7212991
Fax: (92–21) 7221965
E-mail: apwa@pienet.net
http://www.un.org.pk/unic/apwa.htm
Established in 1949, APWA is a nonpolitical organization whose aim is to promote the social and economic welfare of women and children. It has branches in fifty-six districts, as well as fringe urban and rural branches across Pakistan.

Baanh Beli
E-mail: mnj@cyber.net.pk
Operating in Sindh, Baanh Beli focuses on village commu-

nity development, savings and credit, female education, and female health care.

Behbud Association
25 Mehmoodabad Road
St. 9, Block 1, Kehkashan
Scheme 5
Karachi, Pakistan
Phone: (92–21) 5862093, 543552
http://xiber.com/behbud
    The association's efforts concentrate on women's development in health, education, vocational training, and income-generating schemes.

Edhi Foundation
Rangila Street, Boulton Market, Mithadar
Karachi 74000, Pakistan
Phone: (92–21) 2443158, 2413232
    Edhi Foundation's activities include a 24-hour emergency service across the country that provides air and field ambulance service to over 1 million persons annually, in addition to other wide-ranging services, through 250 Edhi centers that provide free shrouding and burial of unclaimed dead bodies; shelter for the destitute, orphans; and handicapped persons; free hospitals and dispensaries, rehabilitation of drug addicts; and national and international relief efforts for disaster victims and refugees in Pakistan.

Edhi International Foundation
42–07 National Street
Corona, NY 11368
Tel: (718) 639–5120
Fax: (718) 335–1978
E-mail: edhi@cyber.net.pk
http://www.paks.net/edhi-foundation

Family Planning Association of Pakistan (FPAP)
www.brain.net.pk/-fpapak
Established in 1953, the FPAP is committed to responsible parenthood and focuses on the complete sexual and reproductive health of the whole family.

Indus Resource Centre (IRC)
2-B Plot #13-C, 37th Commercial Street
Tauheed Commercial Area D.H.A. V
Karachi 62200, Pakistan
Phone: (92–21) 5822239
Fax: (92–21) 5822239
E-mail: karachi@irc-pakistan.com
http://www.irc.pakistan
The IRC is working for poor and marginalized community groups in two districts of Sindh, Dadu, and Khairpur. It particularly focuses on girls' education in rural Sindh.

Kashf Foundation
www.kashf.com
Established in 1996, Kashf Foundation was inspired by the success of the Grameen Bank of Bangladesh in reaching out to poor women and is the first such replication of the Grameen Bank in Pakistan. Its mission is to provide cost-effective and quality micro-finance services to poor women, and to enhance their role in economic and social decision making.

Overseas Pakistanis Foundation
Shahrah-e-Jamhouriat, Sector G-5/2
P.O. Box 1470
Islamabad, Pakistan
Phone: (92–51) 9202457–9
Fax: (92–51) 9224335, 9211613
E-mail: info@opf.org.pk

Pakistan Poverty Alleviation Fund
House No. 1, Street No. 20, F-7/2
Islamabad, Pakistan
Phone: (92–51) 111000102
Fax: (92–51) 2652246
E-mail: info@ppaf.org.pk
http://www.ppaf.org.pk
   Established in 1997 as a nonprofit organization, the fund seeks to alleviate poverty in Pakistan.

SAHIL
Islamabad, Punjab
E-mail: info@sahil.org
http://www.sahil.org
   This is a voluntary social welfare agency operating in rural and urban areas to sensitize journalists on issues of child sex abuse. It also provides shelter for male child prostitutes.

War Against Rape
E-mail: war@super.net.pk
   Operating in Karachi, this NGO provides legal aid to rape victims and counseling for rape.

Advocacy and Research NGOs

Applied Social Research
E-mail: asr@brain.net.pk, asr@lhr.comsats.net.pk
   ASR was set up in 1983 as a multidisciplinary group working toward sociopolitical transformation through reexamining and redefining the political and developmental processes that people themselves identify, articulate, and struggle for.

Association of Business Professional & Agricultural Women
98 Chakllala Scheme 1
Rawalpindi 46000, Pakistan
Phone: (92–51) 5593179

Fax: (92–51) 5506613
E-mail: abpaw@abpaw.cjb.net
http://www.abpaw.cjb.net

Aurat Publication and Information Service Foundation
6-B, LDA Garden View Apartments
Lawrence Road
Lahore 54000, Pakistan
Phone: (92–42) 6306534, 6314382, and 6372839
Fax: (92–42) 6278817
E-mail: apisf@brain.net.pk
www.brain.net.pk/~apisf/main.html

The goals of the foundation are to support women at the community and district levels and to undertake advocacy with public servants and public representatives for gender-responsive development planning, supportive legislation, and increasing women's access to government services. Major projects undertaken with regard to women include establishment of 3,000 information network centers, shelter for women in Peshawar, and strengthening of the democratic electoral process in Pakistan with a focus on women's empowerment.

Human Rights Commission of Pakistan
www.hrcp-web.org

The commission's mandate includes work for Pakistan's ratification and implementation of the Universal Declaration of Human Rights and of other related charters, covenants, protocols, resolutions, recommendations, and internationally adopted norms, and promoting studies in the field of human rights and mobilizing public opinion in favor of accepted norms.

Shirkat Gah- Women's Resource Centre
www.spinifexpress.com.au/pakistan/shirkatgah
http://aphy.ku.edu.pk/resources/res2001/afsheen-kamal/w-organization.htm

The group was set up in 1975 as a pressure cum lobby and

consciousness-raising group on discriminatory customary practices and laws against women. It was later expanded to include women's development concerns, networking, income-generating projects, and nonformal education.

Simorgh
www.spinifexpress
http://aphy.ku.edu.pk/resources/res2001/afsheen-kamal/
w-organization.htm
    A women's resource and publication center, Simorgh was formed in 1985 in response to the promulgation of retrogressive and discriminatory legislation. Major projects undertaken include a study of violence against women and gender equality and the judiciary.

Women's Action Forum
http://aphy.ku.edu.pk/resources/res2001/afsheen-kamal/
w_organization.htm
    This network acts as a pressure group, holds demonstrations, and collaborates with NGOs on issues related to women in Pakistan.

Annotated Bibliography of Recommended Works on Pakistan

The references listed in this section include some of those cited within this book as well as others related to Pakistan. They are organized by categories according to the chronology of the narrative section of this book. They include the most highly regarded, current, and readable sources. In the following sections, certain books and reports are mentioned more than once to assist people with interests in specific areas.

GEOGRAPHY AND HISTORY OF PAKISTAN

Ahmed, Akbar S. 1997. *Jinnah, Pakistan and Islamic Identity: The Search for Saladin.* New York: Routledge. 304 pp.

This well-written and scholarly book provides a historical and biographical analysis of Jinnah's unique position in Pakistan's history, and the unparalleled loyalty to his memory even today.

Alavi, Hamza. 2002. "Misreading Partition Road Signs." *Economic and Political Weekly,* November 2–9. 13 pp.

This article traces the history of the Pakistan movement, arguing that Islamic ideology did not play any part in the success of the Muslim League, the political party led by Mohammad Ali Jinnah, the founder of Pakistan.

Baxter, Craig (ed.). 2004. *Pakistan on the Brink: Politics, Economics, and Society.* Lanham, MD: Lexington Books. 244 pp.

This volume provides information on Pakistan's ongoing conflict with India, its Afghan policy, its economic challenges, the 2002 elections, and education reform.

Blood, Peter R. (ed.). 1996. *Pakistan: A Country Study* (Area Handbook Series). Washington, DC: Federal Research Division, Library of Congress. 398 pp.

Perhaps the most comprehensive volume on Pakistan, this book covers a wide range of topics and issues of Pakistan, including geography, history, society and the environment, government and politics, economy, and national security.

Burki, Shahid Javed. 1991. *Historical Dictionary of Pakistan.* Metuchen, NJ: Scarecrow Press. 254 pp.

This is a comprehensive source of dictionary-style entries on the religious, social, political, economic, and cultural events and prominent figures of Pakistan, both before and after independence.

Jalal, Ayesha. 1985. *The Sole Spokesman: Jinnah, the Muslim League and the Demand for Pakistan.* New York: Cambridge University. 320 pp.

Concentrating on the All-India Muslim League and its leader, Mohammad Ali Jinnah, the book addresses the role of religious communalism and provincialism in shaping the movement for Pakistan. It traces how the claim of Jinnah and the Muslim League to speak for all Indian Muslims, built upon the demand for Pakistan, came to be accepted by the British and by the Muslims in both majority and minority provinces.

Kibria, Ghulam. 1999. *A Shattered Dream: Understanding Pakistan's Underdevelopment.* Karachi, Pakistan: Oxford University Press. 234 pp.

This book traces developments from before the creation of Pakistan in 1947 to 1997, and argues that despite being a viable state at partition, Pakistan was let down by its rulers, crony capitalists, and the privileged classes, leading to a disintegration of Pakistani nationhood.

Talbot, Ian. 1998. *Pakistan: A Modern History.* New York: St. Martin's Press. 432 pp.

Giving a comprehensive and scholarly account of Pakistan's history from 1947 until the 1990s, this book stresses the resilience of millions of Pakistanis living in thousands of towns and cities to counter the gloomy predictions about Pakistan's failure as a state.

Tonchev, Plamen. 2003. *Pakistan at Fifty-five: From Jinnah to Musharraf.* European Institute for Asian Studies. BP 02/03. 8 EUR Series. 53 pp.

This paper analyzes the impact of three main trends that cut across the history of Pakistan: the fundamental role of Islam, the omnipresent military, and the high levels of poverty.

United Nations Development Programme. 2003. *Human Development Report, 2003.* New York: Oxford University Press. 367 pp.

This report provides a good source of data on a host of socio-economic variables for 175 countries of the world, including Pakistan. Data on demographic and migration variables from the report are used in the present book.

Ziad, Zeenut (ed.). 2002. *The Magnificent Mughals.* Karachi, Pakistan: Oxford University Press. 339 pp.

This anthology is an authoritative history of the religious, cultural, economic, political, and military aspects of the Mughal Empire. It contains excellent illustrations.

Ziring, Lawrence. 1997. *Pakistan in the Twentieth Century: A Political History.* Karachi, Pakistan: Oxford University Press. 647 pp.

This book gives a comprehensive and scholarly account of Pakistan's history from 1947 until the late 1990s.

ECONOMY OF PAKISTAN

Ahmed, Viqar, and Rashid Amjad. 1985. *The Management of Pakistan's Economy, 1947–1982.* New York: Oxford University Press. 315 pp.

Though somewhat outdated, this book gives a comprehensive analytical history of Pakistan's economy.

Blood, Peter R. (ed.). 1995. *Pakistan: A Country Study* (Area Handbook Series). Washington, DC: Federal Research Division, Library of Congress. 398 pp.

This book provides an informative and comprehensive description and analysis of Pakistan's historic, political, economic, social, and cultural events and institutions.

Duncan, Ann (with Yasmeen Mohiuddin, M. Habib, and P. Blair). 1989. *Women in Pakistan: An Economic and Social Strategy.* Washington, DC: World Bank. 192 pp.

This report discusses the status of women's health, education, and work in the rural and urban sectors; highlights the issues in these and other areas; and recommends strategies for addressing the issues.

Hasan, Parvez. 1998. *Pakistan's Economy at the Crossroads: Past Policies and Present Imperatives.* New York: Oxford University Press. 376 pp.

This book analyzes the factors that have contributed to the steady growth in Pakistan during the first fifty years of its existence, despite high political volatility, and the reasons for the failure of development to dominate the national agenda over long periods of time.

Hussain, Akmal. 2003. *Pakistan: National Human Development Report 2003: Poverty, Growth, and Governance.* Karachi: Oxford University Press. 176 pp.

This is a comprehensive report on human development in Pakistan that recommends a multidimensional strategy for poverty alleviation, including governance reforms and empowerment of the poor, particularly women.

Hussain, Ishrat. 1999. *Pakistan: The Economy of an Elitist State.* Karachi: Oxford University Press. 451 pp.

The book gives an account of the elitist policies in Pakistan until 1998, regardless of the form and ideology of the existing governments, and lays down an economic and social agenda for reform of the judiciary, educational, and financial systems.

Hussain, Ishrat. 2003. *Economic Management in Pakistan 1999–2002.* Oxford: Oxford University Press. 271 pp.

This book, written by the governor of the central bank of Pakistan, gives a lucid account of three years of economic management of external debt, foreign exchange, the financial sector, and monetary and fiscal policy from 1999 to 2002.

Khan, Shahrukh Rafi (ed.). 1999. *Fifty Years of Pakistan's Economy: Traditional Issues and New Concerns.* New York: Oxford University Press. 506 pp.

This book makes an important contribution to our understanding of Pakistan's economic development in the first fifty years of its existence.

Malik, Sohail J., Safiya Aftab, and Nargis Sultana. 1994. *Pakistan's Economic Performance 1947–1993: A Descriptive Analysis.* Lahore, Pakistan: Sure Publishers. 444 pp.

This book gives a comprehensive descriptive analysis of the key aspects of the Pakistan economy, putting them in a historical and policy context.

Mohiuddin, Yasmeen. 1983. "An Investigation into the Determinants of Farm Employment in Pakistan." Unpublished Ph.D. dissertation. Vanderbilt University. 155 pp.

This study provides an exhaustive analysis of the impact of the green revolution and related factors on labor use in Pakistani agriculture.

Mohiuddin, Yasmeen. 1985. *Women's Employment in the Putting-out System in Sindh.* Karachi: Applied Economics Research Center. Report prepared for the International Labor Organization.

This survey-based study examines the socioeconomic profile of handicraft workers in Sindh and the characteristics of their piece-rate work in the informal sector. 110 pp.

Noman, Omar. 1990. *Pakistan: A Political and Economic History since 1947.* New York: Routledge, Chapman and Hall. 285 pp.

This well-written and interesting book provides a fairly comprehensive and balanced analysis of Pakistan's political and economic development from the early years until General Zia's death and the start of Benazir Bhutto's government.

Pakistan. Federal Bureau of Statistics. Statistics Division. 2003. *Pakistan Statistical Pocketbook.* Islamabad, Pakistan: Government of Pakistan. http://www.statpak.gov.pk/

This work is a good and authentic source of statistical information on Pakistan.

Pakistan Census of Agriculture. 1998. Agriculture Census Organization. Lahore, Pakistan: Government of Pakistan. 357 pp.

This is an exhaustive source of statistical information on Pakistani agriculture.

United Nations Development Programme. 2003. *Human Development Report, 2003.* New York: Oxford University Press. 367 pp.

This is a good source of data on population, income, employment, poverty, education, health, environment, gender, trade, public expenditure, and other variables for 175 countries of the world, including Pakistan.

World Bank. *2004. World Development Report 2005.* Washington, DC: The World Bank. 271 pp.

This 2004 report focuses on a better investment climate for everyone and contains data for selected world development indicators for all countries.

Zaidi, S. Akbar. 1999. *Issues in Pakistan's Economy.* Karachi: Oxford University Press. 462 pp.

This book gives a comprehensive account of Pakistan's economic performance from 1947 to 1997 while addressing institutional issues in the delivery of social services in Pakistan.

POLITICAL DEVELOPMENT SINCE 1947

Blood, Peter R. (ed.). 1994. *Pakistan: A Country Study* (Area Handbook Series). Washington, DC: Federal Research Division, Library of Congress. 398 pp.

A comprehensive source of information for political developments from 1947 to 1990.

Burki, Shahid Javed, and Craig Baxter. 1991. *Pakistan under the Military: Eleven Years of Zia ul-Haq.* Boulder, CO: Westview Press. 212 pp.

This book analyzes the political, economic, legal, and administrative structures of Pakistan as they were formed and transformed by General Ziaul Haq.

Duncan, Emma. 1989. *Breaking the Curfew: A Political Journey through Pakistan.* London: Arrow. 320 pp.

This book, though outdated, gives a well-written journalistic account of Pakistani politics and society.

Jones, Owen Bennett. 2002. *Pakistan: Eye of the Storm.* New Haven, CT: Yale University Press. 328 pp.

This book focuses on the political and social history of Pakistan, not in chronological order, but through a thematic and issues-based approach. The critical issues covered include Musharraf's challenge, the 1999 coup, Kashmir, nationalism, Bangladesh, the bomb, democracy, and the army.

Kux, Dennis. 2001. *Pakistan: Flawed Not Failed State.* New York: Foreign Policy Association. 80 pp.

This book presents a good analysis of chronic political instability in Pakistan, its shaky institutions, uneven economic and social development, and problematic relations with neighbors, as well as its strengths.

Long, Roger D. 1998. *The Founding of Pakistan: An Annotated Bibliography.* Lanham, MD: Rowman and Littlefield. 336 pp.

This source discusses the literature on Pakistan from 1947 to 1997 in the categories of reference works, political studies, provincial studies, biographical studies, and Mohammad Ali Jinnah.

Malik, Hafeez (ed.). 2001. *Pakistan: Founders' Aspirations and Today's Realities.* New York: Oxford University Press. 482 pp.

This book presents a realistic assessment of the country's successes and failures.

Noman, Omar. 1990. *Pakistan: A Political and Economic History since 1947.* New York: Routledge, Chapman and Hall. 238 pp.

This book provides an excellent introduction to Pakistan's political development from 1947 to 1990.

Qureshi, Ishtiaq Husain. 1965. *The Struggle for Pakistan.* Karachi, Pakistan: University of Karachi Press.

This book is a scholarly and comprehensive work on the Pakistan movement.

Weaver, Mary Anne. 2002. *Pakistan: In the Shadow of Jihad and Afghanistan.* New York: Farrar, Straus and Giroux. 284 pp.

This book draws a vivid portrait of the land, people, and clans of Pakistan against the background of the U.S.-sponsored jihad of the 1980s in Afghanistan. It focuses on politics and government under the regimes of Ziaul Haq, Benazir Bhutto, and Pervez Musharraf.

Ziring, Lawrence. 2004. *Pakistan: At the Crosscurrent of History.* Oxford: Oneworld Publications. 400 pp.

This work presents a concise and lucid political history of Pakistan.

PAKISTANI INSTITUTIONS AND CONTEMPORARY CULTURE

Cohen, Stephen Philip. 2005. *The Idea of Pakistan.* Lahore, Pakistan: Vanguard Books. 380 pp.

This informative and insightful book analyzes the role and ethos of the Pakistan Army, its political parties, Islamists, and various ethnic, linguistic, and sectarian minorities. Arguing that Pakistan may be a flawed but not failed state, which can still emerge as a successful and cohesive nation, Cohen makes proposals for a U.S. policy of continued engagement with Pakistan while pressing for real reforms.

Duncan, Ann (with Yasmeen Mohiuddin, M. Habib, and P. Blair). 1989. *Women in Pakistan: An Economic and Social Strategy.* Washington, DC: The World Bank. 192 pp.

This World Bank Country Study contains a comprehensive and scholarly analysis of the role of Pakistani women in the rural, urban informal, and urban formal sectors of the economy, and outlines an economic and social strategy for their development.

Haqqani, Hussain. 2005. *Pakistan: Between Mosque and Military.* Lahore, Pakistan: Vanguard Books. 395 pp.

This book gives a well-written account of the historic alliance between Pakistan's powerful Islamist groups and its professional army, which was forged over time and has changed in character with the twists and turns of Pakistani history.

Kennedy, Charles H. (ed.). 2003. *Pakistan at the Millennium.* Karachi, Pakistan: Oxford University Press. 390 pp.

The authors discuss religious, military, and folk culture in Pakistan; women's movements; literature and sonic arts; and state and nation building.

Mohiuddin, Yasmeen. 1988. "Women and Agricultural Credit." Report, Identification Mission, Pakistan Agriculture Credit VII Project, Agriculture Operations Division of the Europe, Middle East and North Africa Region Country Department 1 (EM1AG). The World Bank. 51 pp.

The author discusses the reasons underlying women's limited access to credit, designs the first major agricultural credit project for women in Pakistan, and outlines a comprehensive strategy for increasing their access to credit.

Mohiuddin, Yasmeen. 1992. "Female-Headed Households and Urban Poverty in Pakistan," in Nancy Folbre, Barbara Bergmann, Bina Agarwal, and Maria Floro (eds.) *Issues in*

Contemporary Economics, Vol. 4: *Women's Work in the World Economy.* Hong Kong: Macmillan. 21 pp.

This article, based on a survey of domestics in Karachi, discusses the working conditions of these self-employed workers and the relationship between their headship status and household poverty.

Mohiuddin, Yasmeen. 1995. "Country Rankings of Women's Status: An Alternative Index." *Pakistan Development Review* 34(4). 15 pp.

This paper develops an index on the gender gap and status of women and ranks 112 countries of the world on that basis.

Mohiuddin, Yasmeen. 1997. "Gender Inequality in the Pakistan Labor Market: Myth and Reality," in J. Rives and M. Yousefi (eds.), *Economic Dimensions of Gender Inequality: A Global Perspective.* Westport, CT: Praeger. Pp. 167–184.

This article analyzes the labor force participation of women in the rural, urban informal, and urban formal sectors of the Pakistan economy; the gender wage gap; and the occupational segregation of women.

Mumtaz, Khawar, and Yameema Mitha. 2003. *Pakistan: Tradition and Change.* An Oxfam Country Profile. UK: Oxfam. 72 pp.

This is a good source of brief information on Pakistan's geography, history, economy, and society, with very illustrative and unusual pictures.

Mumtaz, Khawar, and Farida Shaheed. 1987. *Women of Pakistan: Two Steps Forward, One Step Back?* London: Zed Press. 196 pp.

This book gives a descriptive account of the status of women in Pakistan, particularly during the military regime of Ziaul Haq.

Winter, Dave, and Ivan Mannheim. 1999. *Footprint Pakistan Handbook: The Travel Guide.* Bath: Footprint Handbooks. 688 pp.

This is a good source of information on travel in Pakistan.

Zaidi, S. Akbar. 1999. *The New Development Paradigm: Papers on Institutions, NGOs, Gender and Local Government.* Karachi, Pakistan: Oxford University Press. 321 pp.

This book is a good source of information on local government and NGOs, particularly in Sindh.

PAKISTAN IN PICTURES

Amin, Mohamed, D. Willets, and G. Hancock. 1982. *Journey through Pakistan.* Camerapix Publishers International. 255 pp.

This work presents a good pictorial description of the landscape, culture, and peoples of Pakistan.

Index

About the Author

Yasmeen Niaz Mohiuddin was raised, educated, employed, and married in Pakistan. She is currently the Ralph Owen Distinguished Professor of Economics and past chair of the department at Sewanee: The University of the South in Tennessee. She received a PhD in Economics from Vanderbilt University in Nashville, Tennessee in 1983 and an MA in Economic Development from Vanderbilt in 1978. She earned a BA and MA from Karachi University, Pakistan. She has taught for 23 years at Sewanee and for 10 at Karachi University.

Mohiuddin also works as a consultant to the World Bank, the United States Agency for International Development (USAID), and several United Nations (UN) agencies involving project, sector, and policy work on gender issues, agricultural development, credit and micro-finance, and education and training. In that capacity, she has designed and evaluated projects and programs for Pakistan, Nepal, Bangladesh, Sri Lanka, Yemen, Turkey, Cambodia, the Philippines, and China. She has traveled extensively in these countries as a member of different World Bank and UN missions. She has also conducted considerable field research in Pakistan funded by research grants from Sewanee.

Mohiuddin has published widely in the field of development economics, including rural employment, urban informal sector, poverty and female-headed households, microfinance, agricultural credit, women's employment, gender gap indices, girl trafficking, and strategies for women's development in Pakistan and Turkey. In addition to numerous World Bank, USAID, and UN mission reports, she has co-authored the World Bank report on Women in Pakistan and contributed to the report on Women in Turkey. She has presented papers at conferences in twenty countries and several of her papers on Pakistan have been published in the *Pakistan Development Review*. She has been the associate executive editor of the *Journal of Asian Economics*.

Mohiuddin has received numerous honors, awards, and grants and serves on the boards of several agencies. In 2000, the governor of Tennessee appointed her for a six-year term to the Tennessee Economic Council on Women, a state agency created to assess the economic needs of Tennessee women and to advocate for their advancement.